Sex and Zen
A Bullet in the Head

STEFAN HAMMOND & MIKE WILKINS

A FIRESIDE BOOK PUBLISHED BY **S**IMON & **S**CHUSTER

FIRESIDE
Rockefeller Center
1230 Avenue of the Americas
New York, NY 10020

FIRESIDE and colophon are registered trademarks of Simon & Schuster Inc.

DESIGNED BY BARBARA MARKS

Manufactured in the United States of America
10 9 8 7 6 5 4

Library of Congress Cataloging-in-Publication Data
Hammond, Stefan
        Sex and Zen & a bullet in the head / Stefan Hammond & Mike Wilkins
            p.   cm.
        "A Fireside Book"
        Includes index.
            1. Motion pictures—Hong Kong.   2. Motion pictures—Hong Kong—
Catalogs.   3. Hand-to-hand fighting, Oriental, in motion pictures.
        I. Wilkins, Mike.   II. Title.
        PN1993.5.H6H26   1996
        791.43'75'095125—dc20   96-15210
                                                                      CIP

ISBN 0-684-80341-0

Acknowledgments

All thanks and credit go to the following wonderful people:

Contributing Writers
Richard A. Akiyama: RAA
Keith Allison: KWA
Tod Booth: TB
Michael Helms: MH
Lars-Erik Holmquist: LEH
Andy Klein: AK
Jim Morton: JM
Chuck Stephens: CS
Karen Tarapata: KAT

Production Intern
Carmen Bradley

Chinese Character Wrangler
Andrew Scal

Special Thanks
Helen Soo and Janie Chuck of Tai Seng Marketing, South San
    Francisco
Sandra Lo of World Video, San Francisco

Jackie Chan and Willie Chan of Jackie & Willie
    Productions, Hong Kong
Tom Gray and Elisa Choe of Rim Films, Los
    Angeles
Gere LaDue of Dragon Art, Los Angeles
Le Video, San Francisco
Hung Ming Enterprise, San Francisco
Mike Leeder, Hong Kong
Barrie Pattison
Elliot Levine and Bill Banning of the Roxie
    Cinema, San Francisco
Mike Mallery of World Lithographic Services,
    San Francisco
David Chute
Roberta Chow
Bruce Black
Wendy Van Dusen
Fatal Visions Magazine
Richard Laslet, Chinatown Cinema Complex,
    200 Bourke Street, Melbourne
Lursak Thavornvanit of Cine Group, Bangkok
Sheila Duignan of Awesome Catering, San
    Francisco

Our Editors
Cindy Gitter
David Dunton

Our Agents
Jane Jordan Browne
Danielle Egan Miller

Our Heroes
Golden Harvest Productions, Hong Kong
Shaw Brothers Studio, Hong Kong

Corporations
Apple Computer, Cupertino, California
Kempinski Furama Hotel, Hong Kong
Kirin, makers of Jive Coffee—world's most
    caffeinated beverage

Thanks
Rod Alley, William Bailey, Steve Bodco, Pietro
Bonomi, Jane Caeneddi, Monte Cazazza, Terence
Chang, Chinatown Theater (San Francisco, Cali-
fornia), Bill Connolly, Brad Daniels, Joseph Fierro,
Peter Flechette, Paul Fonoroff, Christopher Fu,
Allan and Cathy G., John J. Gainfort Jr., Colin
Geddes, Stuart Gottesman, Richard Grosse,
Richard Hall, D. E. Hardy, Tim Holmes, Rebecca
Ip, Chika Ishigaki, Alice Joanou, Carol Jokinen,
Richard Kadrey, Johanna Keltner, Regan Kibbee,
Doug Kirby, Mick LaSalle, Frances Loden, Joel
Loree, Felix Lu, Heather Mackey, Jeanette Mak,
Mike Maloy, Brad Masoni, Paul Mavrides, Philip
Metcalf, Hank Okazaki, Pagoda Palace Theater
(San Francisco, California), Carl Parkes, Richard
Petersen, Martha Pike, Leslie Pollock, Kevin Pow-
ers, William Henry Pratt, Timo Rautiala, Cather-
ine Reuther, Lightning-Always-Strikes-Twice
Reuther, Mary Ricci, Jane Ritchie Rice, Ritz The-
ater (Minneapolis, Minnesota), Riverview Cinema
(Durham, North Carolina), Brad Roberts,
Cameron Scholes, Jeff Segal, Dr. Bob Smith, Doug-
lass St. Clair Smith, Ken Smith, Strand Theater
(San Francisco, California), Richard A. Spears,
Terry Thome, Edward Van Sicklin, Dewey Webb,
Jeff Wilkins, Bill Wilson, Declan Wong, Michael
Wong, World Theater (San Francisco).

Contents

Foreword

BY JACKIE CHAN

Finally, an English-language guide to the wonderful films of Hong Kong! It is a great thing that the movies we have been making in Hong Kong are being discovered by people the world over. Video stores around the United States are beginning to carry copies, and Chinese film festivals are occurring regularly. New Line Cinema is now distributing my films in North America, and I was thrilled when MTV gave me a Lifetime Achievement Award at their movie awards show this past year.

I think you'll enjoy Hong Kong films. Because for me, making movies is about making excitement. I've made movies all over the world, but I keep returning to Hong Kong, where the excitement is best. In Hong Kong, although the local police may object, if we want to drive a motorcycle on top of a speeding train, we just do it.

If we want a jeep to explode in fire and ignite the four stuntmen leaping out of it, we just do it. If we want a beautiful female police officer to sweep-kick a bad egg in the chops, we just do it. That's Hong Kong. We just do it.

Here in this book you'll find many of my favorites, which I hope will become some of yours. If you're new to HK films, you are in for some movie-watching experiences beyond your wildest dreams—and nightmares.

If you are already familiar with HK films, you'll still find some undiscovered gems here. Stefan and Mike have included a primer on Hong Kong Noir, a brief history of the Shaw brothers, some "mondo" curiosities, hopping vampires, and lots of unique action films. They even list the addresses of my fan clubs.

I'm proud that they chose to review a dozen or so of my own works. Once you read about them, I hope you'll be tempted to see them in a theater with your friends. Because if you (yes, *you*) go and have a great time at my movies, then I'm really, really happy. Because I make my movies for you. It's that simple.

Please enjoy. *Doh jeh sai!*

Introduction

In describing Hong Kong cinema—its excitement, vitality, electricity—film-school polemics fail. There is no pointy-headed, white-wine-and-baked-brie philosophizing that adequately describes its "scalding propulsion," the force that blasts you out of your seat and rearranges your popcorn, because over-intellectualizing film denies the primary purpose of moviegoing: entertainment. And Hong Kong movies are, simply, some of the most entertaining films on the planet.

Entertaining for everyone, not just for Hong Kong natives. These windows on a culture half a world away teach any viewer what is universal about the human experience: the goodness of a noble heart, the purity of a mother's love, the fear of a giant scaly monster. It also teaches what is not universal to the human experience: an overflowing squid-bucket of only–in–Hong Kong conventions to enthrall the most jaded cineaste. Gunfight opponents quickly shoot each other up, then trade pistols in a ritualistic fashion before the final fusillade. Corpses hop, heroes pee their pants in fright, and beautiful women punch hulking bad guys into submission. The familiar and delightfully unfamiliar are mulched together, creating a fertile mayhem—rich, compelling, and rewarding.

Hong Kong filmmakers capitalize quickly on current events; infamous HK criminal cases are transformed into feature films in a matter of weeks, and sequels are de rigueur. Yet, despite the up-to-the-minute exploitation, the rich history of Chinese culture (sixty centuries or so; the only unbroken link to the ancient past) is also mined for inspiration; a Ming Dynasty fable is just as likely as last month's sensational homicide to serve as template for the afternoon's first-run feature.

Hong Kong movies are not a genre, but the world's third largest film industry, after Hollywood and Bombay. Shanghai served as the Far East's Tinseltown in the 20s and 30s, but Hong Kong took over after World War II, and currently produces hundreds of feature films each year that play throughout Asia and in Chinatowns on every continent.

This industry heralded a "new wave" in the mid-eighties. The Shaw Brothers studio, which dominated Hong Kong films since the 40s, suddenly decided to stop making motion pictures and to concentrate instead on television production. Small independent production companies sprang up alongside more established names, and visionary directors like John Woo, Jackie Chan, and Tsui Hark were given freer rein over their work.

This new, partially Westernized cinema started to receive sporadic attention at film festivals outside Asia—in New York and Toronto, and at Chicago's AFI and Minneapolis's Walker Art Center. A cultlike viewership began to grow. Internet groups and World Wide Web pages appeared. As the new wave crested in the early 90s, the cognoscenti perked up in earnest. But finding a reliable beginners guide to the subject was almost as hard as finding a publisher who wanted to print one.

So we teamed with Fireside to bring you *Sex and Zen & A Bullet in the Head.* This book, which gets its name from two Hong Kong films, is supposed to give you the suss on a hundred and fifty or so movies that we like enough to vigorously recommend. These include the film-festival classics, some lesser-known pearls, and a few buzz-bombs that are kept behind the cash register. There are a lot more movies available and, after getting into the flow, you may find that we don't mention some of your new favorites. So if you've become an *afflictionado,* with a favorite that we don't include, we've done our job introducing you to the subject.

You should know going in that we are not talking about the old kung fu, chopsocky films you see on late-night TV (we do talk about them, a little, but not until chapter 12). Most of the movies we discuss are less than ten years old, and encompass a wide range of settings, situations, and subject matter.

We also want to make it as easy as possible

for you to get access to the films. If you get hyped on a Hong Kong film but can't find it, you'll be pissed, and, knowing you, you'll probably give up right there. Fortunately, Hong Kong movies are growing in their North American accessibility. Because Hong Kong is still a British colony, almost all Hong Kong movies are subtitled in English. And because Hong Kong soon will no longer be a British colony, many Hong Kongers have emigrated to the United States and Canada, and their native video rental outlets have followed. Right-on alternative video stores are also setting up Hong Kong sections with increasing frequency.

Even though subtitled HK films are readily available on videotape, we recommend that you make every effort to see them in a theater. They thrive as en masse experiences. It is entirely possible that there is a Hong-Kong-movie region of the brain that remains a dormant little almond until that initial stimulus, at which point it starts to grow and vascularize. We've seen it happen: people rigid in theater seats, heads cocked agog, mesmerized.

We know that you don't really believe us. You are being polite and giving us a listen only because you need something to thumb through at the bookstore while your date looks for the latest heal-thyself-by-napping guide. Or because some

guy you know—who was right about how great *Mystery Science Theater 3000* was, but wrong about the excellent head one gets from over-the-counter inhalants—goes to see Hong Kong films every weekend. We can talk ourselves blue in the face, but until you see a couple yourself, there will be no gestalt shift. We'd keep pointing, and you'd keep staring at our finger.

It's true; you need an open mind, but not for very long. Just from the video store to your home. Just while you are waiting in line alongside fifteen hundred rabid hardcores at a venue like Berkeley's UC Theater. Once you get ten or fifteen minutes into one of these films, we think that your curiosity and open-mindedness will be well rewarded. The gestalt will shift: The duck becomes a bunny, the lamp becomes two block-jawed twins staring at each other. Go ahead, gamble a couple of bucks for this book, and a couple more for a movie rental.

Why do we pester you like this? Because these movies kick ass. Like power-chord rock, they induce a state of dashboard-pounding, over-the-top euphoria. "Aiyahhh!" as they say in Hong Kong films. Once you've seen the hyper-stylized action of John Woo or Ringo Lam, the exhilarating kineticism of Jackie Chan, or Tsui Hark's alternative planet, you'll start pestering people too.

Ten That Rip

1

We start things off with ten Hong Kong films that rip. The movies in this chapter are all extremely entertaining, well-made, accessible, and like nothing you've ever seen anywhere else. They should also demonstrate once and for all that anyone still thinking in terms of the old chopsocky stereotypes is just plain wrong.

This is not a "Ten Best" list. Picking the ten best is a never-ending flame war best played out over coffee or on the Internet's "alt.asian-movies" newsgroup. Instead, what we have tried to do is pick a great representative movie from some of the categories that we explore in more detail later in this book. As a result, we've included only one film each from auteurs John Woo, Tsui Hark, and Jackie Chan, even though a Ten Best list might contain multiple entries from any or all of them.

Hell hath no fury like Brigitte Lin scorned. From *The Bride With White Hair.*

Not only are these "Ten That Rip" the films that we recommend finding first, they are also among the ones that are easiest to find. Some, like *A Chinese Ghost Story* and *Naked Killer*, are staples of the growing college and art house theater circuit. Most are available on both videotape and laser disc. And all can be found subtitled.

The Bride With White Hair

1993
Starring Brigitte Lin Chin-hsia, Leslie Cheung Kwok-wing, Elaine Lui Siu-ling, Francis Ng Chun-yu, Nam Kit Ying
Directed by Ronny Yu

Psychosexual drama loaded with rich visual textures and fast, furious action. Leslie Cheung plays Yi-hang, a martial arts master condemned to self-exile atop a snowy mountaintop. In flashback, his tale reveals a childhood spent learning sword technique. Young adulthood brings with it a moshpit coif and a bright future as the heir to the Chung Yuan organization—a powerful alliance of eight clans.

But Yi-hang is not fond of the martial life, and longs for freedom from swords plunging through flesh. Into his life swirls a fierce, beautiful warrior (Brigitte Lin), who can rip people apart with her whip. They fall into thunderbolt love, consummating their obsession in a crystalline pool surrounded by stalactites—their deadly careers forgotten in giggling, washed-innocent abandon. Yi-hang finds that his new girlfriend has no name and christens her Lien Ni-chang.

Ni-chang didn't have a name because she was raised by wolves (really) and is now sponsored in her lethal activities by a cult leader named Chi Wu-shuang. Chi is a back-to-back brother/sister Siamese twin, a creature burning with malevolent intent. The male half blisters with unrequited passion for the beautiful Ni-chang, while the female half mocks her brother as an unlovely abomination.

Ni-chang wants out of the cult so she can start a new life with Yi-hang, and offers herself to the male half of the monster in exchange for her release. But she can't even pretend to get excited by his slathering advances (yeesh), and the female twin on his back shrieks with derision as she realizes that Ni-chang will never be her brother's lover in any way, misshape, or form.

As punishment, a barefoot Ni-chang is forced to walk a gauntlet over jagged shards while her rabid fellow cult members club her. She survives, but the scorned Chi Wu-shuang resorts to scorched-earth subterfuge—slaughtering the leaders of the Chung Yuan organization. This bloodletting brings him face-to-face with Yi-hang, with the issue of Trust (the highest virtue these less-than-savory characters can aspire to) at stake. Few things hath greater fury than Brigitte Lin seeking vengeance.

While *The Bride With White Hair* shares elements with other "legend films," like *A Chinese Ghost Story,* it is darker and more erotic than most. The film contains quite a bit of graphic violence, and fans of stage-blood-jetting-out-backlit won't be disappointed. Star Brigitte Lin's ferocious performance drives the film, and seldom have her features (especially her expressive eyes) been photographed to such effect. Unscrolled on the big screen (where it belongs), this epic poem will go a long way toward converting an HK film skeptic.

A Chinese Ghost Story

1987
Starring Joey Wong Jo-yin, Leslie Cheung Kwok-wing, Ng Ma, David Lam Wai
Directed by Ching Siu-tung

A Chinese Ghost Story breathes flesh and nerve as it spins a love story from a cyclone of fantastic action. An ancient Chinese legend married to Western pacing, this cinefable from producer Tsui Hark (see chapter 4) is at once earthy and unearthly, elegant and chaotic, and remains one of Hong Kong's breakthrough films.

Good-natured scholar Ning Tsai-shen (Leslie Cheung) is the most unpopular man in any village: a traveling tax collector making the rounds. Opting for a night at a deserted temple, he steps into the middle of a sharp and angry staredown between the loner misfit, Swordsman Yen (Ng Ma), and itinerant blade-for-hire, Hsiao-hou (David Lam). Ning keeps the swordsmen from carving each other up but receives a chilly welcome. The misanthropic Yen warns him there are things still skulking about "more scareful than a tiger."

We soon see what he means when Hsiao-hou meets a flirtatious, nubile ghostress bathing in a nearby stream and leaps lustfully upon her. After a shake of her belled ankle bracelet, something unseen slithers upon him, rams itself straight down his throat, and sucks out his essence, turning him into a desiccated corpse!

In the temple, Ning pricks his finger, and the basement, which houses a gaggle of these blood-sniffing corpses, stirs to life. Hollow bones crackle as they move in unison toward an oblivious Ning, who wanders off, attracted by the evocative sound of a lute and voice drifting through the window. He finds a pavilion on a serene lake, occupied by the same beautiful nymph who lured Hsiao-hou to his doom: the gorgeous Nieh Hsiao-tsing (Joey Wong). She immediately attempts to seduce him, but finds that he's different from the churls she's previously set up for drainage. Despite her beauty, he tenderly and politely turns her down.

Good move. A ghost and concubine to hell, Hsiao-tsing's job is targeting men for "yang element" absorption by her spirit-world pimp, an awful, dual-gender matron. But Hsiao-tsing gets no fulfillment from her work. Murdered a year earlier, she is now held in bondage by the creepy she-warlock, who has a witching symbiosis with the forest and sports a fifty-foot tongue that she wraps around her enemies like a python's coils. Even worse, Hsiao-tsing is betrothed to her pimp's boss, Lord Black. Given the circumstances, falling in love with the human Ning would be sheer folly. But, as Woody Allen once wrote, "The heart wants what it wants." They go for it.

Ning convinces the cantankerous-but-lovable Swordsman Yen that his new, pale sweetheart deserves a decent reincarnation. So the trio set off to recover the jar of her remains they'll need to accomplish the job.

The pissed-off matron assaults the trio with walls of tongue and other slimy effects. When these fail, she opens the portal to hell itself and drags Hsiao-tsing down. "Scholar! It seems we have to storm hell!" shouts Swordsman Yen, as the pair descend to scrap with Lord Black and his minions. Victory is hard-won, and enormously entertaining, but Ning and Hsiao-tsing's ill-fated man-ghost love doesn't survive the dawn.

Full Contact

1992
Starring Chow Yun Fat, Simon Yam Tat-wah, Bonnie Fu Yuk-ching, Ann Bridgewater, Anthony Wong Chau-sang, Frankie Chin
Directed by Ringo Lam

Drenched in feedback and octane, *Full Contact* revels in outrageous villains, antiheroes, and the hollow rattle of brass casings hitting the pavement. The film's multiethnic soundtrack sparks with crime glamour: psychedelic blues guitar threading together Cantorock, Yankeerock, and Thai Pop. Ace director Ringo Lam cranks up all the knobs to ten in this crime-action fuel-burner.

Full Contact opens with the robbery of an antique shop in Bangkok, Thailand. The robbers are a surreal bunch, led by Judge, an openly gay fashion plate and amateur magician whose colorful pocket-scarves conceal deadly weapons. Judge's

Rim Films

Chow Yun Fat, Hong Kong's leading leading man, looking good in this publicity still from Ringo Lam's film *Full Contact*.

THE SCENE

Not every HK film is a classic. Some have little to recommend them, in fact, *except* for one awe-inspiring bit of business: The Scene. Here are some of our favorites:

FATAL TERMINATION   1990

Paint-by-numbers bloodbath of corrupt customs inspectors smuggling things that go boom.

The Scene: Moon Lee's daughter—a polite eight-year-old—is kidnapped from ballet practice and held two feet out of a moving car window *by her hair.* The car careens down busy city streets as Moon jumps on the hood, then punches out the windshield. Multiple camera angles clearly show the little girl, dressed in a pink ballerina outfit, hanging inches off the speeding asphalt, legs flailing! Oncoming cars, trucks, and walls zoom past as Moon, still on the hood, punches out the passenger-side crook, grabs the driver's tie, and starts pulling him toward her. But he *speeds up,* trying to navi-

accomplices are the gum-chomping harlot Virgin (Bonnie Fu) and her muscleheaded pro-rassler-like beau, Deano (Frankie Chin). This over-the-top trio has barely finished terrorizing the staff, shooting up the local cops, and roaring off with the swag (in a twitch-perfect 64 Fairlane), before the opening credits roll over a funk-removing interpretative striptease by Mona (Ann Bridgewater).

Meanwhile, Mona's squeeze and fellow dance club employee, Jeff (played by Hong Kong's leading leading man, Chow Yun Fat), sets off to rescue their friend Sam (Anthony Wong) from the clutches of a local loan shark and his henchmen. Steel rings as Jeff thumps the thugs, then zooms off with Sam on his Honda-Davidson motorbike.

Discharging the sharks does not discharge the debt, however, so Sam arranges a joint heist with Jeff's troops and those of his cousin, Judge. But when the Jeff gang meets the Judge mob, a squabble brings out the Freudian rods. Jeff's hog-leg .45 dwarfs Judge's nickel-plated automatic, and a tense standoff ends when Judge unabashedly tells him: "Your eyes are so charming and attractive."

Judge's frustrated sexual energy must be sublimated by evildoing when he's contracted by the humiliated loan shark to double-cross Jeff during the robbery. The job—hijacking an arms-laden truck on a crowded Bangkok bridge—starts with Virgin furiously masturbating in Jeff's speeding car and concludes with a half-hearted betrayal, when Sam shoots Jeff through the chest after Judge traps him in a house whose occupants he has just shot and burned. Escaping with fewer friends and fingers, Jeff is slowly nursed back to health by monks at a Thai temple, who are also tending a weird, bug-eyed puppy.

Meanwhile, Sam is busy rising through the criminal ranks in Hong Kong, running guns for Judge and seducing Mona (both believe Jeff was killed in the robbery). When Jeff finally returns to HK and contacts them, this tangled trio struggle with their loyalties, alternately frail and tough.

Caught in the trap of gangster pride, Sam must bite off his leg and help Jeff gain his revenge. They steal Judge's arms cache and hold it for ransom. Negotiations disintegrate, and a "bulletcam" nightclub gunfight ensues—individual shots are followed through plate glass, hands, and necks. In the finale, Jeff puts an end to Judge's incessant flirting, climbs on his iron horse, and thunders off into the distance.

Hard-Boiled

1992
Starring Chow Yun Fat, Tony Leung Chiu-wai, Teresa Mo Shun-kwan, Anthony Wong Chau-sang, Philip Chan, Kuo Chui, Bowie Lam, Bobby Ah Yuen
Directed by John Woo

Hong Kong cinema is a deck full of action aces, but John Woo's *Hard-Boiled* is the trump. This tale of gunrunners, double agents, and innocents caught in between showcases several action sequences that suck your jaw to the floor. *Hard-Boiled* is Woo's most spectacular film and an absolute must-see; it will convert anybody to the HK cause.

Hard-Boiled (like another Woo masterpiece, *The Killer*—see chapter 2) revolves around an intense platonic relationship between two men in a violent world. Loyalty is all, superseding both law enforcement and criminal careers. Either way, you pack a gun and use it when necessary.

Hard-Boiled plainclothesman Tequila (Chow Yun Fat) moonlights as a clarinet player in a neon lounge. Tequila and his drummer, fellow cop Lionheart (Bowie Lam), go for an early morning dim sum in the Wyndham Teahouse, a Hong Kong landmark where customers bring along their own caged birds to sing tableside. In the large, crowded teahouse, gun-smuggling mobsters hide their gats in false-bottomed birdcages. Tequila blows their cover, and a trademark John Woo gun battle steeps the teeming teahouse

gate highway traffic while being choked to death.

The little girl bravely claws at the wild-eyed bearded *gwailo* holding her out of the back window as the guy riding shotgun comes to, climbs onto the hood through the busted windshield of the still-speeding vehicle, and starts beating up Moon. She eventually sends her attacker spinning into the curb with a good kick, then pulls the driver out of the window, and starts beating him up. The scene ends with the child unhurt; but try to pull off stunts like this in Hollywood, and they'd put you in jail.

LEGEND OF THE LIQUID SWORD
1993

Half-comedy, half-costume sliceplay with swordboy Chu traipsing around, flinging steel.

The Scene: Squadrons of monks run on a featureless plain. Those in white robes somersault and leap in unison as gray-garbed ones simply run. Trotting on the gray ones' *heads* are a quartet of white-robes bearing a golden Buddhist swastika fifteen feet across, which in turn supports a white tent

continued on next page

in the shape of a lotus blossom. The martial monks deposit the tent on a hillside, and its portals part to reveal Flowerless (Chingmy Yau), a beautiful woman dressed in white. She issues a challenge to Chu, and the two swordfight on the monks' backs, on the points of upturned spears, while surfing on flying swords, or just plain old flying through the air (their feet are not allowed to touch the ground). The duel ends in a draw as their swords entwine and twist like tinfoil.

BRAIN THEFT   1981

Whole brains aren't being stolen, just the pituitary glands, which means that some goodhearted but unlicensed doctor from the mainland is pilfering pituitaries in a tragically flawed attempt to create a growth hormone potion that will allow his dwarf son to lead a normal life.

The Scene: A mean nurse is the first suspect. She sneaks into the morgue, but not to carve brains out of the cadavers. Instead, she is a frustrated corpse warden, who

in flying slugs and birds. As Lionheart bites it, Tequila chases crooks by sliding sidesaddle down a banister—toothpick in mouth and automatics blazing. In the kitchen, he skids across a countertop and is powdered with flour; white-faced as a ghost, he terminates the villain with a squirting shot to the head.

As the web unfolds, we meet Tequila's apparent nemesis, Tony (played by Tony Leung, who is often called Tony "Hard Boiled" Leung because of his great performance). He's a flamboyant underworld killer working for the powerful Mr. Hoi. His trigger skills are coveted by Hoi's gunrunning rival, Johnny (Anthony Wong), who also covets Hoi's empire. Johnny's men assault Hoi's warehouse in a spectacular battle—slick, violent, and beautiful—with phalanxes of motorcycles, breathtaking tracking shots, and Johnny's top gun-

Airborne combatants (including Tony Leung [left] with the twin hand cannons) get after it in the brisk warehouse sequence from John Woo's *Hard-Boiled.*

man Mad Dog (Kuo Chui) greasing row after row of Hoi's men. Loser Hoi dies stoically, just as lone cop Tequila rappels down from the warehouse ceiling.

More rounds are uncapped as Tequila disassembles what remains of the assembled armies. It ends with Tony and Tequila exploring their psychic bond by pointing guns at each other's heads, but the crucial chamber—for once—is empty.

As it turns out, Tony is also a cop, but he has gone so far undercover that routine hits don't mean anything to him anymore. As the two cops gradually realize they're on the same side, they uncover Johnny's arsenal, stashed in the basement of a hospital. It's in this hospital where *Hard-Boiled* resolves itself.

The entire third act is a half-hour action sequence that dwarfs the offerings of most action movies in their entirety. The battle against Johnny and his legion of "killable dogs" assumes epic proportions as patients are used as pawns and bullets fly like horizontal sleet. Tequila and Tony battle the entire length of a hospital corridor together, step forward as elevator doors close behind them, enjoy a few moments of calm and conference, then start over on a different floor.

And, just when you think the stakes can't get any higher, Tequila and policewoman Teresa (comedienne Teresa Mo in a Betty-and-Veronica flip wig) have to move a nursery full of babies to safety. As cops and crooks die right and left, Tequila cradles a sanguine tyke named Saliva Sammy in one arm while his free hand cradles a warm pistol. Sticking cotton balls in Sammy's ears, Tequila blasts away and prepares to escape, but accidentally catches on fire. Fortunately, the child pees and douses the fire. The underground arsenal explodes, and fireballs blow through the hospital, but the babies are saved, the bad guy croaks, and the audience settles back with a loud "Whew."

Hard-Boiled is easily available, both subtitled and dubbed, even in video chains like Blockbuster or on laser disc as part of Voyager's outstanding Criterion Collection.

stands up a row of the stiff occupants, yells at them until they seem to obey her close-order-drill commands, bites one in the neck, and then, cackling, knocks them over like dominoes. When police suddenly burst in on her, the nurse dies of fright! This sets the brain theft investigation back to square one.

THE CAT 1992

Nutty film about a Blob-type oozing monster, a pair of aliens, and their killer cat.

The Scene: Earthlings release a feisty mongrel to harass the kitty. In a junkyard, the two animals engage in a startling how'd-they-do-that imitation kung fu match that blows away many human martial arts battles! No stop-motion critters here; these are real flesh-and-blood house pets doing nail-to-claw thrust and parry.

QUEEN'S HIGH 1990

Warring Hong Kong clans have too much gunpowder in their coffers.

The Scene: Cynthia Khan's wed-

continued on next page

Till death do us part. After gangsters kill Cynthia Khan's betrothed on her wedding day, she caters her own affair. From The Scene from Queen's High.

ding is crashed by white-suited gunmen who ventilate the wedding party. When her brother and husband-to-be get shot to pieces, she literally goes ballistic with discarded nine-millimeter ordnance:

It's Now or Never

1992
Starring Sharla Cheung Man, Rain Lau Yuk-tsui, Ng Man-tat, Alfred Cheung Hin-ling, Cynthia Khan
Directed by Louis Chan Kwok-hei

It's Now or Never opens in a furious blur. Roving packs of early-sixties teddygirls with big hairdos are out looking for boys and trouble. Soon you realize you're watching a shrewd black comedy whose gags are nasty enough to draw blood. Hong Kong comedies don't usually translate well, but this one, influenced by the films of John Waters, is a crackpot exception.

At a local dance, Chewing Gum (Pauline Chan) puts the moves on the boyfriend of Little Bun (martial arts diva Cynthia Khan). As distorto surf guitar rumbles, Little Bun's best pal—rose-tattooed Rose (Sharla Cheung)—brings in her she-wolves to bust heads. The rhubarb ends when the toughettes are carted off to the cop shop, where Rose finds her sister, fellow delinquent Tracy (Rain Lau), already in stir. When the girls' father, Wong Tat (Ng Man-tat), shows up to bail them out, he pulls a tearful "I try so hard with these kids" speech that has the whole station reaching for their hankies. All in a day's work for "Lady-Killer Tat," who's actually a low-rent gigolo!

The movie is a series of hilarious setups involving this dysfunctional Family Circus and their involvement in the underworld. Rose and Little Bun (who keeps bragging of her "deadly Eagle Claws," only to get her butt kicked repeatedly) get jobs at a cosmetics shop. They just want to shoplift and con the customers, but they're foiled by their police-madam nemesis. Revenge is extracted as Rose's gang rounds up a group of scummy men by promising a live nude show, then sneaks them into the policewoman's flat just as she emerges from the shower.

A bigger problem is Loan Shark Wong, who interrupts daddy Tat's for-profit tryst with a grotesque client to thump him over some unpaid debts. Rose has to enlist the services of Shing (Alfred

Cheung)—a nerdy cop who's fallen for her—to combat the underworld elements, seducing him in the bargain.

What makes *INON* so effective is the humor the film finds in potentially repellent situations. Its warm visual style—embracing beautiful sixties elements (white vinyl skirts and red leather Beatle boots, gleaming transistor radios and Jackie O flips)—butts up against unromanticized violence. Everyone is vengeful and manipulative, except for the mama's-boy copper.

Actor Ng Man-tat is at his scenery-chewing best as he schemes and schmoozes with the typically microscopic outlook of the petty criminal, gulping down aphrodisiacs as he lectures his daughters to venerate their Pa. Rain Lau tops even her over-the-top performance in *Queen of Temple Street* as the shoplifting, pill-pushing schoolgirl Tracy "Big Mouth" Wong. No Chinese-speaking abilities are needed to figure out that every piece of Cantoslang foaming outta Tracy's gob is irreverent and foul! And creamy-perfect Sharla Cheung is excellent as the trash-talking, goldbricking Rose.

Mr. Vampire

1985
Starring Lam Ching Ying, Chin Siu Ho, Moon Lee Choi-fung, Ricky Hui, Pauline Wong
Directed by Ricky Lau

*M*r. Vampire is first and foremost in a long line of Chinese vampire flicks. Our bloodsucking brothers from the East do not traipse about in capes flaunting Old World charm and seductively biting necks—although they do reside in coffins and have healthy incisors. Pale and blue? Heck yes, they're *dead!* Are they as stiff as boards? You bet, and since they can't walk, they *hop.* Well, how scary can a hopping ghost in a Ming Dynasty costume be? If you find one in your face—sniffing for your breath—you'll feel your short hairs stiffen! Funny? Absolutely. There is a fine line between

cut to slo-mo shots of *psychobride* in a long flowing gown—with a lovely corsage—feeding the unwanted guests hot lead.

ANGEL ENFORCERS   1990

Above-average policewomen kick-butt film starring tougher-than-leather Sharon Yeung.

The Scene: An unfortunate young woman is put in harm's way by a psycho villain. He perches her atop a cake of ice, which rests upon a heating coil. A web of taut monofilament lines are looped through to the pullrings of a dozen hand grenades he's attached to her dress. The result? A belief in reincarnation always helps.

ESCAPE FROM BROTHEL   1992

Tedious melodrama about two kindhearted HK hookers, one's inadvertently criminal boyfriend from the mainland, and the sad fate that awaits them all.

The Scene: Naked coed kung fu! Evil Billy Chow and tattooed Sophie Crawford are starting to get it on (she's nude, he's topless),

continued on next page

when in busts Crawford's husband and his crony. They demand money from Chow; instead he starts to thrash them.

Then Crawford's up off the bed and, with a *chi*-concentrating yell, lands a kick to Chow's midsection. She attacks in slo-mo (like Caine in the old TV series, *Kung Fu*) but he defends himself well, delivering a forearm shiver to her chest that sends her reeling backward and out of the scene.

After Chow violently mops up her husband and crony, Crawford returns, swinging from the top of a door frame and catching Chow around the neck with her legs. Upside down and hanging down his back, she grabs his crotch and squeezes. Chow endures long enough to fire a hold-breaking chop to *her* crotch. Crawford keeps fighting, but Chow subdues her, gets a gleam in his eye, and begins doing the nasty, when his beeper goes off!

continued on page 28

horror and humor, and *Mr. Vampire* does everything but jump rope with it.

The film is a series of farcical vignettes involving a Taoist *sifu* (Lam Ching Ying) and his two well-meaning but dorkacious students, Chou and Man Choi (Chin Siu Ho and Ricky Hui). The *sifu* gets a gig reburying wealthy Mr. Yam's father, and must store the freshly dug coffin overnight. Unfortunately, the corpse has become rather cranky during twenty years of burial without the proper *feng shui,* so he busts out, ignoring sacrificial black goats in favor of Yam Junior's throat. Young Yam turns blue and nasty, then kills a few locals. The Taoist is accused of the murders by the local constable, a loathsome bumpkin, but Yam's reanimated corpse proves an effective alibi. The student Man Choi is infected, and must eat, bathe in, and dance on sticky rice to be cured of creeping ghoulification.

The most interesting subplot involves a lovelorn ghost (Pauline Wong) who appears in the forest, riding in an ectoplastic sedan chair. Her theme song is a haunting childlike rhyme with fractured subtitular lyrics: "Her piercing look/Shining bright like the stars/Sure enough to make one chokes/The lady ghost looks for a lover/Who would take a bride so shady?"

Student Chou, that's who. She tempts him with wine and hickeys, then fights fiercely with the Taoist master, who attempts to intervene. After tossing her head from her shoulders and sending it flying toward the *sifu,* she eventually gives up when she realizes that "you two are from different worlds."

But as one goblin is vanquished, another hops onto the scene. Vampire Yam *père* has been lurking in a rat-infested cave, just waiting for the chance to return to his displaced coffin.

Mr. Vampire's appeal is based on its ability to place its characters in just enough danger to straddle the humor/horror balance beam. Ghouls come in various concentrations of evil. The possessed Man Choi never becomes more than a toothy nuisance while Master Vampire Yam takes no prisoners. Fortunately *sifu* has enough Taoist tricks up his loose yellow sleeves to take care of everybody's business.

Naked Killer

1993
Starring Chingmy Yau Suk-ching, Carrie Ng Kar-lai, Simon Yam Tat-wah, Svenwara Madoka, Kelly, Johnny Lo Hwei-kong
Directed by Clarence Ford (Fok Yiu-leung)

Naked Killer arches its back and spits at you for ninety minutes. Stylish, vaguely comprehensible, and entertaining as hell, it's the story of antiheroine Kitty (Chingmy Yau), a woman who really, *really* hates girlfriend-bullying cads. In fact, she grabs a pair of scissors and stabs one in the crotch (and he's her hairdresser, too)! As he screams "I lost one ball of mine!" she makes good her escape, only to be followed by police officer Tinam (Simon Yam). But his attempt to collar Kitty fails, because he vomits whenever he pulls his gun!

Plot shards pile up as Kitty first toys with the copper, then beds him, then falls for him—a bad career move for both. As Kitty explains it: "I'm a professional killer, and you're a cop . . . we have conflicts in our jobs."

Kitty's killer instinct is being developed by her mentor Sister Cindy (Svenwara Madoka), Hong Kong's Svengali of man-hating hitwomen. After much training, the pair takes a commission in Tokyo, which requires nightclub dancing, followed by creep decapitation by garrote.

Kitty's growing affection for Tinam not only softens her edge, but also arouses the jealous ire of Princess (Carrie Ng)—a lethal lesbian assassin with the hots for our heroine. Princess—once trained by Sister Cindy, but now operating as an independent contractor—has a flair for tossing her male victims across the room before blasting their privates to shreds. She is rent with a lust for Kitty that her own muffinbutt protégé, Baby (the vanilla-bean Japanese cutie, Kelly), cannot satisfy. Naturally, this causes friction between Princess and her former teacher—so Princess kills her.

Chingmy Yau flaunts her full-metal evening jacket in *Naked Killer*.

Rim Films

GHOSTS GALORE   1982

Created by a wizard, ghostbusting Buddy and his overweight buddy, Fat Chick, battle evil spirits in the days of yore.

The Scene: A young master is haunted at night by a sexy succubus. Confronted by our duo in the bedchamber, the succubus suddenly stitches together master's collection of naughty 8½" × 11" love position woodcuts into a two-dimensional man, who staggers toward Buddy and Fat Chick like an old sci-fi robot. During the battle, Fat Chick gets enthralled by its sutured sutras. The woodcuts suddenly arrange themselves into a flat wall of temptation, from which the succubus's arm emerges, lengthens across the room, and grabs Fat Chick, slowly pulling him toward certain damnation. Thinking fast, Buddy grabs a magic coin held in a red Jacob's ladder, aims, and fires. A blue blast from the coin sends the sex ghost up in a shriek of smoke.

Carrie Ng plays Princess with cigar-chomping, Harley-humpin', "Gimme-that!" focus, and it's impossible to take your eyes off her. Combat is conducted in the nostalgic format of 1960s secret-agent TV shows (especially Hong Kong's *Rose Noir*), with poisoned lipstick and flying ropes and darts, in masquerade masks and black spandex jumpsuits.

Beginner's Note: Top-shelf HK actresses usually refuse to shed blouse, whether the script calls for it or not, because they know that doing "Category III" (nudie) work puts them in a different category, and the stigma is nigh impossible to overcome. This fact helps explain that while there are the naked *and* killers in *Naked Killer,* the killers are not always naked. The lengths to which some killers go to disguise their nakedness is a silly and disappointing sidelight to this silly—but definitely not disappointing—movie.

The best place to enjoy *NK* is at a theatrical venue like San Francisco's charming Roxie Theater, soundtrack boom-booming and crowd a-howling over the way-loopy subtitles.

Pedicab Driver

1988
Starring Sammo Hung Kam-bo, Nina Li Chi, Sun Yueh, Benny Mok Siu-chung, Fennie Yuen Kit-ying, John Sham, Meng Hoi, Lowell Lo, Liu Chia-liang (Lau Kar-leung)
Directed by Sammo Hung Kam-bo

Sammo Hung's magnificent *Pedicab Driver* is—in many ways—a metaphor for Sammo's career. Sammo is kung fu star Jackie Chan's big brother (see chapters 6 and 10), and has directed or starred in some of HK's finest output, yet he languishes in relative obscurity when compared to his larger-nosed sibling. *Pedicab Driver*—a love story with barbed hooks and exquisite martial action—also remains largely undiscovered, even by HK film fanatics.

Set in postwar Macau (a Portuguese colony just a short ferry ride from HK proper), *PD* tells the story of a quartet of working-class Joes who transport people down Macau's narrow lanes in pedal-powered rickshaws known as pedicabs. Their leader is the stalwart Lo Tung (Sammo Hung), whose chums are Malted Candy (Benny Mok), Rice Pudding (Meng Hoi), and Shan Cha Cake (Lowell Lo.)

Tung lives in a grotty little room next to the local bakery, where the baker, Fang (Sun Yueh, from *City on Fire*), has his eye on plainly-styled-but-stunning Ping (Nina Li). Fang's heart is in the right place, but Ping can't take him seriously as a suitor. Nonetheless, he takes her to pick out a jade bracelet in town, where she's spotted by whoremaster Yu, aka Master 5. Yu is played with apocalyptic villainy by John Sham, who's better known for his light-hearted comedic roles. Master 5's slicked-back hair, gold-capped teeth, and self-centered amorality ooze menace as he comes on to Ping.

Tung shows up and inserts his heavyset, righteous self between the terrified woman and the odious pimp. Provoked, Master 5 hops in his car and chases Tung's pedicab, Ping clinging precariously to the seat. Tung escapes by crashing into a *mahjongg* parlor, but must atone for his table-wrecking entrance by dueling with the proprietor (Liu Chia-liang). The fight between these two masters—accelerating from fists to poles—is breathtaking, state-of-the-razor kung fu. Tung loses, but Liu is so impressed ("Fatty, I've fought with many men, but you're the only one who has scared me") that he lets them go.

Tung and Ping drift toward each other as Tung's fellow pedaler Malted Candy falls for comely youngster Hsiao Tsui (Fennie Yuen). A meal at a local noodle stall brings Shan Cha Cake and Hsiao Tsui face-to-face in a social setting. In a moment of horror, Shan reveals Tsui's secret: not only is she a brothel worker, but he patronized her the night before! Tsui stoically departs the resultant brouhaha, but Ping—who's been quiet and passive until now—

HOLY WEAPON 1993

Dopey all-star comedy with all your favorite stars wearing Ming Dynasty costumes and being silly.

The Scene: Sharla Cheung Man impersonates a famous courtesan, and her beauty causes a local pervert to salivate frantically: "I beg you to eat me right now!" She transforms into a giant half-spider/half-Sharla creature and binds him in an enormous web. Spinning a thread from her gorgeous mouth, she then binds his bodyguards and chops them to pieces with her razor-sharp legs. Then . . . he gets his wish.

THE SEDUCTION AFTER 1979

An unfortunate young woman is cursed and posthumously gives birth to an illegitimate demon that kills monks, housekeepers, blue bloods, and anyone else who gets in its path.

The Scene: A man with a troubling medical malady is seeking help at a foreboding monastery. While a dozen monks rhythmically chant, ring bells, and hit drums in an incense-filled hall, a mystic

continued on page 31

Jackie Chan gets steam-cleaned while hanging from a helicopter's rope ladder as it passes over a steam locomotive, in one of the many thrilling moments from *Police Story 3: Supercop*.

gets in the pedicab drivers' faces, reminding them that they are not the only ones exempt from life's circumstances, and that perhaps humility and compassion are more appropriate responses here. Malted Candy swallows his foolishness and makes amends.

News of Tsui's forthcoming nuptials reaches Master 5, whose apoplexy reaches a zenith upon contemplation of even a single soul escaping his grasp. He dispatches goons to chop up Malted Candy and Tsui on their wedding night. When Tung arrives—too late— he looks at his diminutive friend Rice Pudding and, *without a word,* they go out to seek revenge. At Master 5's opulent hideout, Tung must defeat head goon Billy Chow. The furious pedicab driver smashes most of the furniture, as well as Chow's head. When Master 5 takes that final southward elevator ride—aided by the sword-wielding Rice Pudding—the audience lets rip a hearty cheer.

Police Story 3: Supercop

1992
Starring Jackie Chan, Michelle Yeoh Chu-kheng, Maggie Cheung Man-yuk, Yuen Wah, Kenneth Tsang
Directed by Stanley Tong

*P*olice Story 3: Supercop presents Jackie Chan at the top of his game. As a Hong Kong cop chasing drug smugglers across Southeast Asia, his action partner is the capable and stunning Michelle Yeoh, whose appearance here marked a comeback from a lengthy film hiatus. Driven by a strong narrative and making the most of its striking locations, *Police Story 3: Supercop* propels the viewer with a watch-spring-tight plot and Jackie Chan's trademark: an assortment of ever-escalating, heart-halting stunts.

When a pair of Royal Hong Kong Police officers need a "supercop" to take down the heinous drug czar Chaibat (Kenneth Tsang), they choose the valorous Chen Chia-chu (Jackie). Telling his girlfriend May (Maggie Cheung) that he's going to Special Training Camp, he packs his bags for Guangzhou in mainland China. Once there, he's assigned to the command of Inspector Yang from Interpol (Michelle Yeoh). Yang enlists him in a scheme to spring Chiabat's henchman Panther (Yuen Wah) from a prison labor camp, a feat he accomplishes with derring-do. Panther is impressed and, after shooting the miscreant who landed him on the work farm, gives Jackie a job on his crook-squad. Prior to sailing for HK, they pay a visit to Chen's (nonexistent) family village in Fu Shan. The undercover HK cop is desperate, but he's saved by a family setup engineered by the mainland Chinese cops, who disguise Inspector Yang in pigtails, as his kid sister! The ruse works, but a visit to a Cantonese restaurant ends in a ruckus, as the cops attack the gang with stunguns. Yang proves her mettle by outfoxing both cops and crooks, and Chen takes her along to HK.

Once in Chaibat's lair, the undercover pair realizes just what picaroons they're dealing with as the bodies start to pile up: a bikinied *gwailo* OD's and a double-crossing associate is forcibly drowned in Chaibat's pool. A voyage to the Thai/Cambodian border introduces them to a Khun Sa–type druglord (Lo Lieh). But his poppy auction loses its civility when Chaibat becomes annoyed and bashes a rival's head in with a spiky durian fruit. "Shoot if you have the nerve!" yells a combatant. Everyone's nervy—and heavily armed. The scene erupts in a vicious vortex of violence as competing factions unload hollow-points by the drumload, blasting each other to shreds. Yang, whose bulletproof vest is filled with explosives (another trick by the treacherous Chaibat) must stay out of harm's way; Chen assists with grenade attacks and by serving as an impromptu gun tripod.

Having proven themselves in battle again, Chaibat enlists the duo in a plot to bust his wife out of a Kuala Lumpur jail. But when the gang runs into Chen's gal-pal May—whose job as a tour guide brings her to Kuala Lumpur—she inadvertently blows his cover. Panther and crew kidnap May and force Chen and Yang to carry

The Scene (*cont.*)

healer works his magic. With the man's worried family looking on, the healer solemnly rams long needles into his patient's fingertips. The man screams, and several full-grown frogs plop from his mouth. Working quickly, the healer trephines the back of the man's head and pulls out more live frogs. Head bandaged, the grateful man pays the monks and leaves the monastery in good spirits.

out the hazardous caper, which involves spring-ing the captive from a heavily guarded police van. Chen crashes a car filled with fake poison-gas canisters, and Yang leaps on the side of the speed-ing van as the two factions battle over their respective hostages. The climactic battle involves stunt after hair-raising stunt: Jackie dangles from a helicopter-borne ladder as he swings netless over the exotic Moorish architecture of Kuala Lumpur. Michelle hops on a dirt bike and drives it directly on top of a speeding freight train. Stunt outtakes roll under the closing credits (a Jackie Chan tradition; see chapter 5)—the takes they didn't use are scarier than the actual stunts!

Sex & Zen

1991
Starring Lawrence Ng, Amy Yip, Kent Chung, Mari Ayukawa, Isabella Chow, Lo Lieh, Elvis Tsui Kam-kong
Directed by Michael Mak

Filmgoers expecting staid tantric conjoinings and ethereal advice on meditation from this film adaptation of the seventeenth-century erotic clas-sic *The Carnal Prayer Mat* are in for a pleasant sur-prise. Director Michael Mak's romping *Sex & Zen* is pure Hong Kong hijinks, brimming with both formal, flowing period-piece atmosphere and sex-ual shenanigans of highly improbable postures.

Mei Yang (Lawrence Ng) is a socially promi-nent scholar married to a well-endowed heiress, Yuk Heung (Amy Yip). Despite the availability of the buxotic Yip (one of HK's most notorious soft-core starlets), Mei Yang is not satisfied. Peeping at the athletic ruttings of the large-and-charged silkmaker Kuen and his wife (Elvis Tsui and Mari Ayukawa), he bemoans his own less-than-enormous abilities.

With a scholar's logic, Mei Yang decides to change his lot by visiting a quack who promises to cure his size-complex through surgery. Mei Yang is sequestered in a barrel—its knothole affixed with a miniature guillotine—and submits to having his most precious part replaced with that of a horse. He is locally anesthetized, the guillotine falls, and the procedure begins.

Things quickly and comically spin akimbo as the exposed scholar watches from the barrel. The horse refuses to take *his* anesthesia. The quack spills numbing potion all over his hands and can't grip his instruments well. The quack's dog runs off with the scholar's original equipment. A thun-derstorm hits—the quack is scared of lightning! Terrified, the hapless quack flings the freshly sev-ered horse penis into the air. The camera follows it up, twirling end-over-end, then down, where it lands—Thunk!—in the agape mouth of Mei Yang's page. With time running out, the horse penis is rescued from the gagging page and trans-planted onto Mei Yang. *And it works.*

This outrageous sequence, which takes place during the first reel, sets a tone that is maintained throughout, as our horny scholar—equine mem-ber aloft—successfully pursues the varied objects of his lust. These interludes include a chastity-belt-busting session with Kuen's wife, who cot-

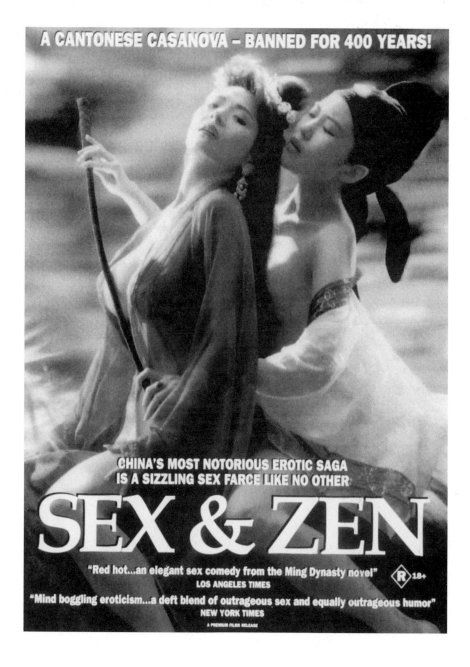

Rode hard and put away wet: Amy Yip and friend in *Sex & Zen.*

tons quickly to Mei Yang's newfound sensitivity, and an upside-down orgy with two restaurant hostesses. Things culminate in a nightmare fantasy sequence, in which Mei Yang must confront the karmic implications of his selfish and unnatural behavior and is led away to comfort the donor horse's better half. Meanwhile, the cuckolded silkmaker schemes a menial job at Mei Yang's court. He then evens the score with a rapacious hot tub coupling with Yuk Heung.

As an inevitable result of their wickedness, all the players eventually get what's coming to them. Yip Heung loses her social standing and ends up turning tricks in a brothel. And in the final scene, a sexually dissipated Mei Yang, resigned to life in a Buddhist monastery, meets and contritely embraces his nemesis Kuen, all lust and vengeance spent and forgotten.

Despite its cornucopia of cartoon couplings, and though some of its erotic particulars—multitongued licking-wheel toys, girl-girl flute manipulations, and Yuk Heung's unusual grip on her calligraphy brush—are played for laughs, *Sex & Zen* retains a high titillation quotient. The women (including a couple of imported Japanese starlets) are nubile, gorgeous, and far from shy. Its high production values and deft creation of mood will impress all.

John Woo

ohn Woo is best known for his unrivaled direction of tightly choreographed action sequences—gunfights of mythic proportions. These multivectored ballistic ballets are brought to life with extended tracking shots: gunmen cover the foreground as light fixtures explode from the left; opponents die in corners as more run in—guns blazing—from the right. The scenes are at once elegant, smooth, and extremely visceral. Fellow member of the *obliterati* Quentin Tarantino once said of Woo, "Yeah, he can direct an action scene, and Michelangelo could paint a ceiling."

Besides spectacular action, Woo's films showcase characters imbued with an audience-pleasing chivalry and spirituality out-of-step with the convenient relativism of the modern world. His central characters are men who experience platonic passion for one

Director John Woo poses with his favorite prop.

John Woo

another through bloody rites of passage (often a passage to the next life), in scenes so emotionally charged they rival the dramatic heights of grand opera. When Chow Yun Fat (Woo's signature lead actor) slowly swaps guns with his opponent at the bloody end of *A Better Tomorrow 2*, the pair is acknowledging that the heroic ritual of the duel is more important than either individual. Woo's heroes are unapologetic modern knights.

John Woo grew up in Hong Kong in the 60s, which he described as a terrific experience for a movie-lover. Rather than watching lousy television in cramped apartments, the young Woo spent his time at the local cinemas, taking in the best of the decade. In addition to first-run Hollywood product, Woo absorbed films from China, Europe, Taiwan, Japan, and, of course, Hong Kong. In HK's international setting, films by Jean-Pierre Melville or Akira Kurosawa were often as commercially successful as Hollywood offerings.

Woo started as an apprentice to the Shaw Brothers Studios' visceraphile director Chang Cheh (see chapter 12), before being promoted to assistant director in the early 70s. By the middle of the decade, he was directing comedies and kung fu films, including an early Jackie Chan film called *Hand of Death* (1975). Woo's skill at constructing humorous situations, honed in his early 80s comedies, would serve him well when he began to craft his intricately staged action material, notable for brief, unexpected sight gags.

Homages to (or imitations of) Woo's trademark action sequences have become part of the

Hollywood lexicon. It was only a matter of time until Woo was wooed by the eight-hundred-pound Tinseltown gorilla and, after the magnificent *Hard-Boiled* (1992), he signed with Fox Studios in Los Angeles. His first project, *Hard Target* (1993), starred Jean-Claude Van Damme—the "Muscles from Brussels." Woo ran into trouble with U.S. censors, who wanted to slap an "NC-17" rating on the film for violent content. Woo had to cut and recut the final version to obtain an "R" rating (a "director's cut" is available on video). In February of 1996, *Broken Arrow,* Woo's second Hollywood feature, opened as the number-one movie in the United States, doing $15.6 million at the box office in its first weekend. (After two weeks in the top spot, it was displaced by Jackie Chan's *Rumble in the Bronx*.)

Compared with most Hong Kong product, Woo's films are widely distributed in North America. Dubbed versions of *The Killer* and *Hard-Boiled* are available at chains like Blockbuster Video, and Voyager has released both films on laser disc as part of its Criterion Collection.

A Better Tomorrow

1986
Starring Ti Lung, Chow Yun Fat, Leslie Cheung Kwok-wing, Waise Lee Chi-hung, Emily Chu
Directed by John Woo

The defining urban thriller of 80s Hong Kong cinema, *A Better Tomorrow* is a raging torrent of blood, sweat, and tears. More than just a hyperstylish, emotionally overwhelming re-creation of Coppola's *The Godfather*, Peckinpah's *The Wild Bunch*, and your choice of Japanese *yakuza* (gangster) flicks, it's the film that put director John Woo and star Chow Yun Fat (HK's Scorsese and De Niro) on the map.

A Better Tomorrow's manic collection of masterfully designed shoot-outs set a new standard for Hong Kong cinema—and cinema in general. But these expertly timed showstoppers aren't simply mindless, lead-pumping gorefests, they're poignant moments of emotionally wrought male bonding, packed full of rapid-fire mood swings. Good-natured horseplay gives way to brooding nostalgia, followed by tear-drenched melodrama—and then a big fight scene.

Never before had the underworld life of the triads (Chinese gangster societies) been so lovingly rendered in scenes of slow-motion mythologizing and bullet-riddled elegizings (not to mention shrill sentimentality). The film's *gwailo*-friendly and grimly ironic title is suggestive of China's impending 1997 takeover, and underscores the film's timely sense of a nation speeding toward uncertainty.

Ho (Ti Lung) and Mark (Chow Yun Fat) are longtime buddies who've risen through the triad ranks to become suave and successful traffickers in counterfeit currency (Chow lights his cigarettes with a bogus C-note). Ho's younger brother Kit (Leslie Cheung), a trainee at the police academy, is unaware of his elder sibling's underworld connections when Ho departs for Taiwan in the company of the inexperienced Shing (Waise Lee) to bring off a "last big score." Inevitably, a convoluted double cross takes shape, forcing Ho to surrender to the Taiwanese cops in order to spare young Shing. Meanwhile, back in HK, a hitman—in a tragic and tightly choreographed episode—murders Ho and Kit's father, despite Kit's best efforts to stop him.

Mark is determined to avenge Ho's misfortune and—in the film's most famous and much-parodied set piece—he sashays into a posh restaurant with a babe on his arm (in slow motion, of course), stashing a small arsenal in a row of potted plants. After bursting in on the collection of do-bad diners and serving them an assortment of lead aperitifs, Mark beats a patient retreat, collecting his potted hardware and continuing to off his adversaries—but not before taking a pair of crippling slugs in his shin and knee.

Three years pass. While Ho has been biding his time in prison, Kit's rise through the ranks of the Criminal Investigation Department is flattened against a glass ceiling due to his brother's notoriety. Mark, now hobbled, has fallen into despair: he earns a meager wage wiping windows and opening doors for Shing, who has become a crime boss, thanks to Ho's sacrifice. Upon his release, Ho attempts to reconcile with Kit, who wants nothing to do with the older brother he believes brought about their father's death.

Determined to go straight, Ho becomes a taxi driver. But when his resistance to Shing's invitations to rejoin the gang result in Kit being shot and Mark being beaten, he risks everything to restore Mark to his trench-coated, two-fisted glory, reunite with the hard-headed Kit, and take his revenge against the smirking Shing—all in a whirlwind of flying bodies and fatal head wounds, backed by a ham-bone strings-and-harmonica soundtrack that will haunt you for days to come.

—CS

Ti Lung (left), Chow Yun Fat, and Dean Shek (right), armed to the gills, arrive at the big party uninvited to begin the end of *A Better Tomorrow 2*. Then everybody dies.

A Better Tomorrow 2

1988
Starring Chow Yun Fat, Ti Lung, Leslie Cheung Kwok-wing, Dean Shek
Directed by John Woo

Determined to cash in on the original's success, the sequel is gorged with Woo's trademarks: slow-motion sentiment, high-caliber chivalry, distracted misogyny, and entertaining excessiveness. If *ABT* set new standards for the intertwining of ultraviolence and evanescent nostalgia, *ABT2* expands the parameters to include self-congratulation. Less a continuation of *ABT*'s narrative than a funhouse exaggeration of its central motifs, *ABT2* mourns its own passing—making history on its way to the wax museum.

In *ABT2*, Chow Yun Fat confirms his position in the pantheon of big-screen stars. Decked out with gangster shades, a well-groomed bowl-cut, and his trademark matchstick jammed into the corner of his grimacelike grin, his nonstop affability seems as equally well-suited to exuberant high-fiving as to stoic deep-sixing: at times it seems likely Chow will simply smirk his opponents to death. Woo transforms him from rustic bumpkin into bullet-dispensing badass through a series of highly theatrical sight gags, the best of which finds Chow sliding headfirst down a staircase on his back while emptying a pair of automatics into his legion of pursuers. At one point, Chow pauses in his goofy, moony stylishness to deliver a brief lesson in tough-guy flair to the uptight Kit (Cheung): "You must learn," he explains, "to act with panache."

With Mark dead and Ho behind bars, Kit is determined to build his career as a detective. When Ho refuses an offer of probation to assist the authorities in their investigation of his former mentor, shipping magnate Lung (a nattily goateed Dean Shek), Kit ignores his home-life (his wife Jackie is pregnant) and goes undercover to romance Lung's daughter, Peggy. Now reformed Lung is being pressured by counterfeiters who want to use his shipyard. When Ho learns that Kit has become involved in the investigation, he agrees to an early release to protect his hotheaded and vulnerable younger brother. No sooner is Ho out than Lung finds himself framed for a gangland hit. Forced to flee to New York, Lung leaves Peggy in Kit's care; she is promptly murdered.

While Ho remains in HK, Lung begins to disintegrate in New York, landing in a padded cell. Fortunately, Mark's identical twin brother (!) Ken (Chow again), a Chinatown restaurateur, manages to tough-love him back to stability—during a series of shoot-outs, natch—and the pair return to HK. In the meantime, Ho has gone undercover to join forces with Lung's betrayer, Ko, who impels Ho to shoot Kit as a test of his fealty. (Kit, of course, miraculously recovers.)

Reunited, Ho, Lung, Ken, and Kit band together to bring down Ko. While Ho, Lung, and Ken plan their strategy, Kit—ever the hard-head—goes solo to infiltrate Ko's headquarters. It's there—in a sequence that confirms Woo's penchant for unwitting misogyny and over-the-edge pathos—that Kit meets his destiny: blown away by a ruthless assassin while his wife, Jackie, in a series of intercuts, gives birth to their child at a hospital across town.

At last primed for a final showdown, Woo's remaining heroes don their *Reservoir Dogs* costumes—white shirts, black suits, and thin ties, with Ken wearing Mark's bullet-riddled trench coat—and head off to Ko's mansion. Hundreds of bodies, tankers of blood, rocket launchers, samurai swords, battle-axes, flying heroes, and flailing flunkies all fill the screen in an orgy of killing that may never be surpassed. Gore-smeared and corpse-clogged, our heroes meet an uncertain end in this cartoon charnel house where nothing—save a visual reference to *Taxi Driver*'s demure-by-comparison climax—can escape. Panache? Aplenty.

—CS

Bullet in the Head

1990
Starring Jacky Cheung Hak-yow, Tony Leung Chiu-wai, Waise
Lee Chi-hung, Simon Yam Tat-wah, Fennie Yuen Kit-ying,
Yolinda Yam
Directed by John Woo

No one who sees John Woo's most intense film, *Bullet in the Head*, can remain neutral: you either love it or you hate it. This epic remains Woo's personal favorite, the inspiration for which he drew from 1989's Tiananmen Square massacre.

Set in 1967, *BITH* tells the story of lifelong friends Paul (Waise Lee), Ben (Tony Leung), and Frank (Jacky Cheung). The financially ambitious Paul suggests that the trio go to war-torn Vietnam for quick-money opportunities. Ben, who is initially hesitant about leaving, changes his mind after his wedding to Jane (Fennie Yuen) is marred by a fight in which he and Frank take revenge against a thug named Ringo. Ringo dies, and the trio decides to leave HK for Nam until things cool off. Their associate, Mr. Shing, gives them a suitcase of penicillin and Rolexes for a Mr. Leong, who runs the Bolero nightclub in Saigon. Jane bids goodbye to Ben amid the chaos of the 1967 HK border riots.

Once in Saigon, the three receive their first look down the muzzle-end of frontier capitalism when their taxi is blown up by a Vietcong

Waise Lee puts blood money ahead of his blood brothers in *Bullet in the Head.*

bomber. Our boys are put in an on-the-spot suspect lineup by the local authorities, tasting pavement and fear. The real perp is discovered and summarily executed, so they are free to go to the Bolero nightclub to meet Leong. The musketeers meet their D'Artagnan in Luke (Simon Yam), a Eurasian hit man working for Leong.

In *BITH*'s most exhilarating gunfight (a classic Woo-choreographed slugfest), the trio joins forces with Luke to unseat Leong and free the drug-addicted torch singer Sally (Yolinda Yam). Using pistols, submachine guns, shotguns, knives, and explosive Havana cigars, they fight off Leong's minions, kneecap the nightclub owner, and abscond with Sally—and a heavy crate of gold.

While Ben and Frank are most concerned with Sally's welfare—she took a round during the firefight—Paul is obsessed with the gold, which becomes an albatross around their necks. Arguments escalate and relationships fray until the boys are pointing their guns at each other's heads. Sally dies of her wound, and the trio is captured by the Vietcong, who find an envelope with CIA-surveillance photos hidden among the gold leaves.

The film becomes extremely harrowing at this point, as the VC force Frank to shoot his fellow prisoners in the head. When Frank becomes unhinged by the horror, Ben takes over to spare his friend, machine-gunning the bound and pleading captives.

As in *The Deer Hunter*, the guns are turned on the VC, and the three escape with the help of Luke and the U.S. Air Cavalry. Frank is seriously wounded with a gunshot to his skull, in a sequence that must be seen rather than described. Brutally intense, this film is not easily forgotten.

The Killer

1989
Starring Chow Yun Fat, Danny Lee Sau-yin, Sally Yeh
Directed by John Woo

The Killer has done more to spark interest in Hong Kong cinema in the West than any film since *Five Fingers of Death*. It's easy to see why. *The Killer* is a stylish, heartfelt action film, made by a wonderfully skilled director whose celluloid paradigm is informed by everything from French New Wave to Japanese gangster classics. Woo cited Martin Scorsese as a major influence on his style, and it shows. But Woo is no mere imitation of Scorsese; his style is rich, well-balanced, and decidedly his own.

The film begins and ends in a Christian church somewhere on the outskirts of town. Here we meet Jeff, a professional assassin played by Woo's favorite leading man, Chow Yun Fat. During a messy gun battle in a nightclub, Jeff accidentally blinds a pretty young singer named Jennie (Sally Yeh). Remorseful over the incident, Jeff decides to give up killing. After one last hit—to help pay for a cornea operation for Jennie—he's going straight.

Of course, the job goes awry, and Jeff finds himself pursued by Inspector Li (Danny Lee), a

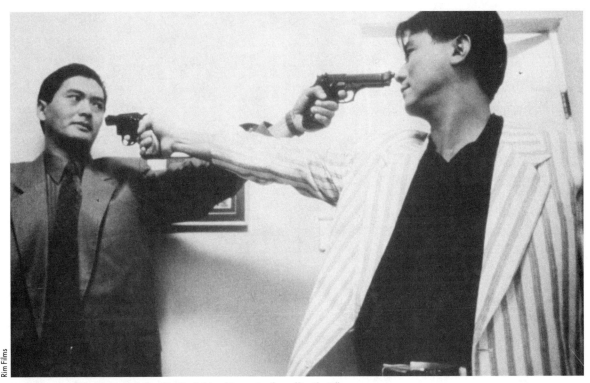

Cordite-based male-bonding ritual: Chow Yun Fat (left) and Danny Lee face off in *The Killer*.

clever and doggedly determined police detective. To make matters worse, Johnny Weng—the gangster who hired Jeff—would rather kill him than pay him. Eventually, Jeff and Li learn to trust and respect each other.

The Killer is best known for the scene in which Jeff and Inspector Li are pointing guns at each other while convincing the blinded Jennie that they are old friends. Unbelievably, Woo says he drew his inspiration for this scene from *Mad* magazine's "Spy vs. Spy" series!

The policeman and the hit man find themselves in the same camp, fighting off Weng's henchmen in an over-the-top shoot-out that takes place in the church. This lengthy, climactic battle takes place against a ritualistic backdrop of flying doves and burning candelabras—cordite gone gothic.

Like other examples of HK films during the late 80s, *The Killer* has a bleak view of the changing face of Hong Kong. Fear over mainland China's takeover of Hong Kong in 1997 and

CHOW YUN FAT

Rim Films

The coolest actor in the world: Chow Yun Fat slides down the banister, guns blazing, in the teahouse sequence of John Woo's *Hard-Boiled.*

*I*n repose, Chow's casual magnetism recalls the glory days of Robert Mitchum, Steve McQueen, or Ken Takakura—great movie actors who can rivet your attention while seeming to do almost nothing. And when he's stepping high, Chow is a unique, ebullient star-presence, a man who embraces life so unselfconsciously that he becomes vulnerable to all kinds of suffering and heartache.

—David Chute, *Film Comment*

*T*he coolest actor in the world.

—R. J. Smith, *Los Angeles Times*

*C*how Yun Fat began his acting career on Hong Kong television in the mid-70s, debuting in 1976 as the young hunk on a prime-time soap called *Hotel.* He became even more popular when he played a white-suited crime boss in the 1980 series *Shanghai Bund,* which was a huge hit all over Asia.

But when John Woo's *A Better Tomorrow* hit, Chow vaulted to superstardom. Hong Kong went mad when it opened in the summer of 1986, and *the* fashion statement in those hot and humid months was a long, heavy coat identical to that worn by Chow Yun Fat's character, Mark. Despite the discomfort, every fashionable young man donned a "Mark Coat," as they were known, and the colony bristled with Chow Yun Fat wannabes.

Although Chow Yun Fat is best known for his partnership with Woo, he's a prolific and versatile actor with dozens of films under his belt. Chow's contribution to director Ringo Lam's body of work is substantial (see chapter 8), and he's also played romantic leads, heroic buffoons, and even a retarded gambling king!

Should you wish to join the Chow Yun Fat fan club, here's the info:

Chow Yun Fat International
   Friends Club, Ltd.
P.O. Box 71288
Kowloon Central
Hong Kong

dismay at the increasingly amoral behavior of the triads are briefly touched upon. "We're outmoded characters," complains Jeff's fellow assassin. "We're outcasts." It is a sentiment this film shares with Peckinpah's *The Wild Bunch*, another masterpiece of violence.

Chow Yun Fat's portrayal of Jeff is charismatic and compelling. Danny Lee, who often winds up playing a cop, does an excellent job as Inspector Li. *The Killer* is an extremely powerful film melding operatic melodrama with bullet hailstorms. Required viewing.

—JM

Once a Thief

1991
Starring Chow Yun Fat, Cherie Chung Chor-hung, Leslie Cheung Kwok-wing, Kenneth Tsang, Declan Michael Wong
Directed by John Woo

Hollywood studios gear up for the Christmas season with a fruit basket of family-oriented product. The holiday cornucopia runneth over with cute-kid movies, big-stupid-dog movies, jerk-brain-comedy movies; whatever it takes to put an entire family's bottoms on cinema seats. In Asia, the big kahuna of holiday seasons is the Lunar New Year—commonly known as "Chinese New Year." This two-week festival usually occurs in February. Businesses shut down, kids get out of school, and families engage in traditional activities, including—naturally—moviegoing en masse.

This is why the John Woo film sandwiched between *Bullet in the Head* and *Hard-Boiled* is, in fact, a romantic action-comedy. The film was made for release during the New Year, and while there are some finely crafted action sequences, *OAT* is not *The Killer*. This may come as a shock to bullet junkies, but *Once a Thief* is not really out of character for John Woo, whose comedic directorial efforts include *Laughing Times* and *To Hell With the Devil*. If you have half as much fun watching this high-glamour, high crimes/no misdemeanors flick as the stars obviously had making it, your time will be well spent.

Shot largely in Paris, the film revolves around three HK art thieves and their romantic links, which, according to Woo, were inspired by *Casablanca*—with a nod to Truffaut's *Jules and Jim*. In James Bond–caper style, the trio steals a valuable painting out of a moving truck. As they celebrate, it's clear that Joe (Chow Yun Fat) and Cherie (Cherie Chung) are lovers while Jim (Leslie Cheung) is the beloved third wheel.

Another heist takes them to a Gothic castle, where Joe and Jim dress in secret-agent black turtlenecks to steal a valuable portrait. They dodge laser-activated alarms, but end up tangling with security on the outside. Weaponry is unpacked. Then a series of terrific car stunts ensues (orchestrated by French motorhead Remy Julien) that culminates with Joe crashing headlong into a speedboat full of shooters. Believing him dead, Jim and Cherie head back to HK and—eventually—drift together romantically.

Cherie Chung (left), Leslie Cheung, and Chow Yun Fat (right) motor through Paris in *Once A Thief*. John Woo's recent Hollywood success has emboldened Fox Television to remake *Once a Thief* for the U.S. small screen. Directed by Woo, this will serve as a two-hour pilot for what may become a weekly one-hour program starring Sandrine Holt (*Black Robe*), Ivan Sergei (*Dangerous Minds*), and Nicholas Lea (*The X-Files*).

Two years later, Joe (allegedly legless, yet cheerful) shows up in a wheelchair, and the three are reunited. He feuds with the trio's scheming adoptive father (Kenneth Tsang), however, and conspires with Jim to blow a high-tech safe and relarcenate the portrait, in order to sell it back to Dad. As paternal duplicity rears its ugly head, Joe (who by now has shed the wheelchair ruse) and Jim retaliate.

John Woo displays a lucid sense of humor by lampooning his own choreographed mayhem, as well as Bruce Lee "duck-call" kung fu, martial polefighting, and whatever gimmicks might send the New Year crowds into uproarious frothing fits. The final villain here is professional magician Declan Michael Wong, who duels with Joe using a deck of razor-sharp playing cards and bursts of fire! You might guess that there's a happy ending, and you'd be right about that.

To Hell With the Devil

1982
Starring Ricky Hui, Fung Shiu Fan, Paul Chiang
Directed by John Woo

As director John Woo's popularity in the West increases, it is certain that many of his earlier films will start showing up at your local video stores. Even if you are a diehard fan of Woo's bloody epics, you should approach *THWTD* with caution. You may find this film either astounding, disappointing . . . or both.

Loosely based on Dudley Moore and Peter Cook's Faustian send-up *Bedazzled*, *To Hell With the Devil* is a comedy about a lonely nebbish (Ricky Hui) who sells his soul to an agent of the devil to get the girl of his dreams. Added to the mix is a drunken priest (Paul Chiang), who is sent by God to rescue the poor slob's soul. Woo—no slouch when it comes to movie lore—also throws in references to *Gone With the Wind*, *The Exorcist*, and *Close Encounters of the Third Kind*, plus *Horror of Dracula!*

Flit—the devil's assistant—and the priest meet briefly and challenge each other on their way to their prospective hereafters. Woo's cosmos is based on boilerplate Christian stereotypes: heaven is up in the clouds, where everyone wears white robes and halos; hell is filled with fire and brimstone. God looks like Hal Holbrook doing Mark Twain while Satan resembles a cross between Jim Carrey and Max Schreck's Nosferatu.

When the action returns to Earth, things slow down as we watch the poor soul (who has the unfortunate moniker of Bruce Lee) suffer one misfortune after another. Fed up with life, Bruce is an easy target for Flit's offer to buy his soul. In a scene that is a direct rip-off of *Bedazzled*, Bruce's first attempt at happiness turns him into a successful pop star. But when the chump realizes the cruelty and selfishness of the devil's vision, he becomes sympathetic to the priest's entreaties. Bruce tries to cancel the contract, setting the stage for the final pyrotechnics.

The priest locks eyeballs with Flit, and the fiend's energy bolts turn the prelate into a bug-eyed mutant with laser beams shooting out of his bulbous blind eyes. Bruce, under attack by emissaries of Old Scratch, hurriedly straps the priest onto a hospital gurney and fights back, wheeling the priest back and forth while whacking his head. This causes blasts of energy to fire from the priest's eyes at Flit, who in turn clones himself, all the while moving forward in rigid geometric patterns. The imitation of "Space Invaders" is complete when a video game scorecard appears on the bottom of the screen!

To Hell With the Devil's strongest resemblance to Woo's other films is in the friendship/hatred dynamic between the good priest and the evil Flit. Woo's concerns with Christianity and redemption are in evidence here, but in the strangest forms they have ever taken.

—JM

Nail-Polished Fists

3

ong Kong cinema may be the only place in the world where men and women fight as equals. Not yammering over domicile hygiene or remote-control control, but toe-to-toe you-bust-my-nose-and-I'll-bust-yours pugilism.

The first time you see this sort of cinematic fury from the fairer sex, initial disbelief quickly gives way to wide-eyed adulation. Your first gasp comes as a burly male opponent punches our heroine in the stomach; the second comes as she immediately lands three quick return blows on the brute, then kicks him in the head, sending him sprawling. Those gentlemen whose nascent longings were fueled by *The Avengers'* Diana Rigg in backzip-kitten leather splendor will be left slack-jawed at the sight of Moon Lee or Yukari Oshima being all lightning-quick and unapologetic. We still are.

Despite what you may have read in picture-less film journals, there is no modern cryptofeminist dialectic responsible for the phenomenon of female fighters in the Hong Kong cinema. China has a tradition of women warriors stretching back fifty centuries or so. Sigourney Weaver said that she drew on these legends for inspiration when gearing up to fight the hideous critters in *Aliens*.

But while action roles in Weaver's Hollywood seem limited to male underwear models or grim-faced blockheads toting golf-bag-sized automatic weapons, revenge is unrestricted by gender in Hong Kong. In films like *Princess Madam*, *Satin Steel*, or *She Shoots Straight*, women are both protagonist and antagonist while men are relegated to peripheral roles—ineffectual simps or "any-minute-now" pistol targets. Fury carries a designer handbag, and knocking about its bottom is a .38 snub.

Davian International, Mike Leeder

In this lobby card from *Black Cat*, Jade Leung, after infiltrating a Japanese hot spring resort, turns a Yakuza kingpin into steamy sashimi.

Black Cat

1990
Starring Jade Leung, Simon Yam Tat-wah, Thomas Lam
Directed by Stephen Shin

A virtual shot-by-shot remake of Luc Besson's *La Femme Nikita*, which was also remade by Hollywood as *Point of No Return*. Of the three, the HK version hits the target hardest. Newcomer Jade Leung's shuddering, animalistic performance as the Pygmalion hit lady makes her American and French counterparts look like Avon salesladies.

The film opens in the States, with spitfire Catherine dispatching a few slobbering *gwailos*, then plugging a cop for good measure. Hauled off to jail, she takes a beating from a porky lesbian guard and enters a state of bruised madness, grabbing the guard's nightstick and raining hell down upon her. The cops turn a firehose on Catherine to cool her off. She uses a bathroom break to slip her cuffs and brain a mysterious assailant with a toilet tank's top. Swiping his gun, she blasts her way out of the cop shop, but is "killed" by a second mysterious assailant.

These mystery guys are in the employ of an equally mysterious CIA-like agency headed by a suave Chinese guy named Brian (Simon Yam).

Brian tells Catherine, "Now you're not a patient, but a dead," and proceeds to train her as a clandestine assassin. A microchip known as "Black Cat" is implanted in her head. Loads of high-tech bahooha (computerized treadmills and EKG simulations) are used to turn Catherine's raw aggression into politically useful controlled lethality. She's even taught to speak German!

Black Cat's first hit occurs when Brian drives her to the countryside to kill the bride at a Jewish wedding (the filmmakers never bother trying to explain *why* the targets need killing). She shoots the bride, the best man, even the caterer . . . as members of the wedding party chase after her (more Uzis here than at most weddings). Despite an intentionally ineffective getaway plan, Catherine eludes her pursuers and passes the last of Brian's tests.

The next assignment takes her to HK, to kill the director of the World Wildlife Fund with a mythic bullet made of ice. She pulls off this improbable stunt, but is photographed by Allen Yeung (Thomas Lam), a local bird lover. Being thorough, she goes to his house to eliminate him, but is touched by his soulful harmonica playing, and falls in love with him instead.

Of course, being close to Catherine is hazardous; a chance encounter with an old friend leads to a natural-gas explosion that terminates the friend! Then, on a business trip to Japan, Allen insists on prying into Catherine's affairs, leading to a violent confrontation with the local cops. The Japanese police are no match for Brian, who shows up to rescue Catherine and take out the meddlesome Allen. Black Cat, meanwhile, lives to kill again.

The Heroic Trio

1992
Starring Michelle Yeoh Chu-kheng, Anita Mui Yim-fong, Maggie Cheung Man-yuk, Damian Lau, Anthony Wong Chau-sang
Directed by Johnny To and Ching Siu-tung

The Heroic Trio is an outrageously uninhibited action movie, and an engaging showcase for three of HK's most talented actresses. Each adds a surprising amount of emotional depth to this film's cartoonish landscape and frequently loony occurrences.

Anita Mui portrays a famous masked superheroine known as "Wonder Woman," who battles the forces of evil when she's not playing subservient housewife to her naive police captain hubby. The city is panicked: someone is stealing male babies, and the cops are stymied by the kidnapper's veil of invisibility. Even Wonder Woman is unable to apprehend the culprit, who is soon revealed to be a beautiful but deadly female named San (Michelle Yeoh). San is following the orders of an evil centuries-old Ming Dynasty eunuch, who is trying to reclaim China's past glory by bringing forth a new emperor from his ever-growing stable of babies.

Enter Chat (Maggie Cheung), a sexy leather-and-lingerie motorbiker, mercenary, and Jill-of-all-trades. She was once a disciple of the

underground-dwelling eunuch, before escaping to a freer and more profitable existence in the above world. Aware of the eunuch's nefarious plans, the reckless Chat dares to reinvade the creature's subterranean turf, thus setting off a wild chain of events that will bring her together with San and Wonder Woman in a life-and-death struggle against both the eunuch and one another.

Some see *The Heroic Trio* as a thinly veiled allegory of a divided China, with the three heroines representing Hong Kong, Taiwan, and the mainland. Yeah, maybe. But even if it isn't, it *is* a delirious comic book fantasy that seems to invent itself as it moves along. Director Ching Siu-tung (*A Chinese Ghost Story*) creates a kinetic combination of campy sci-fi and graceful martial arts: One sequence captures a motorcycle spinning through the air like a top—with its riders still aboard!

The lead actresses remain admirably straight-faced throughout the bizarre spectacle, making their characters' own personal dilemmas wholly believable amidst unbelievable circumstances. Steeped in graphic scenes of childhood trauma and even cannibalism, *The Heroic Trio* is the perfect antidote for those disillusioned by the uninspired or overly tongue-in-cheek fare offered by recent American action cinema.

—RAA

Wonder Woman (Anita Mui) wants to find out who stole all those male babies in *Heroic Trio*.

In the Line of Duty 3

1988
Starring Cynthia Khan, Michiko Nishiwaki, Hiroshi Fujioka, Stuart Ong, Melvin Wong, Sandra Ng, Dick Wei
Directed by Brandy Yuen and Arthur Wong

After action star Michelle Khan (now known as Michelle Yeoh) made three features for D&B Films, she married her boss—Hong Kong tycoon Dickson Poon. The "D" of D&B forbade his new bride the rigors of action filmmaking and cast pixie-faced whirl-wind Cynthia Khan as her replacement. With Michelle's *Royal Warriors* and *Yes, Madam!* considered the first two installments of the *ITLOD* series, Cynthia debuted in number three—with a bullet.

ITLOD3 opens with Rachel (Cynthia Khan) dressed in navy blue HK policewoman-drag, issuing parking tickets. Despite a dramatic, skirt-ripping apprehension of a purse snatcher, she's stuck with her cop-bureaucrat uncle's department of bunglers: a gang of dunderheads trying to increase arrest quotas without getting hurt. The grind of HK police work bores Rachel, who craves action.

Meanwhile in Japan, a couple of crooks—Nishiwaki (Michiko Nishiwaki) and Nakamura (Stuart Ong)—are raising funds for their Japanese Red Brigade arms-gathering activities by knocking off a gala gem exhibition. They kill a few people, including a Japanese cop named Ken, whose partner (Hiroshi Fujioka) vows revenge on the ultrafashionable (dark suits and shades) crime duo. Fujioka resembles a Japanese *animé* character grafted onto Columbo. He resigns his commission and follows the villainous pair to HK, where they're pursuing the foppish jewelry maker Yamamoto in order to punish him for foisting fake gems on them in the arranged robbery.

Fujioka's task is complicated by the buttheaded cops, who handcuff him to a Volkswagen bumper while Yamamoto is past-tensed via Nishiwaki's Uzi. The bumper comes off (but the cuffs remain) as the Japanese cop pursues Nakamura to a shipyard. There

David Chute

The lovely Miss Joyce Godenzi models the flat-black, 7.62-millimeter belt-fed M-60 machine gun. From *Eastern Condors*.

CYNTHIA KHAN

Cute as a bug's ear. Usually found in prosaic jeans and tennies, the pastel Benetton look. Yet this ex-ballerina is one of the most ferocious female fighters in Hong Kong cinema, well-versed in delivering innard-altering kicks to the torsos of hapless thugs. No truth to the rumor that she and Michelle Yeoh (also known as Michelle Khan) are sisters!

Selected Filmography
In the Line of Duty 3 (1988)
In the Line of Duty 4 (1989)
In the Line of Duty 5 (1990)
Sea Wolves (1990)

they duel with pickaxes, lead pipes, pieces of ship, furniture, and flesh-chunkin' gaffs.

Nakamura is set afire but is bandaged by paramedics, only to be stolen directly out of the ambulance by Nishiwaki and her HK accomplice. Nakamura is punctured by bullets from the pursuing HK cops. He vengefully urges Nishiwaki to extract blood, and he slips out of the getaway vehicle, only to be pulped under Rachel's wheels. Fortunately, revenge is unrestricted by gender in Hong Kong cinema. As the smoldering Japanese ex-terrorist obsessively snaps the action on her .45, she murmurs, "I must kill that policewoman." The result is an end battle (conducted in industrial warehouse ambiance) pitting the desperate Rachel against the cucumber-cool, sledgehammer-swinging Nishiwaki, exhibiting a hatred in her heart that only fire can cleanse.

In the Line of Duty 4

1989
Starring Cynthia Khan, Donnie Yen Chi-tan, Yuen Yat Chor, Michael Wong Man-tuk, Michael Woods
Directed by Yuen Woo Ping

The fast and furious fourth installment of the *ITLOD* series is about raw aggression, extended brawling, and kicking one's opponent's guns into the ocean. Jam-packed with *gwailo* talent, *ITLOD4* opens with a shot of the Seattle Space Needle.

The unwitting protagonist here is a Seattle dock worker named Luk Wan Ting (Yuen Yat Chor). Luk has just become a resident alien after seven years of illegal status in the United States and wants to live his simple existence as another hardworking overseas-Chinese-regular-guy in the first-generation melting pot. But like

Cary Grant in *North by Northwest*, he is caught in someone else's dangerous web of deceptions.

Cynthia Khan appears as a Hong Kong policewoman, assisting American law enforcement officers (Donnie Yen and Michael Wong) bust international dope dealers. Luk witnesses the bloody result of a deal-gone-bad, and he's suspected of possessing a crucial film negative. This Hitchcock-style MacGuffin makes him a hot property for John Law and crooks alike.

Luk is collared by Donnie, but escapes from the Seattle cop shop by knocking out a protagonist and putting on his uniform (why this nondescript guy possesses great martial arts skills is unexplained). They're after him again upon his return to his apartment, and his buddy Ming is killed as Luk escapes. Trading his hard-won green card for ship's passage, Luk sadly sets off for Hong Kong—trailed by his growing entourage, who fly over on nice Cathay Pacific jets. There they pick up where they left off: hothead Donnie, cool-hearted Cynthia, and a legion of spontaneously generating *gwailo* heavies scrap over Luk, who gets smashed, bashed, and occasionally shot over a negative he never had in the first place!

There's an intriguing subplot involving U.S. Special Forces troops involved in drug-smuggling for the CIA, and Michael Wong makes an Oliver North–style excuse for his nefarious activities. In the end, though, the *ITLOD* series is about fisticuffs and high-rev tarantellas, and we get plenty here.

Cynthia fights while clinging to a hijacked ambulance: in the driver's seat, on the roof, hanging off the side, even pinned to the grille. Actress Khan reported having repeated nightmares after the filming of this stunt! Donnie Yen performs a dirt-bike jousting match with muscle-bound Michael Woods, using axes and shovels in place of lances; Donnie stops chasing him only after his bike comes apart in pieces. There's some goofy spoofing of Hollywood martial arts styles, but you won't find the likes of Cynthia Khan—bruising a bruiser's Adam's apple with the sole of her shoe—at your local mallplex.

Deadend of Besiegers (1991)
Transmigration Romance (1991)
Forbidden Arsenal (1991)
Thirteen Cold-Blooded Eagles (1991)
Zen of Sword (1992)
Madam City Hunter (1993)
Tough Beauty and the Sloppy Slop (1995)

Davian International, Mike Leeder

"Ow. Quit it. That really, really hurts." Cynthia Khan kicks some Road Warrior head in *Eternal Fist*.

KARA HUI YING-HUNG

Under different circumstances, Kara Hui Ying-hung could be just as famous (in HK circles) as Brigitte Lin is now. Like Brigitte,

continued on next page

Kara has a twenty-year career in films, and she was the main *femme*-fighter for Shaw Brothers in the 1980s. Slithering up a wall in *Legendary Weapons of China*, using a bicycle to attack thieves as the boss-lady in *The Lady Is the Boss*, or busting heads in *Mad Monkey Kung Fu*, she's unforgettable to anyone who sees her in action. Still lovely, still deadly, she's still making movies.

Selected Filmography

Dirty Ho (1979)
Martial Club (1981)
My Young Auntie (1981)
Eight Diagram Pole Fighter
  (1984)
Zen of Sword (1992)

MOON LEE

Indefatigable, doll-faced, and ferocious, Moon Lee has kicked the crap out of more men than any other living actress. Ms. Lee got her start in Tsui Hark's *Zu*, rocketed upward with *Angel*, and has made figuratively billions of action films, often paired with Yukari Oshima or Cynthia Khan.

Magnificent Warriors

1986
Starring Michelle Yeoh Chu-kheng (Michelle Khan), Richard Ng, Derek Yee Tung-shing, Lowell Lo, Chindy Lau
Directed by David Chung Chi-man

Big-budget adventure pictures like *Raiders of the Lost Ark* dominated the 80s, and this Michelle Yeoh vehicle is no exception. Like in *Raiders*, it's the 1930s and the khaki-fascists are up to their usual plans of world domination. Since this is a Hong Kong movie, the bad apples are the occupying forces of Imperial Japan (the title literally translates as "Chinese Warriors").

Michelle is a cute-but-serious barnstormer in a bomber jacket flying a biplane for the Chinese resistance in a Himalayan kingdom. Filmed somewhere in High China, the mountainous desert provides dramatic exteriors. Michelle's cohorts are a handsome resistance leader (Derek Yee), the kingdom's ruler (Lowell Lo), and a shoehorn-faced rogue and hustler (Richard Ng). Despite leaning toward collaboration and self-interest, all eventually prove their mettle.

The Japanese villains are as cartoonish in their evildoing as our heroes are in their heroism; but no matter, we're here to watch the daredevil action. In addition to her de rigueur whipwielding, Michelle performs rope tricks with a length of quarter-inch hemp. Jeeps, biplanes, motorbikes, and belt-fed tommy-guns all get their bearings lubed. A huge, fiery fight culminates with four blazing stuntmen leaping out of an exploding-with-incendiaries jeep.

The 30s rough-fashion look and style of *Magnificent Warriors* is up to the *Raiders* standard, even if the film's budget wouldn't pay for Spielberg's catering. The obligatory end battle features battlement scaling and catapulting (shades of *Beau Geste*!), and even a John Williams–style theme that you'll be tired of by movie's end. The outfoxed Japanese slink off (to Manchuria?), and all our heroes live to fight another day—rare enough in a Hong Kong film.

Royal Warriors

1986
Starring Michelle Yeoh Chu-kheng (Michelle Khan), Michael Wong Man-tuk, Hiroyuki "Henry" Sanada
Directed by Corey Yuen Kwai

Another excellent D&B action vehicle for Michelle Khan (now known as Michelle Yeoh). In *Royal Warriors*, the Japanese are presented as human beings rather than bloodless villains, and national loyalties do not interfere with the gleeful mayhem.

A notorious HK criminal is being extradited from Tokyo's Narita Airport. En route, an accomplice engineers an aircraft takeover with smuggled weapons, and the pair—Tiger and Cockerel—kill the accompanying cops. However, a trio of undercover cops are also on the plane—Michelle, Michael Wong, and Yamamoto (Japanese martial arts star Hiroyuki Sanada). They thwart the takeover, killing both crooks in the process and patching a blasted-out window with crook-ballast.

Back in Hong Kong, Yamamoto is trying to patch up things with his wife and infant daughter; it's obvious that his workaholism has been straining things and he's anxious to become less, well, *Japanese* about his work habits. But there's a third partner-in-crime, who wires a bomb to the underside of Yamamoto's car.

Yamamoto spots the bomb, but not soon enough to stop his wife from turning the ignition, so he watches in horror as she and their daughter are blown to bits. He chases the bomber to a construction site, where the bomber jumps on a bulldozer and starts burying our hero with gravel! Michelle arrives and kicks the bad guy off the dozer, but he escapes as she's rescuing the grief-stricken Yamamoto.

Vengeance on his mind, Yamamoto visits the local arms merchants and picks up a .44 Magnum, then sets up a meeting with Yeoh at a trendy nightclub, hoping to lure the creep. But the bad guy shows up packing a nine-millimeter open-bolt slug-wrench

JADE LEUNG

The compact Jade made her impressive debut in *Black Cat*, a remake of *La Femme Nikita* that eclipses the original. She's not been in many action pictures, though, 'cause her screen persona is just too damn vicious, even for HK filmmakers! Check out her sexy, explosive performance as a suicidal cop in *Satin Steel*, a reverse-gender remake of *Lethal Weapon*.

continued on next page

BRIGITTE LIN

Brigitte Lin Chin-hsia, who retired from filmmaking in 1994, had a twenty-year career beginning in her native Taiwan and continuing in Hong Kong. Her appearance as the Ice Countess in Tsui Hark's *Zu* was a hit with HK audiences. A decade later, her roles in legend films like *The East Is Red* and *The Bride With White Hair* were still delighting the punters. Brigitte is not an agile forehead-kicker like Moon Lee or Cynthia Khan; she prefers to rip opponents apart with a whip, fillet them with a sword, or just give 'em that blood-crystallizing hell-stare.

Selected Filmography

Zu: Warriors from the Magic Mountain (1983)
Fantasy Mission Force (1984)
Police Story (1985)
Peking Opera Blues (1986)
Dragon Inn (1992)
The East Is Red (1993)
The Bride With White Hair (1993)

and—spitting sparks and spewing chunks—shoots up the club, aerating most of the patrons. Amid the acres of broken glass, Yamamoto gets his final-shot revenge. But it turns out there's a *fourth* man!

Michael finds out who he is, but the last villain captures him, shoots him in both ankles, and suspends him from Energy Plaza in Tsimshatsui, twenty stories up. Michael plummets to his death, but even then he's not allowed to rest in peace, as Crook Number Four digs up his coffin and suspends it from a crane in a booby-trapped gravel quarry. Yamamoto attacks and is neutralized rapidly, leaving it up to Michelle (who rides into the fray in a heavily armored Volkswagen bug) to take out the last poltroon and rescue their comrade's mortal remains. Wild!

Satin Steel

1994
Starring Jade Leung, Anita Lee Yuen-weh, Russell Wong
Directed by Alex Leung Siu-hung

Hong Kong filmmakers are notorious for reshaping Hollywood movies, often swallowing an idea whole and spitting out something entirely different. In the case of *Satin Steel*, the movie on the carving block is Richard Donner's buddy-buddy *Lethal Weapon*.

How do you rehab that slab of ham? Make the cops women.

The role of the unbalanced, suicidal Mel Gibson partner falls to the feisty Jade Leung, who first left a trail of broken hearts and heads in *Black Cat*. Jade's wedding night passion is curtailed by mysterious thugs who shoot her husband, leaving her with a savage death wish. She opts for undercover work, buying handguns in a sting operation. When she flashes her I.D., the seller panics and threatens her with a grenade. An opportunity to explode delights Jade, who obligingly pulls the pin for him! The terrified crook capitulates, earning police accolades for Jade, and a new assignment: tracking down Mr. Fowler, an "American Mafia leader" selling weaponry in Southeast Asia.

In Singapore, Jade teams up with Inspector Ellen Cheng (Anita Lee), whose wimpy boyfriend Paul constantly whines about her hazardous police job. Jade wonders what a tough cookie like Inspector Cheng is doing with such a Milquetoast; Ellen responds that since men are scarce in Singapore, you gotta take what you can get! The two make the best of the clingy, spineless Paul by whacking him on the head and flinging the odd cockroach in his mouth.

Efforts to capture Fowler in Singapore are fruitless, but the duo tracks him to Indonesia, where Jade falls for his handsome lawyer, Ken (Russell Wong). Ken is forthright, and when Jade tells him that his client's as rotten as a barrel of sun-baked Borneo cuttlefish, he plans to resign. She convinces him to double-cross Fowler instead, and seduces him in the bargain. The chemistry between Jade and Russell is white-hot, and it's nice to see a Hong Kong action heroine so unabashedly sensual. But when she says, "Promise me you won't die before me," you know it's a promise he can't keep.

A well-choreographed fight ensues, with a bunch of creepazoid, masked witch doctors slicing hanks of hair from Jade's head as she dodges their slashing steel. The shamans are invulnerable to knives, but when Jade parks a .45 slug in the leader's head, the rest scatter. Fowler escapes as Ken gives up the ghost, saving Jade in the process. The revenge-minded policewoman pursues Fowler by grabbing onto the skid of the helicopter he's flying. And, in an only-in-Hong-Kong stunt, you see close-ups and medium-shots of Leung clinging to the skid as the helicopter flies along, dragging her through the water!

Note: Many video copies of this movie list the title as *Stain Steel*.

David Chute

Oh my. Japanese crunch-princess Michiko Nishiwaki in *My Lucky Stars*.

MICHIKO NISHIWAKI

A Japanese import, Nishiwaki's ravishing, menacing good looks have earned her juicy villainess roles more often than not: glowering in shades and male drag in *ITLOD3*, flashing her *yakuza* tattoo in *God of Gamblers*, or smashing up a Thai food-hawker's center in *Passionate Killing in the Dream*. Buffed like a gym rat, Nishiwaki makes an impressive presentation in a sleeveless top: biceps, and triceps, and shoulders . . . oh my.

continued on next page

YUKARI OSHIMA

Oshima appeared in a few Japanese productions, including a cameo in the first episode of the wild *Sukeban Deka*, a series of films depicting Japanese schoolgirls who are also undercover cops. But it was her role as the sadistic villainess opposite Moon Lee in *Angel* that boosted her Hong Kong career. Lee and Oshima have now teamed up in dozens of films. Oshima's popularity in the Philippines, where she appears under the name "Cynthia Luster," has inspired a move to Manila, where she appears in and produces films, and serves as an agent for other talent.

A Serious Shock: Yes Madam '92

1992
Starring Cynthia Khan, Moon Lee Choi-fung, Yukari Oshima, Waise Lee Chi-hung, Lawrence Ng
Directed by Stanley Wing Siu

As the opening credits roll, policewomen Wan Chin (Cynthia Khan) and May (Moon Lee) practice their crimefighting techniques. They unpack nine-millimeter rounds, defuse bombs, stomp on pretend bad guys, and generally validate one another's feminine prowess as instructor Wilson (Lawrence Ng of *Sex & Zen* fame) looks on approvingly.

Wan Chin and Wilson, the happy cop couple, are preparing for their forthcoming nuptials. However, Wilson's ex-girlfriend May is boiling over with jealousy. Spurned, jilted, and irate, she pounds her unsuspecting sparring partner bloody during martial arts practice. Unsatisfied, she then follows Wilson into the men's locker room, screams curses at him, then knees him in the crotch.

Unaware of May's emotional toxicity, Wan Chin offers her friend a lift. But when they get to the car, they find it's in the process of being stolen by cheeky criminal Sister Coco (Yukari Oshima in one of her better roles). The police madams chase Coco down and bust her at gunpoint. But when she's taken to the station, Brother Boy (Waise Lee) promptly bails her out.

The two small-time crooks then head for a Houdini-like grudge match sponsored by their motorcycle gang. In an excellent piece of rumble business, Coco and some *gwailo* woman strip to their skivvies, shackle their ankles with heavy chain, and dive into an enormous water tank. Naturally, the keys are on the bottom; the boys shout and bet on the winner (one guess).

May discovers that Wan Chin and Wilson plan to emigrate to London, nixing any possibility of swiping her beloved from her friend's clutches. She dolls herself up in a black miniskirt and red top and appears at his apartment to plead her case. Clearly, Wilson's made his choice, and May goes ballistic. The diminutive, baby-faced actress slams her knee-high leather boots repeatedly into Wilson's midsection, howling, "I hate others cheat me most!"

Wan Chin arrives and fires her revolver in the air, but May grabs the snub-nose from her, cuffs her to the railing, and proceeds to ventilate Wilson—who croaks shortly. A serious shock indeed! May runs to Kent, a fellow cop who's got a crush on her. Together, they frame Wan Chin for the murder. Now a fugitive, her ex-fiancé's ashes in a jar, Wan Chin joins forces with Sister Coco.

This trio moves toward their inevitable final battle in nonlinear fashion (frankly, a few expository scenes might have been left on the cutting-room floor), but there are plenty of opportunities for these women to work out. May's character becomes more malevolent by the frame; during the final engagement, she booby traps Coco's cute son with a backpack full of TNT! Nobody wants to see May survive, and everybody leaves the theater happy.

She Shoots Straight

1990
Starring Joyce Godenzi, Carina Lau Kar-ling, Tony Leung Kar-fai, Yuen Wah, Agnes Aurelio, Sammo Hung Kam-bo, Sandra Ng
Directed by Corey Yuen Kwai

She Shoots Straight opens with the wedding of policewoman Mina Kao (Joyce Godenzi). Mina's husband, Tsung-pao (Tony Leung), is also a cop. On Mina's next assignment, she foils an attempted abduction at a fashion show, jumping atop cars and commandeering dirt bikes in the process. Mina's athletic bravery earns her a medal, but Tsung-pao's sister Ling is unhappy. It seems that Tsung-pao is the only male heir in his family, a position that carries a grave responsibility in patriarchal Chinese society. Everyone else in the family (Ling included) are policewomen, and they're concerned

continued on page 64

Selected Filmography
Angel (1987)
Godfather's Daughter's Mafia Blues (1989)
Kung Fu Wonder Child (1989)
Brave Young Girls (1990)
A Punch to Revenge (1991)
The Story of Ricky (1991)
Hard to Kill (1992)
Deadly Target (1994)

CYNTHIA ROTHROCK

Cynthia is a blue-eyed, blonde-haired, All-American girl from Pennsylvania whose martial arts prowess led to roles in Hong Kong movies. Her early HK work is among her best: *Righting Wrongs* (also known as *Above the Law*) and *Yes, Madam*. She has also appeared in American films (*China O'Brien*, *Martial Law*) and Indonesian-made actioners (*Angel of Fury*, *Rage and Honor*).

Selected Filmography
Righting Wrongs (1986)
Yes, Madam (1986)
Shanghai Express (1987)
The Magic Crystal (1989)
Blonde Fury (1989)
City Cops (1990)

This Thai poster for *She Shoots Straight* features muscular villainess Agnes Aurelio.

that Mina's success will cause the only Jack in this Jill-hierarchy to lose face!

When the law gets wind of a plot to rob the swank New World nightclub, they enlist the policewomen as undercover nightclub hostesses. Their nemesis, though, is a capable and ruthless Vietnamese dissident (Yuen Wah), whose gang cuts the power and uses night-vision goggles to assault the darkened nightclub. The attack is repelled by Mina and her troops, who kill one of the Viet men. The remaining gangsters flee the scene, swearing revenge on our heroines.

They get it by luring Mina, the feisty Ling, and Tsung-pao to the edge of a forest, which they've prepared with Cong-style booby traps: nets, bamboo spears, flying nooses. To the women's horror, Tsung-pao is pierced by a veritable forest of sharpened bamboo and dies right in front of them. Their misery is compounded when they then must attend a celebratory banquet with the rest of the family, pretending that nothing's wrong. They choke back tears as others praise Tsung-pao and speak fondly of the future. Only when Tsung-pao's mother sees the news of his death on television do they crumble, but (as a group) tearfully swear revenge. This powerful sequence—raw with an emotion rarely seen in "feminist" cinema—lends a sharp edge to the resultant fracas.

Mina and Ling track the Vietnamese to a hideout aboard a ship and thrash them soundly with chains, machetes, and .357 Magnum slugs. But the final confrontation comes when Wah's girlfriend (Agnes Aurelio) snatches him from under the cops' noses. Mina pursues them on a police bike and cancels his contract, pissing off his girlfriend, who whips off her coat and displays a physique honed by hours of ironwork. As each has killed the other's mate, their duel is savage and unsentimental. The Vietnamese strongwoman hurls Mina sideways like a whirligig and boots her in the crotch. Mina responds with a right hook to the jaw (repeated like Jake LaMotta's in *Raging Bull*) and kicks to the steroid queen's chest, forcing her into submission. This end fight is more macho than anything Steven Seagal or Chuck Norris has ever put on film.

A note of warning: some video copies of *SSS* are unsubtitled, so it pays to check before plunking down the rental money.

MICHELLE YEOH

Malaysian-born Michelle Yeoh started her career as Michelle Khan, filming *Magnificent Warriors*, *Royal Warriors*, and *Yes, Madam* for Dickson Poon's D&B Films in 1986. Khan subsequently married Dickson (one of Hong Kong's foremost tycoons) and gave up the hazards of filmmaking. She did not step in front of the cameras again until her divorce years later. Khan became Michelle Yeoh, and her first post-Poon feature—Jackie Chan's awesome *Police Story 3: Supercop* —cemented her rep for good.

Selected Filmography
Magnificent Warriors (1986)
Royal Warriors (1986)
Yes, Madam (1986)
Police Story 3: Supercop (1993)
Project S (1993)
The Tai Chi Master (1993)
Butterfly and Sword (1993)
The Heroic Trio (1993)
Wonder 7 (1994)

CAPSULE REVIEWS

ANGEL   1987

The original GWG (Girls With Guns) flick that helped launch the careers of Moon Lee and Yukari Oshima, not to mention inspiring about a dozen other flicks with "Angel" somewhere in the title. A straight-ahead action picture with Moon as a policewoman trying to bust pan-Asian crime syndicates. Producer/director Teresa Woo throws in plenty of fists 'n' guns, uses hunkcake Hideki Saijo (the Japanese Bryan Ferry) to good effect, and casts Yukari Oshima as a sadistic villainess.

ANGEL 2   1988

Director Teresa Woo brings back Moon Lee and Elaine Lui as badass policewomen in search of a good kick. A vacation to Malaysia turns sour when Elaine falls for a local guy, Peter. Unfortunately, Peter has become a Hitler freak and is assembling a jungle paramilitary brigade to help him achieve world domination. These delicate personal matters can only be solved by the liberal application of gunpowder.

BLACK CAT 2: ASSASSINATION OF PRESIDENT YELTSIN   1992

Jade Leung reprises her role as technologically tweaked carnage-goddess Erica—aka Black Cat. Tinkering with the microchip implant in her head has given her a Terminator-like visual display. She attempts to thwart the dreaded AYO (Anti-Yeltsin Organization), which is trying to kill Russia's "Fearless Liter."

When her CIA employers discover that AYO goons are shooting up with performance-enhancing radioactive isotopes, they inject the same into Erica so she can detect decay from the rotten guys. The techno-enhanced Black Cat rushes into a shopping mall and gets the wrong vibe from a grandmotherly type. She hauls out a blued-steel .44 magnum Desert Eagle automatic and blasts the granny right between the eyes, splattering blood on a horrified mall clown.

Performance-enhanced anti-Yeltsinite in disguise? No, a real grandmother after radiation treatment for cancer! Despite this goof, they send Black Cat to Moscow to track down those pesky Nyetskis.

BLONDE FURY   1988

Cynthia Rothrock—Pennsylvania's most furious blonde—uncovers corruption in the HK legal system and takes it out on various creeps with a variety of weapons, including a deadly one—her own spike heel! The end fight is great, with Rothrock battling fellow *gwailo* Jeff Falcon on a complex, weblike rope structure. But the real "blonde fury" in this movie is Cynthia's hair, which keeps changing lengths between shots!

DREAMING THE REALITY   1991

Moon Lee and Yukari Oshima (sporting a fetching, boyish haircut) are raised as trained killers by the ruthless Mr. Fox (Eddie Ko). Rather than forming a support group, they go on to brilliant careers in their field, until a business trip to Thailand leads to a bout of amnesia for Moon. She's adopted by the feisty, beer-chugging, cig-huffing Sister Lan (Sibelle Hu) and her brother Rocky, an ambitious young kickboxer. She recovers her memory, but in the meantime Fox has sent his henchman Scorpion to track down and eliminate his girls, whose loyalty he now doubts.

Moon and Sister Lan must make a stand against Fox and his men, booby-trapping a forest compound and blazing away with various bangsticks. They reject Fox's ruthless code and leave him crippled, yet alive—the worst of all fates for a HK film villain.

KICKBOXER'S TEARS   1993

Johnny Lo, a Hong Kong kickboxer, fails to survive a vicious match. He is avenged by his sister (Moon Lee), who seeks a rematch with Billy Chow, the boxer who killed him. Despite Chow's cheating tactic (rubbing irritating oil on his gloves), she breaks his spine, crippling him. His criminal boss is pleased; the boxer had been having an affair with his wife (Yukari Oshima). Oshima is not pleased, and demands a death match with Moon. Although this ferocious grudge duel is not the film's culmination, it's definitely the highlight of *Kickboxer's Tears*; Moon/Yukari freaks will not be disappointed.

MISSION OF JUSTICE   1992

Shot-in-Thailand actioner featuring Moon and Yukari busting up a drug syndicate. The jungle locations are fun, and the requisite number of kicks to the head and auto-emptied, full-metal-jacket magazines aren't left out. Best of all, Carrie Ng appears as a dominant policewoman, strutting about in fetching paramilitary garb, ordering boy-cop flunkies around like the spineless worms they are.

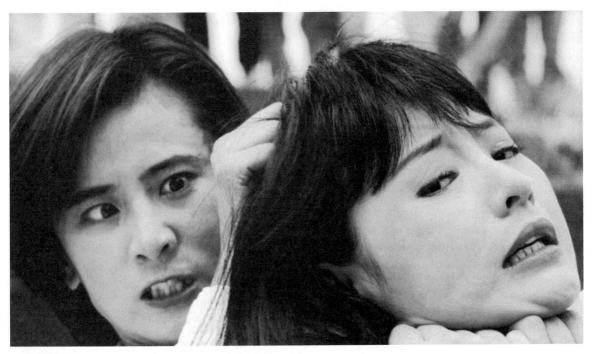

Yukari Oshima (left) and Moon Lee (right) nurture one another in *Kickboxer's Tears*.

PRINCESS MADAM   1989

Buddy film about the adventures of two police-women (Moon Lee and butch-styled Sharon Yeung) popping caps on bad guys. Males in this film are ineffectual pantywaists who must be protected or shot by our tough heroines.

When Moon kills the husband of villainess Michiko Nishiwaki in a botched assassination attempt, the Japanese woman stalks, seduces, and torments Moon's wimpy husband. "I'm scared stiff of you!" he shouts into the phone, as he rubs the bite marks Michiko embedded in his shoulders. On the other end of the line, she smolders in front of a poster of a snarling cat, throwing darts at a photo of Moon.

Michiko kidnaps the couple and ties the police-woman—spread-eagled—five feet off the ground. Moon watches helplessly as Michiko administers more painful bites and busts liquor bottles against her husband's knees. "Do you have the guts to fight with me?" shouts Moon. "I don't have the mood," replies Ms. Nishiwaki.

Dames. Who can figure 'em? Many rounds later, justice triumphs.

STORY OF A GUN   1991

Gun-running flick featuring Philip Kao as the big boss and Gordon Liu as a copper trying to bust the ring, aided by *gwailo* policewoman Sophia Crawford. Mark Cheng and Yukari Oshima play a couple on the other side of the law—just trying to make a buck pushing deadly metal. During shooting, Crawford attempted a hazardous stunt and broke her foot. Of course, the show must go on and, when it was noticed that she was limping during the subsequent action scenes, the thoughtful filmmakers changed the plot so her character is shot in the leg!

WIDOW WARRIORS   1989

As even a casual viewer of HK films knows, turning the men into worm food just makes the women that much crankier. This is certainly the case in *Widow Warriors*. Elizabeth Lee and Tien Niu (who are not noted for their martial abilities) team up with Kara Hui Ying-hung and Michiko Nishiwaki (who are). A bleak and violent look at survival in the male-dominated triad world.

HEX ERRORS

Hong Kong films are usually sub-titled in both Chinese and English. The Chinese is for natives, like Mandarin-speakers, who don't understand the spoken Cantonese dialect. The English is there because Hong Kong is a British Crown Colony until 1997, and British law mandates it.

However, translating Chinese into English isn't simple, and multiple gaffes are the inevitable result. Especially when you are translating at the breakneck pace demanded by cost-conscious HK producers. Director Tsui Hark claims that his feature *Peking Opera Blues* was subtitled in two days for less than a hundred dollars.

This splintering of the Queen's English adds additional—if unintended—entertainment value for those of us who have no idea of what to make of the rapid-fire Cantoflow. We've collected our favorite "hex errors," divided them into categories, and sprin-kled them throughout the rest of the book.

If you are like us, some of these epithets will stick in your head, springing from long-term memory at the oddest times. Drop a cup of coffee, and out pops "Damn you, stink man" (*Caged Beauties*); when someone cuts you off in traffic, you spit "You bastard, try this melon" (*Gunmen*); and for no good reason, you'll find yourself whispering "Suck the coffin mushroom now" (*The Ultimate Vampire*).

Original punctuation, capital-ization, and spelling has been preserved. To do otherwise would be cheating.

BATTLE OF THE SEXES

Dammit it! You are crazy for sex! Why should I be the exception?
—*Lewd Lizard*

I know it, he is not an idiot, he is sexual detour
—*Black Panther Warriors*

Same old rules, no eyes, no groin
—*Bloody Mary Killer*

Sex fiend, you'll never get reincar-nated!
—*Banana Spirit*

He's Big Head Man, he is lousing around
—*Close Escape*

Catherine is a nasbian!
—*Passionate Killing in the Dream*

Men are somehow abnormal
—*Call Girl 92*

You're bad. You make my busts up and down
—*The Love That Is Wrong*

Don't shout. Balls are not broken yet.
Yeah? My iron balls are like marshmallows now!
—*Devil Cat*

I have piles. You won't be comfort-able.
—*Ghostly Vixen*

Apparently, sex makes him mad
—*Robotrix*

I've told you, men with beard are
  anxious in sex
—*Girls in the Hood, Part 1*

She's adulterated and cuckolds
  me
—*Flirting*

What you need is a canned
  woman.
—*To Hell With the Devil*

Got it, love machine!
—*Dreaming the Reality*

For him, every day is a moral holiday.
—*The Missed Date*

I'll jelled if you ask me out
—*Ghostly Love*

Nicked named Little-bun, also
  named Bitchy-bun.
—*It's Now or Never*

All men are sex maniac they
  deserve death
—*Spiritual Love*

No, it's bad if she's seriously
  twisted
—*Kickboxer's Tears*

She's terrific. I can't stand her.
—*Rouge*

From your tiny eyes, I can tell you
  won't be lazy in bed.
—*Holy Weapon*

I've checked, you are suffered
  from "Big Penis."
—*Ghostly Vixen*

Don't do anything perverted, we
  are in a hurry.
—*Holy Weapon*

Tsui Hark 4

Producer/director Tsui Hark (pronounced "Choy Hok") is one of modern Hong Kong cinema's guiding lights. Tsui was born in Vietnam and moved to HK as a teenager, but relocated to the University of Texas to study film. After graduating, he spent time in New York before returning to HK.

Zu: Warriors from the Magic Mountain (1983) was the first film to showcase the fantastic, madly paced Tsui Hark look and feel. But when Tsui began to have creative conflicts with *Zu*'s parent company, Golden Harvest, he was inspired to create his own production company, Film Workshop. FW was designed to nurture young filmmakers and give them an outlet for expression, a task it has accomplished quite well. Tsui, who is more than a bit of an obsessed workaholic, becomes deeply involved with everything he produces.

Hark's stable of directors (including Ching Siu-tung and Raymond Lee) continue to expand upon Film Workshop's tradition of innovation.

After *Zu*, Tsui went on to produce John Woo's *A Better Tomorrow* (1986) and Ching Siu-tung's *A Chinese Ghost Story* (1987), two of the seminal HK "new wave" films of the mid-eighties. After Tsui produced Woo's *The Killer* (1989), Woo went ahead and formed his own production company. Tsui's *Once Upon a Time in China* series, which reintroduced Wong Fei-hong to modern audiences, has also proved extremely popular.

Dragon Inn

1992
Starring Brigitte Lin Chin-hsia, Maggie Cheung Man-yuk, Tony Leung Kar-fai, Donnie Yen Chi-tan, Lawrence Ng, Elvis Tsui Kam-kong
Directed by Raymond Lee

Buoyed by the success of the Tsui Hark productions *Once Upon a Time in China* and *Swordsman II*, HK filmmakers responded with an avalanche of action epics dressed up in period costume. These movies—often flashier, pumped-up remakes of martial classics—have done much to sustain the current worldwide appreciation of contemporary HK cinema, well beyond the scope of John Woo's gangster films.

Dragon Inn, a remake of director King Hu's 1966 film *Dragon Gate Inn*, is one of the more impressive efforts to come out of this revival. A clever reworking of Hu's film, it takes the basic premise and deepens its approach to character while seizing on the story's opportunities for swashbuckling swordplay.

The film draws its title from an isolated rest-house located in the middle of a vast desert. Business is surprisingly good for the inn's crafty female owner, Jade (Maggie Cheung), who earns a little pocket money by luring horny bandits up to her room with the promise of sexual favors. Before the poor bastards can even undress, however, they're quickly dispatched and left dead on the ground with blades protruding from their foreheads as Jade rifles their wallets. Not one to let fresh meat or a business opportunity go to waste, Jade sends the warm corpses down to the basement, where her enthusiastic cook uses them to prepare the inn's specialty dish of "spicy meat buns." Shades of *Sweeney Todd*.

Jade's carefree and isolated existence is interrupted, however, when her inn becomes the rendezvous point for a virtuous government official named Chow Wai-on (Tony Leung) and his swordswoman lover, Yau Mo-yin (Brigitte Lin), who's disguised as a man. Both are on the run from a power-crazed eunuch (Donnie Yen) intent on their destruction. When the eunuch's murderous underlings abruptly arrive at the inn, the couple's plans of escape are thwarted. But the killers are unsure of what their quarry look like, so they are forced to proceed with caution as they attempt to pinpoint their assigned targets. With both sides confined to the inn during a stormy deluge, a tense game of cat-and-mouse ensues.

Jade cleverly takes advantage of the situation by bouncing like a pinball between the antagonistic factions and gleefully accepting bribes in exchange for empty promises.

Maggie Cheung has the meatiest role here, playing Jade with a perpetual twinkle in her eyes and effectively mixing the character's ruthless materialism and sly sexiness with a reluctantly blooming conscience. Maggie delivers one of her most colorful performances, full of spontaneity and understated humor. A scene in which a suspicious Jade and Yau Mo-yin acrobatically attempt to snatch off one another's clothes is one of the film's highlights.

The action is technically superb, with bouts of expertly choreographed swordplay and spectacular wirework that allows characters to leap or somersault several feet in the air or soar off a cliff and slice the necks of rival swordsmen down below. The climactic duel occurs in the midst of a sandstorm that nearly buries its participants, and in the end the villain gets his comeuppance when an arm and a leg are carved to the bone. TKO!

—RAA

A power-crazed eunuch (Donnie Yen) leaps for his life in the middle of nowhere, as Yau Mo-yin (Brigitte Lin) and Jade (Maggie Cheung) slash at him, in *Dragon Inn*.

Green Snake

1993
Starring Joey Wong Jo-yin, Maggie Cheung Man-yuk, Wu Hsin-kuo, Zhao Wen Zhou
Directed by Tsui Hark

This gorgeous Tsui Hark production is based on one of China's most famous folktales, *Madam White Snake*. This tale of two female snakes who have achieved the power to assume human form after centuries of training is irresistible, and has been brought to the Chinese screen several times before. This latest version pulls together some intriguing ideas about humanity, religion, and sexuality as a base for Hark's scintillating visuals, which include an enticing eroticism not usually seen in his movies.

Of the two snakes who aspire to womanhood, elder sister White (Joey Wong) is by far the more accomplished mimic: her training has encompassed ten centuries. Kid sister Green (Maggie Cheung) is irrepressibly curious about humans, like a teenybopper anxious for her first date. But Green has been practicing for only five centuries and is still prone to dropping to the ground and scooting around corners in search of juicy bugs. Despite White's stern admonitions, Green is susceptible to lapses of concentration, during which her legs revert back to a snake's tail.

The two creatures live in a ghostly mansion on the edge of town, slithering in to observe human behavior when the mood strikes. White is more devoted to the idea of living out her life as a human and, better able to keep her shape, she seduces, falls in love with, and then marries a nerdy scholar named Hsui Xien (Wu Hsin Kuo). The pesky and inquisitive Green tags along with the couple, anxious to discover why her sister is so attracted to the idea of being human. Unfortunately, the romance between White and Hsui Xien is mostly shown in flashy montage, depriving the voyeuristic viewer of any reptilophiliac shots of ravishing Joey Wong's scaly skin or quivering rattles.

The sisters' nemesis is a self-righteous and sexually repressed monk (martial artist Zhao Wen Zhou), who gets bent out of shape at the idea of snakes mating with human beings. The monk tries to tell Hsui that his beautiful new bride is actually a monster. He does not find a receptive ear. Green spars lustfully with the annoyingly pious prelate, teasing him mercilessly. Jealousy flares when Green tries to seduce White's naive hubby (to experience love), but the serpentine sisters eventually unite to do spectacular battle with the irked monk.

Green Snake boasts a superbly diverse musical score that incorporates everything from Hindi-inspired rockin' pop to New Age ether. The film's main drawbacks are its dime-store special effects, which look jarring juxtaposed with the seamless fantastic landscape of the film as a whole. Viewers entranced by the undulating groove of Hark's big, bad *Snake* will barely notice.

—RAA

That old Buddhist monk has extra-honking-long earlobes and hates the secular world steeped in greed and sex, none of which endears him to sword-bearing younger snake sister, Green (Maggie Cheung). From *Green Snake*.

Once Upon a Time in China

1991
Starring Jet Li, Rosamund Kwan Chi-lam, Jacky Cheung Hak-yow, Yuen Biao, Kent Cheng
Directed by Tsui Hark

Tsui Hark's *Once Upon a Time in China* is one of those rare productions that sparks latent interest in a perennial favorite, then transforms it into an instant franchise. The film quickly spawned four sequels, a prequel, numerous imitations, and it was parodied in several comedies. Yet, *OUATIC* is not the first movie to chronicle the adventures of Wong Fei-hong, a legendary martial artist from the Ching Dynasty of the late nineteenth century (see pages 78–79).

Tsui Hark's most significant contribution was the casting of Jet Li as Wong Fei-hong. Li, a Beijing native and youthful martial artist, achieved fame in a series of early 1980s Shaolin Temple movies. Jet's infectious grin and dazzling martial arts skills made him an excellent choice to revive the legend. Although Jet Li has moved on to star in a variety of other roles—including the Wong-like folk hero Fong Sai-yuk—most of his fans still associate him closely with the virtuous Wong.

OUATIC has our hero running an herbal clinic with his associates Porky (Kent Cheng) and Buck Tooth Sol (Jacky Cheung). Like all Wong Fei-hong movies, *OUATIC* chronicles Wong's battles with corrupt local officials and the encroaching effects of Western civilization on China.

As with its sequels (and many other Hong Kong films), *OUATIC* is imbued with a strong anti-European sentiment. British, French, and American troops have invaded China and are portrayed as foolish, self-righteous imperialists who impose themselves, their beliefs, and their technology upon the Chinese without any regard for how it will affect the native culture.

In spite of this, there is a strong Christian theme running through the film. The one *gwailo* who comes to the aid of Wong and his men is an American priest. A young admirer of Wong's plays Judas by joining forces with "Iron Robe" Yim, a nearly invincible character who has sworn to defeat Wong. In a takeoff on David and Goliath, Wong flicks a bullet at an evil American with his finger, striking him in the forehead and killing him.

The action is so furious that it is sometimes too fast to follow, even in slow motion. In one fight, Jet Li, armed only with an umbrella, defeats a dozen opponents. He uses the umbrella in every conceivable way: tripping people with the hook,

stabbing them with the point, and opening it to evade projectiles. It's like a cross between *Enter the Dragon* and *Singin' in the Rain*. The final duel between Wong and Yim has the two foes fighting atop ladders, bouncing off the walls, and dodging swinging cargo flats. Of course, Wong Fei-hong emerges victorious, ready for any possible sequels.

—JM

Peking Opera Blues

1986
Starring Cherie Chung Chor-hung, Brigitte Lin Ching-hsia, Sally Yeh, Mark Cheng, K. K. Cheung, Ng Ma, Ku Feng
Directed by Tsui Hark

For many American viewers, *Peking Opera Blues* was the very first taste of the explosive, kinetic experience known as "new wave" Hong Kong cinema. Sitting through *POB*'s astonishing combination of high-flying acrobatics, hilarious comedy, excruciating torture scenes, and unabashed heroism from powerful female characters is like watching one of the old-style martial arts movies through a kaleidoscope.

The film is set in 1913, a politically chaotic period when competing warlords were jockeying for power with foreign governments in the newly established Republic of China. When corrupt General Tun chooses to recoup his gambling losses by neglecting to pay his troops, he's run out of town. His replacement, General Tsao, signs a covert document with a cabal of foreigners and secretes it in a wall safe. Unfortunately for Tsao, his daughter Wan (Brigitte Lin) is a dedicated revolutionary (sporting a manly haircut to go with her military regalia) who must conceal her idealism from her father.

Also bound into this twisted web of political intrigue is Pat Neil (Sally Yeh), a stagehand at her father's Peking Opera theater who yearns to perform but is stymied by the rigid tradition of excluding women from the stage. Sheung Hung (Cherie Chung) is a jobless servant chasing after a stolen jewelry box, although her greedy materialism gradually melts away in the heat of more substantial concerns. This trio of unlikely women unites to protect their nascent republic not only from renegade officers and sneaky foreigners but also from the local officials, a gang known cryptically as the "Ticketing Office."

Throughout *POB*'s running time (best described as "120-compressed-into-90"), identities are mistaken, genders rent and bent, and the laws of gravity constantly amended. The action sequences are masterfully choreographed, but so are the slapstick comedy routines, and together they create a giddy, unbelievable spectacle.

Director Tsui Hark has often featured strong female roles in his movies, and *POB* features a trio of delectable performances from Hong Kong's finest. Cherie Chung does a delightful comic turn with just the right dose of sexiness, callowness, and compassion while the wide-eyed Sally Yeh is a feisty but endearing inspiration for oppressed women everywhere. Brigitte Lin's portrayal of

Tsao Wan provides the picture's emotional center, illustrating the conflict between human and political desires. She is torn between her duty to her country and her unwavering love for her father—a dilemma perfectly symbolized by a scene in which she tearfully embraces him while his jacket slides off a chair and the key to his safe (containing the documents she needs to expose him) slips from its pocket. Lin's forceful performance gives the film much of its dramatic weight, particularly when we see this tough and unyielding woman gradually thaw when she recognizes the toll her actions are having on both herself and those around her.

—RAA

Swordsman II

1992
Starring Brigitte Lin Chin-hsia, Jet Li, Rosamund Kwan Chi-lam, Michelle Reis (Lee Kar-yan), Lau Shin, Fennie Yuen Kit-ying, Waise Lee Chi-hung
Directed by Ching Siu-tung

Swordsman II gleefully pours a twisty plot into a sprawling, brawling spectacle of delirious swordplay. *S2*'s densely packed frames riot with exploding bodies as antagonists are torn apart by whips, swords, huge bifurcated hooks, and other exotic weapons. Those with solid knowledge of Chinese history and martial arts philosophies might try to follow the breakneck plot; all others, just let 'er rip.

FROM NO-SHADOW KICKS TO ELECTRIC-SHADOW KICKS:

Jet Li leaps from ladder to ladder in a dockside warehouse, a blur of speed dodging deadly blows from dozens of attackers. The audience sits spellbound. "Waaaahh!" they manage to breathe as he springs up to the rafters, whirls around, and sweeps back down upon his adversaries.

The film is Tsui Hark's *Once Upon a Time in China*, and Jet Li is the star. But make no mistake, the audience has not come to the "electric shadows" (a literal translation of the Chinese characters for the word "films") to see Jet Li. They've come to see the character he portrays, the legendary Wong Fei-hong. For more than forty years, no individual has dominated the history, ethics, and culture of Chinese martial arts more than Wong Fei-hong.

Think of him kind of like Wyatt Earp. Both were real people who achieved fame as kickasses during periods of change and upheaval: Earp during the last days of the Wild West, Fei-hong in the fading light of the Chinese Empire. And both were mythologized well past their actual deeds—first by tabloid writers, then by screenwriters.

The legend of Wong Fei-hong, however, has a much more direct connection to the cinematic world, as well as to the political climate of today, than the legend of Wyatt Earp could ever have. Wong Fei-hong is much, much more than a revenge-maddened mayhem-wreaker or high-jumping hero. He is the spirit of kung fu in the real world, a scholar-fighter steeped in restraint and respect, battling the forces that oppress the Chinese everyman.

The real Wong Fei-hong lived from 1847 to 1924. He was a master of such kung fu as the no-shadow kick, drunken boxing, hong ("flower") fist, and the lion dance. He learned his skills from his father, Wong Kei-ying, one of the Ten Fighting Tigers of Kwan-tung. In fact, there is an unbroken lineage of *sifus* and students from the founding of the Southern Shaolin Temple to many of Hong Kong film's current kung fu stars.

One of Wong Fei-hong's favorite students was Lam Sai Wing, a heavyset pork vendor known as The Magnificent Butcher. Lam went on to teach his own students, and his favorite pupil, Liu Chan, moved to Hong Kong and got work in the movies.

After World War II, the Hong Kong movie industry found itself in need of fresh material and turned to the popular pulp novels and newspaper serializations, which were filled with tales of Wong Fei-hong. In 1949, Liu Chan found himself playing The Magnificent Butcher in the first WFH film, opposite Kwan Tak-hing as Wong Fei-hong.

Many other WFH films followed over the next two decades: fifty-nine of them, all starring Kwan, all directed by Wu Pang, and most relying on a stable of actors (called Wong's Troupe), which included Liu Chan's sons. Two of them, Liu Chia-liang and Liu Chia-yung, went on to successful careers, first in the ranks of the Shaw Brother studio (see chapter 12 for more on the prolific Shaw Brothers), and later out on their own.

Liu Chia-liang (aka Lau Kar-leung) has been directing his own films about Wong Fei-hong since 1976. Recent Hong Kong movie converts have probably seen the Liu-directed *Drunken Master II* (1994), starring Jackie Chan as WFH, but few appreciate that it is Liu himself fighting with Chan on a train track, *underneath a train*, and that they, the audience, are watching a living, breathing link to China's martial arts past.

WFH movies petered out in the mid-eighties, as modern-day hit men dominated the big screen, with criminal carnage outselling costume drama. When Tsui Hark made a new WFH movie (*Once Upon a Time in China*) in 1991, no one predicted its phenomenal success. It would be a mistake to think that *OUATIC*'s popularity was merely the result of an appreciation for this continuing martial arts tradition; the skull-cracking stunts certainly helped. But as the monumental changes of 1997 draw nearer, Hong Kong movie fans might well see more films featuring Wong Fei-hong and his heroic, anticolonial exploits.

—KAT

Rim Films

Jet Li strikes the classic Wong Fei-hong pose in *Once Upon A Time In China II*. Although Li is the Wong best known to Western audiences, the Chinese folk hero has been portrayed by Hong Kong cinema stalwarts from Liu Chia-liang to Kwan Tak-hing.

NAMING
CONVENTIONS

Nothing, and we mean *nothing*, caused us as many problems in cataloging and reviewing these films as the names of the actors and actresses. Chinese names don't translate easily into English. Chinese names sound different in Cantonese than they do in Mandarin. Sometimes people change their names. It's confusing, complicated, and frustrating.

Take Joey Wong Jo-yin (*A Chinese Ghost Story* and *Green Snake*) as an example. "Joey Wong"—as she's often listed—is an Anglicization of her Chinese name, Wong Jo Yin. "Wong" is the family name, which traditionally comes first, because a person's family name is considered more important than his or her personal name. Using the Western convention, "Wong" would appear last while "Jo-yin" is (very roughly) her first name. So far, so good. But we have also seen this same actress listed as Joi Wong, Wang Chu Hsien Joey Wang,

The opening scene finds the protagonist—known as Asia the Invincible—wrenching the head off a powerful opponent. But for a fierce, macho warrior, AI is strikingly feminine. Though we don't discover the details until later, it turns out that AI has learned from the Sacred Scroll that the way to achieve supreme power is to supernaturally castrate oneself. To elevate his shadowy Sun Moon Sect to supreme power, he has made that oh-so-personal sacrifice: he is slowly transforming into a woman as his power increases. AI is played by stunner Brigitte Lin.

We then meet the beautiful tomboy Kiddo (Michelle Reis) and the carefree drunkard Ling (Jet Li), two martial arts students from the Wah Mountain school. The pair meet up with their fellow students (who have names like Smart Ass and Scum Bag) so they can go into seclusion as a group, retiring from martial arts. Kiddo has a crush on Ling and tries constantly to doll herself up so he'll notice her, but she's better at handling a sword than a jar of rouge.

It's useless; the hedonistic Ling thinks only of AI's niece, the Highlander girl Ying (Rosamund Kwan). Ying's father, Wu (Lau Shin), is the Highlander Sect's proper leader, but he's been imprisoned by his ambitious brother-slowly-turning-into-a-sister, AI.

While Ying and her assistant Blue Phoenix (Fennie Yuen) wait in their Highland lodge for Ling to show up, they are attacked by one of the Japanese martial arts clans hiding out in this part of China. The ninja assassins hurl live scorpions through the windows and fly in on rotating blades. Blue Phoenix plays a flute, which calls forth bushel baskets of venomous snakes, but Ying's guards are slaughtered, and Ying and Blue Phoenix are forced to flee.

Ling goes searching for the besieged Ying, but finds AI instead, bathing in a lake. Although her appearance is female, her voice has still not changed, so she communicates with sweet smiles alone. She can still drink like a man, however, and the wine gourd she proffers causes Ling to spin hysterically out of the water with delight. He's smitten.

Ling attacks AI's encampment single-handedly, but he's overpowered and tossed in a dungeon. Fellow inmate Wu has been rendered powerless by enormous hooks through his shoulders. Ling and Wu escape; freed of the hooks, Wu regains his strength by sucking the life force out of the jailers with his Essence-Absorbing Stance.

The time in jail seems to have taken a toll on Wu, who has become obsessed with dreams of bloody revenge. AI distracts Ling by disguising her faithful girlfriend as herself and sending her to seduce Ling in a darkened room, then slaughters all of Ling's Wah Mountain brothers except Kiddo.

In the final confrontation, Ying, Kiddo, Ling, and Wu attack AI, who, thoroughly feminized by now, fights them off with sewing-needle kung fu. The evil woman is eventually defeated by Ling but, as the film ends, Wu—now clearly over the edge—has taken up the bloody trail where AI left off.

—AK

Zu: Warriors from the Magic Mountain

1983
Starring Adam Cheng Siu-chau, Brigitte Lin Chin-hsia, Yuen Biao, Sammo Hung Kam-bo, Moon Lee Choi-fung, Meng Hoi, Tsui Siu-keung, Judy Ong
Directed by Tsui Hark

Tsui Hark's frenetic, nutty, fantastic *Zu: Warriors from the Magic Mountain* helped spark an 80s boom in HK supernatural films. *Zu* serves as a bridge from the manic Shaw Brothers supernatural films of the same period to Hark's more Westernized *Chinese Ghost Story* series.

Aemy Wong, Wang Zu Xian, and Wong Tso Hsien. This confusion is due to attempts to reproduce the sound of spoken Cantonese or Mandarin using English characters.

While the written Chinese language is complex, there is only one basic form. Spoken Chinese is a different steamer of fish; dialects number in the hundreds. Fundamentally, there are two main branches of dialect: Cantonese and Mandarin. While Mandarin is considered the official spoken Chinese language (and is spoken widely in Taiwan, Singapore, and mainland China), the main dialect spoken in southern China—including Hong Kong—is Cantonese. This is a major cause of problems in assigning English names to HK film personnel.

Some players adopt an English first name for just this reason. Brigitte Lin Chin-hsia is easily recognized as Brigitte Lin by her English-speaking fans, but we do not know why Benny Mok Siu-chung is known as Max Mok on occasion nor why Michelle Li is known as Michelle Reis half the time. Further clouding matters are the directors who name their characters after

continued on next page

the actor or actress playing them (if they've decided to give the character a name at all).

What we do know is that we've picked one name per person and tried to use it throughout the book. We list the full name in a movie's credits, then use the shorter English version in the review. So please don't send us mail telling us Leslie Cheung Kwok-wing should be listed as Leslie Cheung Kuo-hweng—we know.

HEX ERRORS

CURSES AND INSULTS

More fractured English subtitles from your favorite Hong Kong movies (see chapter 3 for a full explanation).

Noodles? Forget it! Try my fist!
—*Final Victory*

Take my advice, or I'll spank you without pants.
—*The Seventh Curse*

Beat him out of recognizable shape!
—*Police Story 2*

Armed men clash pointlessly in one of the tenth century's numberless clan wars. A young warrior named Ti (Yuen Biao) climbs into a cave to escape the carnage, but is immediately besieged by fiendish thingies with glowing eyes. His bacon is saved by *sifu* Ting Yen (Adam Cheng), who attacks the monsters with a pride of magic swords that shoot out of the scabbard slung across his back. Ti, grateful he's still in one piece, offers to become Ting's student.

The loner *sifu*, however, merely heads off for another evil-filled cave. But Ti wants to prove his mettle, so he joins Ting, rival *sifu* Hsiao, and Hsiao's student, I-Chen, to do battle with the "Evil Disciples." Who are they, this surreal troupe of hellish jokesters whose white faces are adorned with red forehead tridents?

"They're the bad guys and we are the good guys," explains I-Chen to new boy Ti, and that's all we need to know, really, as the screen detonates into an ultrakinetic, razor-edited battle featuring nets of blue electricity, huge flaming logs that are waved like wands, concentric circles of spinning steel death-frisbees, and twitchy video game action.

Hsiao is poisoned by the Blood Monster (who is kept in check only by the eyebrows of the well-named guardian, Long Brow) and must be taken to the Ice Fortress to be cured by the Countess (Brigitte Lin). In a scene of near-orgasmic—yet asexual passion, the Countess spars martially with Ting, then cures Hsiao.

Then Ting becomes possessed, turning spooky-silver in the process. Without enough energy left to effect his cure, the Countess freezes everyone with an ice spell so Ti and I-Chen can go to heaven's Blade Peak to unite the mythical Twin Swords and duel with the hideously possessed Ting. Are ye with us?

Doesn't matter. *Zu* is a fantasy—Hark burning into celluloid what Georges Méliès, the father of cinematic gimcrackery, would have if he could have. But it's also about passion, loyalty, self-sacrifice, and saving the Earth from certain destruction by The Forces Of Evil. Few films set so ambitious an agenda, but *Zu* manages to pull it off, largely because the thing is so visually breathtaking and Brigitte's scowl of concentration makes you damn well *believe* in ice spells and blasting demonic possession outta people's bodies.

David Chute

From *Zu: Warriors from the Magic Mountain:* A powerful supernatural guy with angry white hair and porcupine pullover (Tsui Siu-keung) chained to a giant rock. Just another character in Mr. Hark's neighborhood.

Damn you, stink man!
—*Caged Beauties*

Well! Masturbate in hell!
—*Full Contact*

Beware! Your bones are going to be disconnected.
—*Saviour of the Soul*

You daring lousy guy
—*Satyr Monks*

I'll cut your fats out, don't you believe it?
—*It's Now or Never*

You're stain!
—*Taxi Hunter*

Bump him dead.
—*Police Story 3: Supercop*

Get out, you smurk
—*Aloha Little Vampire Story*

You won't die in one piece
—*Eastern Condors*

Damn, I'll burn you into a BBQ chicken!
—*Pedicab Driver*

You bastard, try this melon!
—*Gunmen*

Your dad is an iron worder, your mom sells beans
—*Legend of the Liquid Sword*

CAPSULE REVIEWS

A BETTER TOMORROW 3: LOVE AND DEATH IN SAIGON 1989

Despite the title and the starring presence of Chow Yun Fat, this is *not* a John Woo film. This is a romantic actioner that serves as a prequel to the first *ABT*, depicting the adventures of Mark (Chow Yun Fat) in Vietnam. He goes to Saigon to meet his pal Mun (Tony Leung), who's getting out of prison. These guys fancy themselves arms dealers, but they need the connections of cool-as-ice Kit (not *ABT*'s Leslie Cheung, but Anita Mui), who's got an upcoming transaction with corrupt General Bong.

A big deal turns sour and it's Kit who does the slo-mo, double-fisted slug-pumping while Mark fumbles with an M-16. Tsui—always fond of powerful and competent female characters—includes a scene of Kit teaching Mark how to shoot accurately!

Mun, Mark, and Mun's elderly father leave war-torn Saigon for HK and start an auto repair garage. Kit has fallen for Mark and follows them to HK, but things get complicated when Kit's former lover, a ruthless gangster named Ho (Tokito Saburo) takes umbrage and delivers a flower-bomb to the garage, killing Mun's father. Amid many plot twists and turns, Ho takes Kit back to Nam, forcing Mun and Mark to return to Saigon for revenge on Ho. But they must also dodge the vicious Bong, who chases our heroes around in a tank!

THE EAST IS RED (AKA SWORDSMAN III)   1993

Supposedly the sequel to *Swordsman II*, but mostly an opportunity to resurrect the fascinating character of Asia the Invincible (Brigitte Lin), a powerful martial artist who castrated himself to attain the full mystical force of the Sacred Scroll, transforming himself into a woman in the process. Lin's multifaceted performance fuses macho swagger with feminine mystique, combining the antics of a spoiled child with the destructive force of a vengeful god.

The East Is Red chronicles AI's search for her identity amidst a landscape beset by political turmoil in which Japanese and Spanish invaders do battle against Chinese warships. Nothing is quite what it seems: an armor-clad Japanese general is exposed by AI as a midget ninja, while AI's former lover Snow (Joey Wong) has assumed her master's masculine identity and is herself attacked by a disguised Japanese nemesis.

During lulls in the fighting—which include a barrage of gravity-defying martial arts as well as levitating warships, jet-powered boots, lethal needles and threads, and ninjas flying through the sky like kites of prey—AI beds down with Snow in a sensual quasi-lesbian scene. The sexual personae implode when the frustrated AI batters the masochistically faithful Snow to near-death, realizing all too late that her redemption lies within the purity of Snow's unwavering love.

Girls will be boys: Brigitte Lin (left) and Joey Wong (right) are cross-dressed to kill in *The East Is Red*.

I LOVE MARIA (AKA ROBOFORCE) 1988

The Hero Gang, led by a ruthless cyborg called Saviour and his vicious girlfriend Maria (Sally Yeh), attempt to take over Hong Kong using a gigantic robot called Pioneer I. They are foiled by a trio of inept losers: Whiskey (Tsui Hark), Curly (John Sham), and a clumsy photographer. Cyborg Saviour feels that flesh is imperfect and that only machines are worthwhile, since they have the potential to live forever.

To prove his love for Maria, Saviour builds a robot version of her called Pioneer II. When that robot is destroyed, Curly, the original inventor, fixes it and sends it into battle with the monstrous Pioneer I. Whiskey longs for the human Maria and has trouble accepting the fact that she is trying to kill him—even after an amazing outdoor chase scene, with the evil Hero Gang swinging through the trees on cables in pursuit of Whiskey, who is swinging on vines and yelling like Tarzan.

Saviour recalls the mad robotmonger Rotwang from *Metropolis*, and the Maria robot owes a nod to *Metropolis*'s Maria, but the film has more in common with goofy fare like *Infra-Man* than Fritz Lang's classic.

ONCE UPON

THE FATE OF A NATION
IS IN HIS HANDS

A TIME IN

GOLDEN HARVEST PRESENTS JET LEE IN ONCE UPON A TIME IN CHINA II
STARRING JET LEE, ROSAMUND CHAN, MAX MOK, DONNIE YEN, JOHN CHIANG, ZHANG TIE LIN EXECUTIVE PRODUCER RAYMOND CHOW PRODUCED BY TSUI HARK, NG SZE YUEN
DIRECTOR OF PHOTOGRAPHY WONG NGOR TAI HKSC ORIGINAL MUSIC BY RICHARD YUEN, JOHNNY NJO SCREENPLAY BY TSUI HARK, CHAN TIN SUEN, CHEUNG TAN DIRECTED BY TSUI HARK

Golden Harvest

CHINA II

The U.S. poster for *Once Upon a Time in China II.* Its hyphenate director appears on a CD by the band Sparks called *Gratuitous Sax and Senseless Violins,* where he sings about himself on a dance number entitled "Tsui Hark."

We'd like to reprint the lyrics, but the suits at Sparks' record company were unresponsive to our repeated requests for permission.

ONCE UPON A TIME IN CHINA II   1991

OUATICII is just as entertaining as its predecessor. Benny Mok takes over for Yuen Biao as Wong Fei-hong's show-off sidekick Leung Fu, Rosie Kwan continues as Aunt Yee, and Jet Li returns as Wong Fei-hong.

The fanatically xenophobic White Lotus Sect, led by the apparently supernatural Master Kung, is urging the local citizenry to kill all foreign devils. At the same time, a noble revolutionary movement (led by Dr. Sun Yat-sen) has sprung up, in the hope of replacing the Chinese Empire with a republic. When Wong's entourage arrives in Canton for an East/West medical conference, Aunt Yee is injured by White Lotus adherents who spot her Western garb and mistake her for a foreigner. Luckily, a kind stranger steps in to translate; he turns out to be Sun Yat-sen.

Wong wows the *gwailos* at the medical conference with his acupuncture technique, but the White Lotus gang attacks again, burning down the Foreign Language School and massacring the teachers. When Regional Commander Lan (Donnie Yen) refuses to shelter the now-homeless kids, Wong takes them to the British Consulate, where he joins forces with Sun Yat-sen and his revolutionary comrade Luke (David Chiang). Eventually, Wong and Luke find themselves at the White Lotus Temple, where Wong duels with Master Kung atop a teetering array of precariously balanced chairs, and exposes him as a fraud. But it's not over yet, fight fans. There's still the villainous Lan to be dealt with!

ONCE UPON A TIME IN CHINA III   1992

Tsui Hark's third Wong Fei-hong epic concentrates heavily on the martial art of lion-dancing. The notion that both East and West have to learn to adapt to each other's cultures is emphasized even more in *OUATICIII,* and the sociopolitical overtones are downplayed. The Empress Dowager decides to hold a Lion Dance competition to cause friction among the various foreign nationalities settling in China. Unfortunately, it causes greater strife among various Chinese factions! As Wong Fei-hong travels to Beijing (Peking) to visit his father, Wong Kei-ying, Dad spars with his enemy, the evil Chiu Tin Bai, who is determined to take the prize.

Yee (now Wong's fiancée) meets Tomansky, a Russian who has been infatuated with her since they went to school together. He gives her one of those newfangled motion-picture cameras, making Wong furiously jealous. After he calms down, Wong does a martial arts demonstration for the camera while Fu barks out orders through a megaphone. Later, the camera accidentally records footage that fingers Tomansky as a spy involved in a plot to assassinate the Dowager's President Li at the Lion Dance contest.

Chiu's men try to defeat Wong by pouring oil on the floor, throwing off his carefully honed balance (the bad guys are wearing cleats). Wong prevails, however, and enters the Lion Dance competition in order to win the crown, defeat Chiu, frustrate the Russian assassination, produce more film evidence against the Russians, and lecture President Li on how his policies are dividing the country.

The Supernatural

There are two kinds of people in this world: those who like movies in which the witch takes her head off and throws it at you, and those who don't. We hang solidly in the former camp, and are pleased to report that HK boasts some of the creepiest, most spookamous-jookamous flicks ever cranked out.

Inspiration is drawn from centuries of Chinese legend, in which legions of hopping vampires are a common part of daily life, and whose existence is put up with as one might tolerate bad weather. Instead of appearing as scheming Eastern European guys in formal wear, charming the ladies and biting their pale, innocent necks, these vampires are corpses in Ming Dynasty garb. Rigid in death, *Kyonsi* ("hopping ghosts") are scary, but they have a cute, playful side to them as well. And child-vampires are always cute.

ALOHA LITTLE VAMPIRE STORY
1988

A cute l'il child-vampire, Hsiu Long, grows tired of the endless bickering of feuding vampires Uncle Black and Uncle White, and runs away from home. Discovered by real kids pretending to be vampires, he camps out at the home of the feisty Dong Dong, who feuds with Fu, a bullying neighborhood kid. Dong Dong is scared of Hsiu Long, but when the cute little dead tyke magically heals the bruises D.D. got from fighting with Fu, they become friends.

Fu's uncle is an unscrupulous Taoist who's hired by a rich mobster to cure the gangster's brother, who's fallen under a rare vampiric spell. The afflicted brother wears a Victorian cloak to go with his fangs and hangs out in trees, gibbering like a monkey. The Taoist feeds him vampire blood straight from a cold blue neck, but it's ineffective; only the blood of a thousand-year-old

But vampires are often just foot soldiers for more powerful demons and witches. These monsters aren't cute at all. They use their powerful magic to transmogrify into all sorts of beclawed and squiggly red-eyed forms in their constant effort to enslave the souls of mortals.

Standing in their path is the Taoist priest. Wearing yellow robes and a wedge-shaped headdress imbedded with the yin/yang symbol, the Taoist is forever constructing altars festooned with candles and incense sticks, mixing black ink with blood, making reams of paper charms, playing with fire, and performing laser-blast tricks with eight-sided *feng shui* mirrors. When the Taoist is not involved in life-and-death struggles with the underworld's yawning maw, he's bailing his dunderhead students out of vampire-inspired snafus.

The priest often will explain the rules of engagement to participants and audience alike. This helps befuddled *gwailos*. Not knowing what to expect next, though, is—like the first trip through a thrill ride—a positive part of the experience.

A Chinese Ghost Story II

1990
Starring Leslie Cheung Kwok-wing, Joey Wong Jo-yin, Jacky Cheung Hak-yow, Michelle Reis (Lee Kar-yan), Waise Lee Chi-hung, Ng Ma, Ku Feng
Directed by Ching Siu-tung

This sequel commences with a montage of scenes from the first *A Chinese Ghost Story* (see chapter 1). Ning (Leslie Cheung, reprising his original character) finds himself thrown in jail in a case of mistaken identity, and is locked up long enough to grow a long beard. However, one night his jailers bring him a rice bowl topped with a succulent soy-sauce chicken leg—unusually fine jailhouse tucker. Ning eagerly sinks his teeth into the fowl but loses his appetite

She's dead and he isn't, but love conquers all. Joey Wong and Leslie Cheung in A Chinese Ghost Story II.

child-vampire will effect a cure. Of course, Hsiu Long qualifies as a source. The human kids team up with the adult vampires to fight the evil gangsters and rescue the kidnapped kid-vamp. Absurd as can be. Despite the title, there are no Don Ho singalongs or parasoltopped rum drinks.

DOCTOR VAMPIRE   1991

A Hong Kong doctor is vacationing in England when he gets bitten by a lovely vampire named Alice (Ellen Chan). He gets away, but when her British master-vamp gets a taste of his Alice-filtered blood, the *gwailo* bloodsucker goes bananas for it: "Don't you understand? His blood is like your Chinese ginseng!"

Back in HK, the doc finds he's lost his taste for garlic shrimp and starts going around with sunglasses and an Edwardian cloak, like Nicolas Cage in *Vampire's Kiss*. His fellow M.D.'s thoughtfully exsanguinate patients to feed him, and the kindhearted Alice tries to cure him by reanimating a fresh corpse, which rambles round the hospital corridors with priapic intent!

when his cellmate (whose beard is even longer) tells him that the dish is known as Headless Chicken, because one's beheading takes place the day after the meal! The cellmate, Chu (Ku Feng), gives him a lucky medallion and helps him escape. Ning takes refuge in a deserted villa containing eight coffins. But after dark, when the coffins open up and their spooks come out, Ning flees.

He is set upon by flying white-sheeted spirits, but Autumn (Jacky Cheung), a monk also taking shelter in the villa, freezes them in midair. The spirits are revealed to be fakes. They are actually a group of patriots, led by Windy (Joey Wong) and Moon (Michelle Reis), who are planning to free their father, Lord Fu, who has been unjustly taken prisoner by the emperor's men. Because of the medallion, the idealistic young patriots mistake Ning for the wise sage Elder Chu, who's still happily scratching on his cell walls.

Ning protests, but they interpret his remarks as wise riddles.

continued on next page

Ellen Chan digs in, while the loyal hospital staff armed with hypo-bandoleros tries to stop an epidemic of vampirism in *Doctor Vampire*.

The doc's meddling girlfriend and her nosy gal-pal make matters worse by bringing in a Taoist priest, whose spells cause our blanched hero to puff up with latex-bladder buboes, veins a-throbbin'. When Count Master-vamp shows up in the hospital, he's zapped with a surgical laser and pumped full of corrosive green fluid from log-sized hypo-dermics. This only slows him down, but he's finally defeated by the supernatural force of reani-mated Chinese opera heroes!

Please note: Chan's perfor-

They attach profound significance to his every word and interpret a poem about Sian—his ghost lover from *ACGS*—as a hint that they should intercept Lord Fu's captors at the Ten Mile Pavilion. Since Ning is smitten with Windy, his ghostly love's lookalike, he too goes to the Pavilion. Unfortunately, the place is haunted. Autumn teaches him the suspended-animation spell, but before he can show him how to break the spell, Ning accidentally freezes Autumn. He attempts to figure out the right defreezing command, unaware that an ani-mated ten-foot zombie is peeking over his shoulder! The frustrated Ning drags the rigid, sweating Autumn around the Pavilion as the monster freezes and thaws with each of Ning's attempts at re-creating the spell.

Windy and her gang arrive, but when the towering zombie reappears, they flee. They run smack into Hu (Waise Lee), the war-rior who is escorting their father back to court. Hu carves the beast up, but in the process, Windy is possessed by evil spirits, leading to some Linda Blair–like cursing and spewing. She turns into a mon-ster, but Ning rescues her with a yang-infusing kiss (*awwww. . .*). Hu then goes to enlist the aid of the High Priest to vanquish the spirits.

The High Priest turns out to be an evil impostor—he has a woman's voice, which, given HK filmic conventions, should have blown his cover already—and is the source of all the dissension and chaos in the empire. His chanting voice hypnotizes everyone but Autumn, who plugs his ears and rescues the others. After a romantic interlude with Windy, Ning goes off to find Swordsman Yen (Ng Ma), the misanthropic-but-lovable monk who saved him in the first *ACGS*. Hu (who now realizes that Lord Fu is a victim of the High Priest's treachery), Autumn, Yan, and the others must destroy the evil priest, who reappears in numerous forms, including a huge centipede.

After evading him through some nifty air-surfing on flying swords, Autumn and Yan are swallowed by the oversized bug. They must leave their bodies temporarily to survive; after the beast is killed, Yan rejoins his physical being, but Autumn's soul overshoots his body and careens off into the sky. But fear not—Jacky Cheung returns in Part 3.

—AK

A Chinese Ghost Story III

1991
Starring Tony Leung Chiu-wai, Joey Wong Jo-yin, Jacky Cheung Hak-yow, Nina Li Chi
Directed by Ching Siu-tung

The third and final installment in the *A Chinese Ghost Story* series eschews Leslie Cheung and his character in favor of a callow young monk named Fong (Tony Leung, bald as a cue ball). Fong and his *sifu* are pursued by thieves who covet their golden Buddha statue. The harassed duo head for the deserted Orchid Temple, unconcerned about any lurking ghosts. After all, they're monks.

Needless to say, the temple houses its share of lovely lady ghosts. Lotus (Joey Wong) and Butterfly (Nina Li) trap the pursuing thieves and turn them over to the evil Tree Demon (the half-man/half-woman/all-evil witch with the the fifty-foot tongue in the first *ACGS*). Sluuuuuurp! Lotus then surprises Fong, who drops the Buddha into the temple's basement. The devilish cutie tries to seduce him while he struggles to maintain his monastic vows. Despite her evil, he lets her leave.

When his master returns, he lies about losing the Buddha, then tries to search the basement in the light of day, but is scared off by snakes. Lotus returns that night and helps him look for the Buddha, accidentally breaking it in the process. The master returns from a trip to the village; since night is approaching, he starts to seal off the temple with prayers and holy beads. Lotus is trapped, imperiled by his prayers. Moved, Fong saves her by dispersing the beads and tricking his master into leaving.

mance includes one of the most sensual bloodsucking sequences ever put on film.

EVIL CAT 1987

Veteran actor-director Liu Chia-liang (Lau Kar-leung) appears as a sorcerer whose family has been cursed by an evil cat-spirit. It returns every fifty years to wreak havoc as it has for the last four hundred years. Do the math: only one more cat life to go! Mark Cheng helps Liu forever ice the feline. Stuart Ong performs creepy cat kung fu, and Tai-wanese sex bomb Tsui Suk Woon (*The Ghost Snatchers*) does a *Terminator* number, wiping out an entire cop shop with her bare claws. Blue-lit and spooky.

THE GHOST SNATCHERS 1986

A new high-rise office building in Hong Kong starts experiencing problems: giant hands are reaching through the air-conditioning system and abducting people and possessed secretaries are biting off executives' ears. An attractive female geomancer (Joyce Godenzi) is called in to diagnose and exorcise.

continued on next page

The problem? A legion of dead Japanese soldiers is buried beneath the foundations, and they're continuing their imperial efforts at world domination from beyond the grave! As wild as it sounds, the film is based on a true story. In the 70s, the Hong Kong Department of Public Works main building was diagnosed as suffering from Japanese World War II ghosts. Civil servants refused to work overtime, and a geomancer had to be called in to perform an exorcism. *The Ghost Snatchers* contains one of Joey Wong's earliest roles, as Godenzi's assistant.

THE GOLDEN SWALLOW 1988

*T*GS is a rip-off of *A Chinese Ghost Story*, but a *good* one. Cherie Chung plays Hell's Handmaiden, snaring souls for consumption by the extremely scary black-eyed Old Witch who delivers bon mots like "there's only one type of man: the *edible* ones." Chung falls for a cute traveling tax collector and shields him from edi-

But just when you make things easy for the sexy nice ghosts, the evil ones always seem to cash in. Sans holy beads, the Tree Demon attacks. And with the protective Buddha statue broken, he's got enough stuff to trap the *sifu*. But thinking quickly, the resourceful holy man grows his earlobes out and—covering his eyes with the fleshy appendages—goes into suspended animation.

Fong heads into town to get the Buddha fixed. He fails, but hires the avaricious swordsman Yin (Jacky Cheung) to help rescue his *sifu*. Back at the temple, Lotus rescues Fong from another assault by the Tree Demon. The jealous Butterfly—whose long red fingernails can shoot out like knives—betrays Lotus to the Demon. The

Rim Films

Ask any demon—kicks just keep getting harder to find. The smokin' ogre with his hairless harem in *A Chinese Ghost Story III*.

grisly witch threatens to marry Lotus to the Mountain Devil. Lotus escapes, but the Tree Demon binds Fong in a web of red silk and has Butterfly attempt to lasciviously suck out his yang energy. Finally, Yin and Fong's *sifu* unite with Lotus to wipe out the Tree Demon with their combined powers. But then they have to contend with the Mountain Devil—comprised of a glowing animated pagoda and a huge disembodied head with sharpened teeth. After vanquishing his horror, the humans emerge battered but victorious. Lotus, however, looks forward only to another shot at reincarnation.

—AK

bility, but complications occur. Lots of beautiful photography, flying silk, and extra-creepy human-freezing effects in this one.

THE HOLY VIRGIN VERSUS THE EVIL DEAD   1991

The moon turns red as the Moon Monster (Ken) visits Hong Kong and slaughters the students of nerdy professor Donnie Yen. Scholarly attempts to defeat the Monster prove futile, as do various forms of killing him! All parties involved must take a holiday in Cambodia, where the Holy Virgin and her tribe vanquish the Lazarus-like green-eyed Monster with sacred steel. Lots of martial action and witchy-nudie stuff, but a dearth of (needed) bugs and slime.

continued on next page

With the song of the Moon Monster in the air, a captive Miss Sha (right) kneels in front of an imposter One-Breasted Goddess With Moustache. A censored lobby card image from *The Holy Virgin Versus the Evil Dead.*

MR. VAMPIRE PART III   1988

One of the best of the *Mr. Vampire* series. Lam Ching Ying returns as World's Greatest *Sifu*, and bespectacled Billy Lau plays his addle-brained student. A black-lipped demon girl proves a formidable foe—healing her slain henchmen's wounds by pulling demon-healing maggots from her mouth and attacking with vats of cockroaches and baskets full of vicious demon-bats. Shoehorn-faced fellow *sifu* Richard Ng befriends a benign vampire and his cute vampire son and burns some baby-blue robes for them so they don't have to wear those scary traditional vamp costumes.

ONE EYEBROW PRIEST   1987

Even for hyperkinetic HK vampire-comedies with blue-faced ghouls and scrappy Taoists hopping on screen, this one is *really* weird. It's got everything—a *sifu* and his pair of oafish assistants, mean master-vampire, cute kid-vampire, husband-seeking ghostress—and it all comes at you

Deadful Melody

1994
Starring Yuen Biao, Brigitte Lin Chin-hsia, Carina Lau Kar-ling, David Lam Wai, Ng Ma, Elvis Tsui Kam-kong
Directed by Ng Min-keng

After Brigitte Lin gleefully stole the show as the she-male villain(ess) of *Swordsman 2*, she appeared in a succession of films as mighty witches, deadly swordswomen, or cold-blooded assassins. As Lin herself put it, "I seem to fulfill some fantasy the audience has about a beautiful girl performing violent acts." In *DM*, she is perfect in another role demanding toughness and invincibility as a musical martial artist who dresses in manly garb and wields a magical lyre that blasts her opponents into plumes of colored smoke.

Lin plays Snow, a character with a likable air of menace. As told in flashback, Snow's parents were slain by rival martial arts masters intent on possessing the lethal lyre. Seeking vengeance, Snow concocts an elaborate ruse to lure the killers out in the open. She hires a naive but headstrong security guard named Lun (Yuen Biao) to transport a case containing the lyre to the Mo Yee mountains.

This turn of events is perplexing and worrisome to the rival martial arts clan leaders, who are a bizarre lot. There's Master of Ghost (David Lam), a tall and scary pale-blue demon; Fire (Ng Ma), who is bald, portly, and bright red; and, of course, Ha Ching Fa, the Hard-Hearted Witch—a comely young woman with a penchant for ripping people's heads off with a whip. Master of Ghost's twin sons are pale blue and twitter about like the Wicked Witch's flying monkeys. In fact, the entire assemblage is something like a Clive Barker re-creation of *The Wizard of Oz*.

Naturally, the villains still want the magic lyre and pursue Lun with a vengeance. Snow shadows him to ensure his well-being and to see her plan come to bloody fruition. Eventually, she discovers that Lun is her long-lost brother, whom she thought had perished with her parents.

Lun, however, remembers nothing of his tragic past, and he vows revenge against Snow when his foster father becomes a casualty of her vendetta. The two siblings finally reconcile, but their long-delayed reunion is interrupted as the evil martial arts masters rally their forces for the final showdown.

The hell-bent Snow pulls back the strings of the musical instrument like a hunting bow and fires bursts of energy that lead to some imaginative carnage. Master of Ghost watches his men blasted into smoke and body parts, but he's still standing as Snow takes a breather to play a soft melody on the deadly instrument. She then informs him that he's been hit internally by the Eight Magic Keys of the lyre, and his body will explode if he takes two steps forward. M of G lets loose with hearty mocking laughter, takes one step, takes a hesitant second step . . . BOOM! Ha Ching Fa fares no better, as Snow's tuneful *fu* penetrates the Hard-Hearted Witch's inner organs and causes her to spew out a geyser of blood prior to her own detonation. Snow survives the ordeal, but she and her hardheaded brother Lun part at movie's end to pursue their separate martial goals.

Hello Dracular

1988
Starring Choi Yeung-ming, Chan Chun-leung
Directed by Wong Chi-chung

There is a custom in China: those who die in foreign lands must be brought back home for proper burial, or else they'll wander around aimlessly forever. A necromancer conducting one such

at a pace that would exhaust a six-year-old. The soundtrack is an aggressive montage of video game effects/Herbie Hancock synthesizer/*Terminator* soundtrack/garage-sale records . . . and right in the middle you get an honest-to-God *dance production number*, with Pauline Wong leading a bunch of kid-vamps in suspenders to the garbage disco beat of League Unlimited Orchestra.

A cute girl is bitten and turns blue, and when the dumbbell assistants rub boiled eggs on her body to cure her, the yolks turn blue. Trapped under a table by the breath-sniffing master-vamp, assistant number one fools the ghoul by farting repeatedly in his face. A rogue *sifu* feeds the master-vamp brackish centipede extract from a test tube. And few films made for general release have ever placed such importance on the magical properties of small boys' urine.

This nitrous supercharger is also known as *New Mr. Vampire Part II*, although it has no relation to the *Mr. Vampire* series, and is not part two of anything.

continued on next page

An exorcism ceremony gone wrong in *Possessed II*. The possessed woman breaks her chains from the wall, electrifies a do-gooder, and then rips his arm off. (The arm, by the way, continues to hold a gun, post-traumatic amputation, which starts to fire after the arm hits the floor, only adding to the confusion.)

POSSESSED II 1989

An HK cop moves his family into a flat facing a cemetery. Of course, they immediately become possessed by demons. The daughter turns on the schoolyard bully with a face full of fangs and pop-

corpse-drive, wrangling a half-dozen hopping undead through the woods, comes upon a kid-corpse who is looking for playmates to relieve his loneliness. Not surprisingly, the necromancer wants no part of his antics.

Five orphans in a wagon, out to bury their recently deceased Master, are also traveling through the dark blue, smoky woods this night. Kid-corpse steals the charms off Master's coffin, which shoots out the back of the wagon, hangs in midair, then explodes. Master's undead now, too, angry with everybody and lurking in the forest.

If that's not enough headache for the local townspeople, a *gwailo* priest, a young nun, and a cigar-smoking capitalist named Mr. Robert show up looking for corpses. Mr. Robert wants to exhibit them in America, where he'll make a fortune.

Back at the orphans' home (a mortuary), girl-orphan Ten-ten (who must be all of nine) teaches the newly arrived corpses some happy dance numbers. But the overweight bespectacled boy orphan still misses his Master. Worse, he is rebuked in his efforts to romance Ten-ten, and the three other boy orphans mercilessly make fun of his failure.

Meanwhile, you'd think the locals would be happy that *gwailos* want to buy the town's vampires and take them off their hands, but in fact they're upset that foreigners are disrupting Chinese traditions, and refuse the offer. So the sneaky *gwailos* decide to steal the corpses.

In danger of being caught halfway through the polterheist, the nun hides in a coffin with a tubby corpse. When their lips accidentally meet, electricity flies, reanimating the corpse, who begins to follow the nun's every move—monkey see, monkey do—even into the bathtub.

Sneaking the corpses out of town, the three body snatchers witness the lonely kid-corpse playing baseball by himself, using bones as bats and a skull painted orange as a ball. He cracks the skull outta the yard, which cracks Mr. Robert's skull on the fly.

A baseball-playing kid-corpse? Mr. Robert knows an American-headline attraction when he sees one and heartlessly resolves to grab him.

Dousing the skull with holy water, Mr. Robert tosses it back to the kid. When the kid picks it up, lightning zaps through his hands and starts him screaming. The screams reach the Master ghoul and send him over the edge.

Coming to kid-corpse's rescue, undead Master makes short work of Mr. Robert. He's no welcome liberator, though, and he soon abducts Ten-ten. Soldiers' bullets cannot stop Master as he returns to the forest, and the soldiers themselves are too frazzled to make full use of their dynamite.

Sensitive Overweight Boy rescues Ten-ten, but still does not win her heart. So he comically tries suicide, even as the other orphans are turning themselves into sacred burial pots—with legs to better do battle with Master. Master crocks the orphan-pots; kills the nun, priest, and lots of soldiers; and menaces Ten-ten again.

When all looks lost, Sensitive Overweight Boy straps the army's dynamite to his midsection, lights the fuse, then leaps into the arms of the Master, yelling, "I'm going with you!" And he does. The movie ends freeze-frame on Ten-ten crying, a most unhappy and unexpected—and therefore cool—ending.

Hello Dracular has a little downtime in between weirdnesses. But just when it gets a little slow, a kid-corpse starts playing skull baseball, or a bumbling troop of soldiers falls all over itself comically peeking at a comely nun's legs while she takes a pee.

ping red veins. The wife becomes a Suzie Wong vamp and sets out seducing weirdos. She traipses in Central Market, finds a porky meatcutter hacking up a huge oinker and lures him into the back of a truck hung thick with hog carcasses. Aiyahhh! She transforms herself into a hairy monster and fries his bacon.

A jive-talking' 1973-style fly-guy shows the wife his African snapshots and holds a lighter to his foot to prove his mettle; of course, he's toast. The exorcist can't get the job done, because he's really a beat cop named Dick who performs demonic duels only as a hobby. It's up to a traveling *gwailo* Hare Krishna to decode the demonology and bust the ghosts. Looks like the makers of this flick stayed up all night watching *The Exorcist*, *Altered States*, and *An American Werewolf in London*—and ate waaaay too much congee.

SPIRITUAL LOVE   1987

Your typical love story: girl dies, boy meets girl's ghost centuries later, they fall in love, boy loses

continued on page 102

TEN THINGS WE'VE LEARNED WATCHING HONG KONG

1 Fierce ghosts and vampires can be subdued by affixing Taoist charms—written in red ink on yellow paper—to their foreheads. But the temptation to play with these immobilized ghoulies (push them, insult them, etc.) is completely irresistible and completely unadvised . . .

2 . . . Because if you taunt or belittle a subdued ghoul, the chances that the charmed paper will come off—restoring the monster's lethality—are 100 percent.

3 Witches' heads just won't stay on. If they're not getting accidentally chopped off in battle, they're purposely being shucked with a neck-toss. In either case, witch opponents get preoccupied with the disembodied heads, which fly around howling and trying to bite. But you also can't ignore the headless body, which always hops up and gets into the fight!

A corpse drive from the movie *Jumping Corpses*. Yellow charms can be seen affixed to their foreheads.

SUPERNATURAL FILMS

4 Humans have *yang* energy; the undead are *yin*-heavy. Since human men have more yang energy than human women, they are a prime target for the seductive powers of female ghosts. Whether the ghost's motives are noble or duplicitous, this kind of love never ever works out. As a Taoist priest put it in *The Golden Swallow*, "There's no love between man and ghost, Sonny."

5 Born under a bad sign? Stars crossed in your horoscope? Sorcerers and Taoist priests shrug their shoulders; they can predict your fate, but can't change it. Even if you started out as the hero of the film, if the geomancer says trouble ahead, you better stock up on incense and Hell Bank Notes, because you are done for.

6 When the exorcist asks for sticky rice, he damn well means *sticky* rice. Sticky rice is the active ingredient in poltergeist poultices. Regular rice is a spurious (and dangerous) substitute, often sneaked into the rice bag by dishonest salesmen because it's cheaper. The consequences can be dire.

7 The Chinese word for the number four sounds like the word for "death." So don't count on finding any room number four in Hong Kong hospitals or dining at a restaurant called the Four Seasons! On the other hand, the number eight is considered quite lucky, and you'll spot it everywhere, from billboards to personalized license plates.

8 If your pet fish die, expect trouble.

9 Ghoul knowledge:
a) Ghouls can't see humans, but they can spot them by smelling their breath. If you hold your breath, you are invisible to a vampire. But he will put his blue face about an inch from your nose and sniff furiously!

b) The undead hop (or glide) only in straight lines along the floor. This is why Chinese temples often have a threshold you must step over, and why pawnshops have a screen directly in front of the entrance. Many a terrified human has received a reprieve when the vampire chasing them simply couldn't hop a log or high curb.

c) Chinese zombies are Chinese first, and zombies second. They'll help repel unwanted foreigners before biting the locals.

d) Chinese child-vampires are children first, and vampires second. Human children recognize this, befriend them, and shield them from meddling adults. In *Mr. Vampire Part II*, kids try to protect a kid-corpse by claiming that he's an illegal alien from the mainland.

10 No monster is ever really finally dead until it explodes.

girl's ghost—it never works out. The lovers here are megastars Chow Yun Fat and Cherie Chung, but the show is stolen by Chow's vengeful, bitchy girlfriend May (portrayed with exquisite malice by Pauline Wong).

"Jealousing" over Cherie, May sets up a sympathy-evoking tableau for Chow to stumble upon: at midnight, she perches on a stool with her head in a noose, wearing a red dress. Dying under such circumstances turns a soul into a virulent, vengeful ghost, but the set-up is all for show—until May's cat jumps at her and knocks her off the stool! She strangles, then returns from the dead in pissed-off mode to take a bite out of Chow. Cherie sends for reinforcements from Hades: her ferocious, feral ghost hubby, who rips May in half. Neither half goes quietly.

THE ULTIMATE VAMPIRE   1991

Taoist hijinks with Lam Ching Ying and Chin Siu Ho of *Mr. Vampire* fame. Watch for the "Hell Police"—four undead constables in monochromatic shinyl-vinyl

Red Spell Spells Red

1991
Starring Tong Chun-yip, Pun Lai-yin, Leung Chi-hung, Eling Chan
Directed by Titus Ho

Red Spell Spells Red's blend of sorcery and warped travelogue takes you back to the glory days of Manhattan's 42nd Street grindhouses. You can almost hear the Times Square faithful hollering for more gore or staring in dope-addled disbelief at the screen. Creepy-crawly and aggressively strange, *Red Spell* will find no favor with hard-core PETA-philes; its scenes of pig-sticking, chicken-geeking, and scorpion attacks are rough and raw. Its Southeast Asian locations are appealing, though (as in many HK flicks) non-HK Southeast Asia is portrayed as a mighty wild and unruly place.

Stephen, a director of *mondo*-style documentaries, takes his onscreen host/offscreen girlfriend Stella to Borneo. His next film will explore Borneo's legend of the Red Dwarf Ghost, an evil dwarf-sorcerer who was assassinated and buried in a large jar by a quartet of righteous sorcerers. The film crew sneaks into the forbidden cave and busts open the cursed sarcophagus, which boils with red smoke. Film in can, Stephen heads back to HK while Stella and crew continue upriver to an Iban tribal village to gather more footage.

The Iban housemaster, Dairoma, seems affable, and the crew looks forward to "trial marriages" with the local girls, who—the portly Dairoma assures them—are free of "herres." But when the house sorcerer touches Stella's hand, he knows with electric certainty that she's got a big red birthmark on her shoulder and . . . well, red spell spells red.

The crew starts dying one by one. In the jungle, one member gets a small cut; his spilled blood bubbles furiously, animating surrounding bamboo stalks, which grab, toss, and pierce the poor man. Back at the long house, a large black scorpion suddenly falls on Stella's shoulder. She flicks it off—stinger-first—into the arm of Dairoma's son Rumbang, who starts screaming in pain. The irked housemaster has to chop Rumbang's arm off with a machete. Dairoma immediately suspects that Stella's got a scorpion curse, but the sorcerer fingers local gal Satali as the curse-carrier. They prepare to sacrifice her to appease the gods, a move scotched by the more civilized Lau—an overseas Chinese representing a local development council.

When Stella passes by the town's cockfighting pit, the birds stop their fighting, then attack her as *Omen*-style music wells up. The villagers now regard Stella in a different light, especially when they realize that the now-teeming scorpions are spontaneously issuing from Stella's red birthmark!

The house sorcerer puts two and two together, recognizing Stella as his own illegitimate granddaughter, on whom he put a scorpion curse many years ago, after she was taken away to Hong Kong by her biological father.

Distraught, he summons a Tibetan Lama from Thailand. The sorcerer sets up an elaborate exorcism, which features Stella tied to a revolving waterwheel—needless to say, wearing a sheer white blouse—while the sorcerer throws a powder at her made from her late mother's ground-up skull.

The Red Dwarf Ghost's spirit—which has had nothing to do with the entire scorpion-curse mess—possesses Satali, and she skewers Lau with just-sprouted sharp fingernails. But then the Lama steps in and puts the kibosh on the whole witchy gang.

garments; their muttering is only made intelligible when *sifu* chews on a ball of mud. Carrie Ng appears as an impudent young ghost ("You don't look thirty-seven." "I died when I was twenty, and it's seventeen years ago!") lusting after *sifu*. Be sure to stay tuned for end-credit outtakes, which demonstrate some spectacular flubs in wirework.

HELL

BANK NOTES

What happens to stuff when you burn it? It goes up in smoke, right? But where does it *go*? The answer is that it goes to the spirit world. Prayer-directed, it reaches the hands of one's departed loved ones.

With this direct pipeline, wouldn't you want to make your relatives' afterlife as comfortable as possible? You'd like to see them enjoying their time in the after-world with a nice house, luxury automobile, servants, and pots of money.

Well, here's your chance to help. Buy a wad of Hell Bank Notes and burn them ceremoni-ally. Since the notes are legal ten-der only in hell, you can buy a large packet of them at your local Asian grocery for about eighty-nine Earth cents. Every Hell Bank Note is a heavy piece of change—burning denominations of less than ten or a hundred mil-

continued on page 106

The Seventh Curse

1986
Starring Chow Yun Fat, Chin Siu Ho, Maggie Cheung Man-yuk, Dick Wei, Elvis Tsui Kam-kong
Directed by Lan Wei-tsang

Secret lives of the HK rich and famous are explored in this splat-terific yarn. It starts in the posh poolsides of Aberdeen Harbor but quickly shifts to the jungles of northern Thailand, which are lousy with preternatural worm tribes and fetid monster breath. *TSC* features the characters of Dr. Yuan and Wisely, a pair of cognac-sniffing adventurers created by pulp novelist Ai Hong. Dr. Yuan is played by *Mr. Vampire*'s Chin Siu Ho while Wisely is given Peter Cushing pipe-puffing authority by Chow Yun Fat.

As *The Seventh Curse* opens, Dr. Yuan defuses a cop/hostage drama despite the meddling of a spoiled-brat cub reporter, Tsai-hung (Maggie Cheung). His triumphal celebration with his girl-friend is stopped ante-coitus as Thai witch doctor Heh Lung (Dick Wei) busts into his apartment uninvited, warning Yuan that his "blood curse" is about to relapse. His final advice: "Keep away from sex." The good doctor gets after it anyway, and is rewarded with cork-popping spurts that burst from his limbs!

The proto-venereal phenomenon is explained in flashback: Dr. Yuan goes to Thailand on a medical expedition and tangles with a Worm Tribe headed by Sorcerer Aquala (Elvis Tsui), a baby-grind-ing, cackling heathen. The tyrant silences dissenters with a flying alien-baby—a reptilian-killer-Hello-Kitty-fetus—that rips into victims, then chews through their torsos.

Yuan saves a native beauty, Betsy, from sacrifice to Old Ances-tor—an animated skeleton with a penchant for biting open necks and sucking out spinal cords! But Yuan is captured and receives a "blood curse": a handful of magic bullets, which he's forced to swallow, will come blasting out at regular intervals. The last bullet to go off will kill him.

The grateful Betsy slices a benign tumor from one of her ample breasts and feeds it to him, but this peculiar antidote lasts only a year. Dr. Yuan must return to Thailand to retrieve sacred "grains" stored in the eyes of an enormous subterranean Buddha statue to effect a permanent cure. Yuan and Heh team up to battle the villainous Aquala; gorehound-spelunking commences as the duo encounter Old Ancestor in his grue-drenched cave.

The skeleton transforms into a rubberized, slimy-fanged Godzilla/Alien critter that survives attacks by bullets and the now-on-our-side reptilian-killer-Hello-Kitty-fetus, before being blown into chunks by Wisely, who arrives on the scene packing an RPG rocket launcher! Yuan heals himself by consuming the sacred grain,

Dr. Yuan (Chin Siu Ho) fails to heed the witch doctor's warning—"Keep away from sex"—so stuff starts bursting from his leg in *The Seventh Curse*.

lion is an insult. Hell Bank Notes are ubiquitous in HK supernatural flicks.

But you don't have to stop with money. HK funerals often feature elaborate houses, servants, and Mercedes-Benzes, which are constructed of brightly colored paper and then torched. Although the Chinese concept of hell is not one of fire-and-brimstone, colored-paper air-conditioning units have been spotted going up in smoke as well.

and the two heroes return to Hong Kong to plan further adventures.

The Seventh Curse is a show-stopping midnight movie, which seems to have flown under the radar of even dedicated HK fans. This film marked a possible development for HK films (gore/fantasy/Wisely) that never really panned out. Viewers copping a Wisely jones from *TSC* should also check out *The Legend of Wisely* and *Bury Me High*.

Jackie Chan

Trying to describe a Jackie Chan film is like trying to describe a dream. Descriptions bog down in accounts of "this happened" and "that happened," until you can't be sure if your mind is adding details, making logical connections in place of more elliptical ones.

There's almost a tendency to want to file Chan's films away under the category of each picture's big stunt, if only to make his talent more comprehensible. But then another Chan film comes out, and he's at it again, somehow beyond language—too fast, too perfect, and too full of nuance to be nailed down by words or memory.

—Mick LaSalle, *San Francisco Chronicle*

JACKIE CHAN

FILMOGRAPHY

Master With Cracked Fingers
   (1971), aka *Snake Fist Fighter*
Hand of Death (1975)
New Fist of Fury (1976)
Shaolin Wooden Men (1976),
   aka *36 Wooden Men*
Half a Loaf of Kung Fu (1977)
Killer Meteors (1977)
To Kill With Intrigue (1977)
Eagle Shadow Fist (1977)
Snake and Crane Arts of Shaolin
   (1977)
Magnificent Bodyguards (1978)
Dragon Fist (1978)
Snake in the Eagle's Shadow
   (1978)
Spiritual Kung Fu (1978)
Drunken Master (1978), aka
   *Drunken Monkey in the Tiger's
   Eye*
Fantasy Mission Force (1979)
The Fearless Hyena (1979)
The Young Master (1980)
The Big Brawl (1980), aka *The
   Battle Creek Brawl*
The Fearless Hyena II (1980)

It cannot be said too many times: nobody on this Earth makes movies like Jackie Chan. He manages to combine a disarming charm with ferocious athleticism to create the finest physical action sequences ever put on film by anyone, anywhere, period. Dizzying physical stunts are choreographed and rehearsed by Jackie and his cadre of stuntmen, then performed in adrenaline-soaked exuberance on the razor's edge of peril. Intensely serious about his craft, Jackie consistently pushes the action envelope farther than anyone else has, or can. Singer James Brown may be a legend, but he is *not* the hardest-working man in show business.

Born in 1954, Jackie grew up as the ward of a school for Peking Opera, where he was rigorously instructed in acrobatics. He performed publicly as a member of a school troupe called The Seven Little Fortunes (see chapter 10 for the film work of other SLF members).

He began his film career in the early 70s, touted as "the new Bruce Lee" (he was once Lee's stunt double), but his spirit is closer to that of silent film comedians Harold Lloyd or Buster Keaton, who performed hazardous stunts for a laugh. What Jackie Chan went on to create was a distinct brand of martial slapstick highlighted with film stunts of masochistic intensity.

It's comedy pushed to the point of pain. Jackie falls twenty feet and hits the ground. Jackie jumps into a bed of hot coals. Jackie hangs dangling from a flying helicopter or hot-air balloon.

If you can, see his movies in a crowded theater. An audience locked into a big screen Jackie Chan experience melds together into a unified organism obsessed with a single rabid thought: What's next? Oh my God! *That's* next!

The stunts have turned Jackie into a one-man legend, and 'most all of it is true. Yes, he was almost killed on the set of *Armour of God;* he hit his head during a stunt and went into a coma. Yes, he has a plate in his skull. Yes, he can't get insurance. Yes, hordes of teenaged Japanese girls are fanatically obsessed with Jackie: they attempt film-set break-ins wherever he's filming and have even been dragged—distraught—off train tracks or rushed to hospitals

Your host for this chapter, Jackie Chan. From *Dragons Forever*.

continued on next page

Should you wish to join Jackie Chan's fan club, write to:

(Headquarters)
Jackie Chan International Fan Club
The J. C. Centre
145 Waterloo Road
Kowloon
Hong Kong

(USA)
Jackie Chan Fan Club, USA
P.O. Box 2281
Portland, OR 97208
(503) 299-4766
chanfansus@aol.com

(Canada)
3007 Kingston Road
Box 109,
Scarborough, Ontario M1M 1P1

(Japan)
#1001 Nagatani Mansion
26 Banchi
Sakamachi, Shinjuku-ku
Tokyo 160

(Australia)
P.O. Box 1668
Bondi Junction
New South Wales 2022

(United Kingdom)
92 Ambleside Road
Kingsway, Bath
BA2 2LP

to have suicidal toxins pumped out. Yes, Japanese video-game maker Kaneko created a *Mortal Kombat*–style game featuring a digitized Jackie Chan in gold kung fu clothes. Yes, superstar Maggie Cheung got seventeen stitches in her head making one of Jackie's films. Yes, yes, yes.

Don't ever, EVER leave a Jackie Chan movie early. He often uses outtakes of stunt mishaps over the closing credits—shocking stuff. You'll see him laugh over light mistakes, or mug over slight injury. But when he gets this real serious look—holding a broken finger or the back of his head—and you see him bleed, you understand that for all the joking and fun of a Jackie Chan movie, this is not Industrial Light and Magic and a bunch of blue screens and computerized legerdemain, but real flesh-and-bone filmmaking.

At the MTV Movie Awards in 1995, at age forty-one, Jackie became only the third person ever presented with a Lifetime Achievement Award. Accepting the award, Chan said "I'm honored but surprised, because I'm still so young. I have a long way to go yet."

After seeing several Jackie films, you realize that this guy is driven to keep topping himself, to make the ultimate Jackie Chan movie . . . and one wonders what that would be.

Armour of God

1986
Starring Jackie Chan, Alan Tam, Rosamund Kwan Chi-lam, Maria Delores Forner, Ken Boyle
Directed by Jackie Chan

Armour of God's main claim to fame is not its shameless appropriation of *Raiders of the Lost Ark*, nor that it's one of Jackie's highest-grossing films, nor even the presence of 80s Cantopop superstar Alan Tam as Jackie's dopey sidekick. Nope, *Armour of God* is famous as the film that almost killed Jackie Chan.

A relatively innocuous stunt went awry, and Jackie plummeted twenty feet to the ground, hit his head on a rock, and went into a coma. But he lived and even returned to filming after a brief hospital visit!

Plate in Jackie's skull or not, *Armour of God*, which was filmed in Yugoslavia, is a marvelous action-adventurer. Jackie plays a Robin Hood character named Asian Hawk. His link with Alan (Alan Tam) is explained with a schlocky Partridge Family–style rock video starring a group called The Losers (a play on Tam's popular 70s band, The Wynners). One of the background singers, Laura (Rosie Kwan), comes between Hawk and Alan by dumping the former in favor of the latter. But when a group of hooded monks busts into a Paris fashion show and abducts Laura at AK-47-point, the two put their differences aside to rescue her.

The hooded figures belong to some sort of satanic Franciscan order that's determined to obtain God's Armour: an antique five-piece set that possesses special properties. They hold Laura for ransom, hoping Alan and Hawk will deliver the three pieces they lack and bring their evil plan to fruition.

Our heroes convince a pipe-sucking European nobleman to lend them the pieces, but they have to accept the aristocrat's beautiful daughter May (Maria Delores Forner) as their apprentice on the caper. Off roar the unlikely trio in Hawk's Mitsubishi sports car (off camera, Jackie Chan is a Mitsubishi pitchman).

The funky monks are flushed out with a bag of fake God's Armour. Bullets rain from the battlements as Alan and Hawk fight with the friars. Despite her haughty, spoiled-rich-girl demeanor, May proves to be a trouper when it comes to providing suppressing fire; it turns out she was a European women's shooting champ.

The heroic trio is overwhelmed by a crowd of villains driving off-road vehicles and dirt bikes and beat a retreat in the Mitsu. Wild car-and-bike stunts (choreographed by France's Remy Julien Action Team) end with a jump over a two-lane divided highway as traffic proceeds underneath them. The baddies still pursue, eventu-

HEX ERRORS

PHILOSOPHY AND WISDOM

More fractured English subtitles from your favorite Hong Kong movies (see chapter 3 for a full explanation).

What is a soul?
It's just a toilet paper.
—*To Hell With the Devil*

What is it that drills your nerves?
MONEY!
—*The Last Message*

The human sense is nonsense.
But human blood is superb.
—*The Golden Swallow*

The fart of God.
What does it mean?
With a remarkable sound.
—*The Informer*

The petrified trees testify to rages
   of thunder
—*Bury Me High*

Don't pee onto the burning pot.
—*Magic Cop*

If you don't waste time, time
   wastes you at once
—*The Avenging Quartet*
continued on next page

People scare people
And people are scared to death
—*One Eyebrow Priest*

Not any nuts will admit they are
   nuts!
—*Naked Killer*

The bullets inside are very hot.
Why do I feel so cold?
—*Lethal Panther*

A toad is no match for a swan
—*Robotrix*

My world is to companion with
   calabash till drunk
—*Shaolin Drunkard*

You're petulant, but not concen-
   trated enough
—*A Chinese Ghost Story*

To generate the greatest power,
   we'd be heartless.
—*Zen of Sword*

Man! Why beat! Take it easy
—*The Nocturnal Demon*

Bastard, an inch longer, an inch
   stronger
—*Fong Sai Yuk*

I'm not . . . I'm!
—*My Neighbours Are Phantoms*

ally trapping our heroes on a narrow suspension bridge. But the car transforms into a micro-racer—a sort of motorized skateboard with just enough room for the three-diamond Mitsubishi logo—and they scoot out of harm's way!

Hawk and Alan then disguise themselves in robes and hitch to the hilltop monastery. They rescue Laura from the mad monks, but she's been drugged and programmed to return with hostage Alan and the Armour. It's up to Hawk to rescue them, and this is where *AOG* really starts to shine.

In a fight with a hall full of monks, Hawk battles his opponents with a flaming ten-foot timber and uses long wooden tables as ramps and springboards. A face-off with the evil head monk (Ken Boyle, with odd eyebrows) brings out a quartet of eccentric assassins: high-heeled 70s blaxploitation vixens. A battle with

Jackie tries to blow himself out before he blows himself up in *Armour of God*.

these opponents (in action, it's obvious that they're Jackie's stunt-men in blackface drag) leaves Hawk on top, but he still has to dyna-mite his way out, with TNT strapped to his body. A leap onto a hot-air balloon completes the adventure, but stay tuned for the *scary* outtakes.

Armour of God II: Operation Condor

1991
Starring Jackie Chan, Carol "Do Do" Cheng Yu-ling, Eva Cobo Garcia, Shoko Ikeda
Directed by Jackie Chan

*A*OG's sequel came five years after the original. The film was shot in Barcelona and the Sahara Desert, and quickly went past sched-ule and over budget. But Jackie fans come out ahead since many of the effects are quite spectacular. Indeed, *AOG2:OC* eclipses the original in many respects.

Jackie plays another Lost-Ark-raiding type named after a bird of prey: Condor. As the film begins, he arouses the ire of some fierce tribesmen and escapes by climbing into an enormous clear plastic inflatable ball and rolling down an almost-vertical hillside.

Condor's next mission involves a trip to Spain, where he befriends a Japanese hippie-girl trinket-hawker (Shoko Ikeda). Summoned there by "the Baron," Condor's given a UN-sponsored mission: liberate a stockpile of gold bars from a secret World War II Nazi desert base. He's also given an ornate key to the gold vault, and a partner who is an expert in desert travel, Ada (played by comedienne Do Do Cheng).

World War II Nazi gold-seekers are everywhere, as Condor discovers when he goes to a locksmith to have the key checked out. As he leaves, a group of thugs accost him at gunpoint. When he escapes on a dirt bike, a frenetic chase ensues. Stuntmen are set up like pinball bumpers as choreographed cars and motorbikes slide

If you don't eat people, they'll eat you!
—*We Are Going to Eat You*

When the tree falls, the monkeys run.
—*Fantasy Mission Force*

Thanks, Monk.
—*Ghostly Love*

THE BIG BRAWL (*AKA* THE BATTLE CREEK BRAWL)   1980

Jackie's first Hollywood film. Directed by Robert Clouse (*Enter the Dragon*), it uses Jackie's comedic skills to good effect. Jackie plays a hardworking guy who enters a fighting competition in Battle Creek, Texas. Perky Kristine DeBell (better known for her antics in *The X-Rated Adventures of Alice in Wonderland*) chastely plays the love interest here as Jackie scraps against a legion of guys who look like they have escaped from the World Wrestling Federation.

THE CANNONBALL RUN   1981

Dean Martin as a drunk! Sammy Davis Jr. as a priest! Farrah Fawcett's nipples poking up under her Lurex jumpsuit! In the middle of all this, you briefly get Jackie Chan as a Japanese race car driver. Directed by Burt Reynolds's

around and crash through stacks of boxes—a giant LEGO village invaded by hurtling metal. Condor finds time to save an imperiled baby in the frantic race toward the docks, where he drives off a pier, leaps off the bike, and clings to a midair block of netted cargo as the pursuers' car flies past into the ocean!

Condor and Ada head off to the desert, the suspected location of the gold hoard. They join forces with the Japanese hawker and her pet scorpion Ding-Dong, then fight off bandit slavers—as well as a pair of idiotic Arabs—before finally locating the secret base.

Unfortunately, a wheelchair-bound Nazi named Adolf has tracked them down, and they must fight a pitched battle against his band of mercenaries for control of the stacked gold bullion. The fight takes place in a secret underground gold dump filled with a wealth of equipment that doubles as a kung fu playground—girder jungle gyms and seesaws crawling with combatants. The gold-sniffing mercenaries turn against Adolf, and the final duel takes place in a wind tunnel, with a massive fan turbine (controlled with wind-baffles by the now-on-our-side Adolf) blowing people around like rag dolls. What *won't* Jackie Chan utilize in his never-ending search for new cinematic thrills? Finally, the good guys are blown out of an air shaft by the fan and the bad guys (and gold) are simply blown up.

City Hunter

1992

Starring Jackie Chan, Joey Wong Jo-yin, Kumiko Gotoh, Chingmy Yau Suk-ching, Richard Norton, Gary Daniels, Leon Lai Ming, Johnny Lo Hwei-kong, Michael Wong Man-tuk
Directed by Wong Jing

Jackie Chan is not only a pan-Asian phenomenon, but Japan's most popular HK film star. There's a Japanese tilt to this fluffy, sprawling comedy, which is based on a *manga* (a Japanese comic book

Rim Films

City Hunter: Chingmy Yau juggles a nickel-plated nine-millimeter fashion accessory from Italy's Pietro Beretta.

series) about a rakish private eye named Ryu Saeba. Teen idol Kumiko Gotoh costars along with the lovely Joey Wong, famous in Japan thanks to the series *A Chinese Ghost Story.*

The film re-creates the comic book style in live action, and viewers should be prepared for ninety minutes of ridiculous sight gags and goony slapstick. Director Wong Jing is famous for his populist, goofball comedies, and *City Hunter* is similarly loaded with absurdities. Still, this *is* a Jackie Chan movie, and action fans won't be disappointed.

The glossy opening sequence has Ryu's partner Makimura (a

former stunt coordinator, Hal Needham, who also directed the screamingly godawful *Megaforce.*

CRIME STORY   1993

Jackie plays it straight as a police lieutenant trying to crack a kidnapping case. Directed by ace action director Kirk Wong, *CS* features Jackie turning over a car by hand and brawling with his turncoat partner (Kent Cheng) in a burning, collapsing building!

DRUNKEN MASTER   1978

Jackie plays folk hero Wong Feihong as a headstrong youngster who runs afoul of his father, Wong Kei-ying. Wong the Elder sentences Junior to tortuous martial training under his uncle Sam the Seed. Fei-hong flees but runs into a tough who thrashes him into submission. The chastened Wong returns to his rigorous *sifu*—and starts taking his training seriously this time. *Drunken Master* was very popular in HK and throughout Asia, going a long way toward turning Jackie into a star.

continued on next page

FIRST MISSION   1985

Jackie stars as a cop who must care for his mentally retarded brother (Sammo Hung, who also directed). When Sammo is kidnapped by criminals to force Jackie to hand over a police informant, the screen explodes into its usual riot of martial lava. Dramatic and well acted.

TWIN DRAGONS   1992

A raucous send-up of Jean-Claude Van Damme's *Double Impact*, this film was codirected by Ringo Lam and Tsui Hark as a benefit for the Hong Kong Directors' Guild. Jackie plays a dual role as separated-at-birth identical twins: one's a classical pianist raised in the West, the other is a streetwise HK punk. When the pinky-raiser meets the hell-raiser, the congee hits the fan. Among the most confused are the pair's unwitting girlfriends: Maggie Cheung and Nina Li. Some excellent stuntwork and a hilarious endbattle in a carmanufacturing plant make this silly film at least twice as good as most Jean-Claude flicks.

cameo by Michael Wong) expiring in a hail of bullets and making Ryu promise to care for his cousin Kaori. The girl grows up to become beautiful Joey Wong, and the two become partners. They end up chasing after runaway teen Kiyoko (Kumiko Gotoh) aboard a luxury cruise ship bound for Japan. Also on board are a card shark (Leon Lai) with a deck of razor-edged aces, a sexy undercover cop named Saeko (Chingmy Yau), and a passel of *gwailo* bandits that includes Australian baddie Big Mac (Richard Norton) and British wunderkind Gary Daniels.

Jackie plays the womanizing Ryu as a declawed tomcat, mugging over the occasional babe while overtly lusting after a bowl of wonton noodles. But when the bad guys shoot the captain and take over the ship, *Die Hard* style, Ryu's full attention turns to the crooks (who dress in natty red ninja getups).

Action is presented in a series of comic set pieces. Ryu wanders into the ship's theater (which is showing that weird Bruce Lee versus the seven-foot-two-inch Kareem Abdul-Jabbar kung fu duel from *Game of Death*), then finds himself confronted by an actual pair of real-life seven-foot black fighters! Taking cues from Bruce's onscreen actions, he vanquishes the giants, only to swing from plastic porpoises attached to the ceiling.

In a powerfully twisted sequence, Ryu gets thrown into a video game machine and emerges as a series of characters from *Streetfighter II*. Ryu and his nemesis fight in a speeded-up and tweaked sequence that resembles those from the video game (Jackie Chan as Kung Fu Sue spinning on her head—buff the mind's eyeball with that).

When he joins forces with Saeko, she spins around in Ryu's arms, firing from twin thigh-holsters, and they finish with a brief, delirious dance routine! Finally, Ryu and Big Mac go hand-to-hand—Mac with a couple of meter-long steel shafts that transform into sectioned whips and Ryu with a pair of police batons and a pole filched from the ship's decimated decor. Triumph. Outtakes. Your ninety minutes are up. Add more coins for additional time.

Dragons Forever

1987
Starring Jackie Chan, Sammo Hung Kam-bo, Yuen Biao, Deanie Yip, Yuen Wah, Pauline Yeung, Shing Fui-on, Benny "The Jet" Urquidez
Directed by Sammo Hung Kam-bo

Sammo Hung is a great stunt coordinator and action director, but this 1987 Jackie Chan vehicle once again proves what a terrific comedy director he is as well. There are fights throughout the film, but—until the final fifteen-minute sequence—the main emphasis is on humor. All three leads are terrific, with Yuen Biao particularly hilarious as a verbose neurotic (his therapy scenes are great).

Lawyer Johnny Lung (Jackie Chan) has a client list so seedy it rivals a Burpee catalog. As the film starts, he is having lunch with a rape victim, offering her money on behalf of his client—the rapist—to drop the charge. When she refuses the money, the rapist's henchmen interrupt the lunch and attack her. Lung rescues her, but she believes he was in on the setup. He gets his client off anyway but, beset by guilt, decks him in the courtroom immediately afterward.

Meanwhile, another sleazy client—that guy with the cigar—polluting industrialist *and* drug smuggler Hua (Yuen Wah) is sued by fish hatchery owner Miss Yeh (Deanie Yip). Lung defends him but, being an inveterate womanizer, he also puts the moves on Miss Yeh's cousin, Wen Mei-Ling (Pauline Yeung). He enlists his old buddies Fei (Sammo Hung), a small-time crook, and Tung Te-Piao (Yuen Biao), a neurotic tech whiz, to help him spy on the two women. Unfortunately, the two sidekicks can't be in the same room together without getting into a fight.

Lung keeps trying to have a romantic meal with Mei-Ling, but something always gets in his way. In one case, Fei and Te-Piao go after each other in Lung's apartment mid-date; in another, a gang of hit men tries to polish Lung off. Two-thirds of the way through, the action slows down to let this romance develop, trading thrills for winsome courtship. Yeah, yeah, yeah.

Finally, Fei and Te-Piao break into Hua's plant and discover his big heroin refinery. Hua's men give Fei an overdose, and Te-Piao runs to gather Lung and Mei-Ling to help rescue him. And then . . . there's a big battle.

Lung must square off with both the twitchy, tricky Hua, who gets dumped in a vat of toxic waste, and his awesome assistant (Benny "The Jet" Urquidez). Urquidez sports a makeup job giving him a face like a shark's: pale with beady, doll-like eyes. The two launch into a fierce fistfight that recalls their stalwart duel in *Wheels on Meals*. Finally, as both are ready to collapse, Jackie pulls out the victory.

—AK

Drunken Master II

1994
Starring Jackie Chan, Anita Mui Yim-fong, Ti Lung, Liu Chia-liang, Ho Sung-pak, Wong Yat-hwa, Johnny Lo Hwei-kong
Directed by Liu Chia-liang (Lau Kar-leung)

Chinese martial arts can take many different styles. Some styles are based on the movement and nature of different wild animals, like the monkey, the crane, or the praying mantis. But one of the more eccentric techniques is based on the erratic movements of a *sifu* long adrift in Sot's

Bay: the Drunken Master. One's fingers hook into imaginary wine-cup supports, and the face freezes with the determination of the terminally potted trying to stay upright as the body sways violently.

Drunken Master style is highly effective, as Jackie Chan first demonstrated in 1978's *Drunken Master*. In *Drunken Master II*, Jackie reprises his role as folk hero Wong Fei-hong. Shaw Brothers veteran Ti Lung (with a touch of gray) plays Fei-hong's father, Wong Kei-ying, and Anita Mui comically portrays his stepmother.

It's pre–World War I China, and Wong Fei-hong and his fellow student Tsao attempt to avoid paying duty by smuggling a valuable ginseng root through customs before boarding a train home. The contraband root gets switched with a valuable seal, the property of some rotten imperialist Brits. The mix-up leads to Wong's first meeting—and a breathtaking spearfight in the cramped space *under* the train—with Chinese loyalist General Fu (Liu Chia-liang).

It turns out the Brits, along with a few collaborating Chinese, are smuggling curios out of the country and exploiting Chinese labor for profit besides. In round one, Fei-hong battles the evildoers and, reddened up with a smorgasbord of liquor, soundly thrashes them Drunken style. Unfortu-

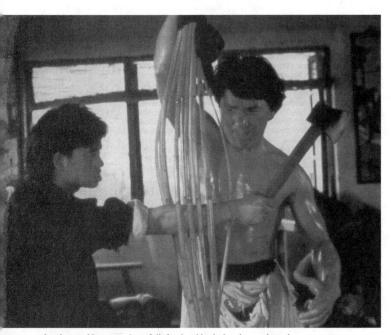

A hatchet-wielding greenhorn falls for the old split-bamboo trick. Jackie wins again in *Drunken Master II*.

nately, his enthusiasm (and likkered-up befuddlement) causes him to assault his own father.

Banished from the household, Fei-hong seeks solace in a bigger bottle at the local pub, where he becomes maudlin and ineffectual. The bruised bad guys track him down, tie him up, and leave him dangling—passed-out and naked—in the town square, with a sarcastic banner reading "King of Drunken Boxing." The disgraced Fei-hong tearfully swears off any more martial adventure benders.

Doesn't really matter. *DMII* provides a showcase for one of cinema's most physically gifted actors to demonstrate a wide range of on-the-wagon styles. A multilevel battle pits General Fu and Fei-hong against long odds—fifty or so hatchet-wielding thugs. Fu spits oil on Fei-hong's buffed torso—purely for its cosmetic coolness—as the pair trash ruffians out of second floor windows and carry the day.

But when Fei-hong, white-robed and fan in hand, walks solemnly to face the turncoat Brit-Symps at the steel foundry, the audience is put at collective seat's edge. First, he and a second-tier toady go at it—literally—with hammer and tongs.

After the penultimate killer goes down in a faceful of flames, number one Bad Dude Ah-jan (played by the lethal Johnny Lo) leaves the on-deck circle. The tall and muscular Ah-jan—in impeccable 1913 Eurodress—raises one leg high above his head while he calmly removes his glasses. Then, still standing on one leg, he rains a barrage of kicks down with the other!

Fei-hong is backed up against an enormous bed of glowing coals and, well, even though you know what's coming, you *still* can't believe he's gonna do it. He does. The gloves come off now, and Fei-hong swigs a mouthful of industrial alcohol to spit fire at his adversary. He accidentally swallows the poisonous fluid and gets a jolt of his old technique. Realizing it's do-or-die, he chugalugs and enters a realm of Über Drunken Master hitherto unwitnessed, thrashing Ah-jan into submission.

This last blackout has some unforeseen side effects, and those shocked by the last scene should notice the word "temporary" in the subtitles . . . and don't you dare miss the outtakes!

My Lucky Stars

1985
Starring Jackie Chan, Sammo Hung Kam-bo, Sibelle Hu Hui-ching, Michiko Nishiwaki, Richard Ng, Lam Ching Ying, Eric Tsang, Yuen Biao
Directed by Sammo Hung Kam-bo

Shot partly in Japan, *My Lucky Stars* is primarily a comedy. It contains some remarkable action sequences and marks the HK debut of Japanese crunch-princess Michiko Nishiwaki, but those who gnash their teeth at extended buddy-buddy gag sequences should be forewarned.

Jackie plays a cop known as Skinny Monkey in HK, but as Muscles in Japan. He and Ricky (Yuen Biao) chase a pair of shady types out of a Japanese subway station. Pursuers and prey hop into vehicles and smush them together a bit.

Then it's off to the amusement park, where ninja warriors in powder-blue suits mess with Muscles and Ricky. As Muscles is distracted by a shutterbug couple, the bad guys lure Ricky into the funhouse and kidnap him. The crook they're chasing turns out to be a rotten-apple HK cop who fled to Japan after absconding with $100 million in contraband diamonds, and is allied with a criminal syndicate called the Scarecrow Club.

Muscles calls Inspector Tsao (his boss in HK) and requests backup. Tsao heads to the local prison, frees greasy thief Kidstuff (Sammo Hung), and gives him the job. Kidstuff rounds up his orphanage buddies Roundhead, Rawhide, and Herb. Then, with undercover cop Miss Woo (Sibelle Hu) in tow, it's off to the land of bullet trains and Hello Kitty. Once in Japan, the buddy-jokes start to pile up: The gang orders lunch by pantomime and Roundhead tries to get a sausage by surreptitiously displaying a part of his anatomy to the waiter. The bemused but polite waiter brings him a plate with . . . a single tiny mushroom.

This is about as funny as it gets, but Jackie starts mixing it up. He disguises himself as a huge-headed mascot and enters the amusement park's funhouse, only to find that the exhibits are genuinely lethal.

My Lucky Stars kicks into gear as Muscles fights his way through the surreal funhouse into the Scarecrow Club's headquarters. He squares off against the fierce Dick Wei as Kidstuff takes on some nasty joker with an eye patch.

But the best duel occurs as Miss Woo faces Nishiwaki, who's in a kimono. She sheds the Japanese dress, displaying a brick pagoda physique that earns her a heartfelt AIYAH! from the audience. Former powerlifting-champion Nishiwaki executes a few posedown moves before bruising up the HK policewoman and tossing her through a shoji screen.

Woo raises up on one elbow and says to Kidstuff, "She's tough," before collapsing. Kidstuff admires another posedown, then KOs the Japanese woman with a single punch!

Police Story

1985
Starring Jackie Chan, Brigitte Lin Chin-hsia, Maggie Cheung Man-yuk, Bill Tung, Kenneth Tong, Chu Yuen
Directed by Jackie Chan

Jackie Chan plays a reckless cop named Kevin Chan, who is intent on putting a ruthless gangster (Chu Yuen) behind bars. After a spectacular opening sequence in which automobiles chase each other down a steep hillside, blasting a destructive path through a shantytown's shanties, Chan manages to snag his quarry. But Mr. Big is released from custody, and his arrogant lawyers vow to clear him of all charges.

Testimony from the gangster's secretary Selina (spunky Brigitte Lin) could send her boss up the river. Selina, though, is uninterested in turning state's evidence. She ignores Chan's warnings, but changes her tune after she's attacked by a knife-wielding assassin and saved only by Chan's timely intervention.

At this point in *Police Story*, theater carbon dioxide levels fall dramatically as the audience holds its collective breath.

The shaken Selina confesses to Chan about her boss's illegal doings, then recants after discovering that the attack was staged by Chan and his buddy. The case is destroyed, and the gangster wins in court. The ungrateful thug decides to have Selina silenced anyway, and it's up to Chan to save her neck—and his own—after he's framed for the murder of another cop.

Stunt highlights include Chan's treacherous ride hanging onto the outside of a speeding bus, then standing defiantly with his gun pointed while that same bus bears down on him. The bus screeches to a halt just short of pancaking the unflappable Chan, throwing a couple of its outlaw passengers through the front windshield and onto the pavement. It's a remarkable bit of stuntwork that reportedly resulted in serious injuries for its participants.

But what viewers will remember most about *Police Story* is the film's extraordinary final fifteen minutes, when Chan lays waste to the gangster, his henchmen, and the shopping mall in which they do battle. In an extended sequence of incomparable physical mayhem and pain, characters are kicked, beaten, and hurled through panes of glass. The action culminates with Chan performing a death-defying slide down a sixty-foot pole covered with sparking, squibbing live electrical wires and holiday decorations. This stunt is shown three times in a row, from three different camera angles.

Police Story stands as a landmark for Jackie Chan, who proved for the first time that he could bring his style of martial arts wizardry to a contemporary setting and still achieve the commercial and artistic success of his previous period-chopsocky films. *Police Story* won the Hong Kong International Film Festival award for Best Picture in 1985 and spun off a pair of equally entertaining sequels.

—RAA

Project A

1985
Starring Jackie Chan, Sammo Hung Kam-bo, Yuen Biao, Dick Wei, Bill Tung
Directed by Jackie Chan

This turn-of-the-century period piece, which features three of the Seven Little Fortunes—Jackie Chan, Sammo Hung, and Yuen Biao, dressed up in wacky costumes—doesn't have much of a plot,

but the action is furious and bruising. It also showcases Jackie's appreciation for and homage to silent film, particularly during *Project A*'s hyper bike chase scene.

Jackie, decked out in a British tar ice cream suit, plays a sailor called Dragon Ma. Led by his commanding officer, Captain Chi (Bill Tung), Dragon Ma and the crew are preparing to set sail against the forces of Lo, a notorious pirate (played with tattooed Manchurian machismo by Dick Wei). Before shipping out, the sailors stop by the local tavern for a farewell bash, and end up brawling with an arrogant group of police led by Inspector Tzu (Yuen Biao).

Then as the crew assembles prior to departure, fire blooms in the night sky as their ships are blown up. Their fleet sunk, Dragon and his salty dogs are desalinated and turned into a police unit by Captain Chi. Bad enough to be a landlubber, but the new boss is Inspector Tzu! Tzu puts them through rigorous training exercises in their new uniforms (which include conical "mollusk" hats) before they eventually patch up their differences.

First assignment: ferret out a hirsute thug who's trying to sell 100 stolen Enfield rifles to pirate Lo. Tzu and Dragon adopt Western garb and wreck a private club trying to rein in the crook. So many stuntmen execute painful-looking floor crashes, you can almost smell the liniment.

They fail, but Dragon and fellow sailor-turned-cop Fei (Sammo) steal the rifles. Dragon is nabbed for the theft, though, and his old boss Captain Chi handcuffs him. But Dragon slips the cuffs and launches into one of the exquisitely paced, over-the-top action sequences that have cemented Jackie Chan's place in the pantheon.

Dragon takes off on a purloined bicycle. His pursuers are also on bikes, and he leads them through a rabbit warren of narrow alleys with more than their share of ladders and Dutch doors. As his attackers close in, Dragon passes a Dutch door and knocks on it. The top-half of the door swings open just in time to scrape off an attacker.

Recaptured and recuffed, he deftly shimmies up a flagpole and leaps into a clock tower, where he uses the huge gears of the clockworks as a jungle gym in a fight with one of the arms smugglers. Hanging on to one of the clock's hands, he drops through two awnings and hits the ground head-first. Merry bike chase, hanging from a huge clock like Harold Lloyd, and an awe-inspiring, head-crunching fall. Rewind and call in your roommates!

None of this impresses the pirates, who are bulldog determined to get those rifles. So they shanghai a ship full of foreign dignitaries and hold them for ransom. Dragon kidnaps, then impersonates, the arms dealer, top-hatted dandy Chou, earning a journey to the pirates' island hideout.

And then . . . there's a big battle. The combined talents of Dragon, Tzu, and Fei are used against pirate chief Lo and his forces. But once victorious, our heroes must attempt to return to the mainland by raft and, unfortunately, their navigational skills don't match their martial arts skills . . .

Project A, Part II

1987
Starring Jackie Chan, Maggie Cheung Man-yuk, David Lam Wai, Rosamund Kwan Chi-lam, Carina Lau Kar-ling, Elvis Tsui Kam-kong, Ray Lui, Bill Tung
Directed by Jackie Chan

This sequel is arguably Chan's finest work to date. In form, it isn't much different from its predecessor or from the *Police Story* movies; it simply has the most sustained sense of inspiration, in both its comic and action elements.

Project A, Part II picks up literally where the first film left off. It opens with a montage of the most memorable moments from the original. On the beach of the island where coast guard officer Dragon Ma (Chan) vanquished the pirate king, the remaining pirates are vowing to avenge their leader. Back in Hong Kong, police officials realize they must curtail the power of corrupt policeman Chun (David Lam), so they bring in Dragon to take over Chun's Sai Wan district.

All but one of the Sai Wan cops are corrupt and lazy. With the honest Ho and his old navy buddies, Dragon decides to earn the respect of his men by apprehending crime boss Tiger Au. The brave but ill-conceived attack on Au's stronghold leads to a pell-mell fight sequence; only the arrival of more navy troops saves the policemen's skin.

Licking their wounds, Dragon and his men are called in to provide security at a party for a general's daughter, Miss Pai (Rosamund Kwan). In league with Chun, a group of revolutionaries—including Maggie (Maggie Cheung) and Carina (Carina Lau)—arrives to steal a priceless necklace from the general's mansion. When Dragon tries to nab head revolutionary Man, Miss Pai plants the stolen necklace on our hero, and Man walks. Still later that night, spies of the empress kidnap Carina. A complex farcical sequence ensues as the empress's spies drag Carina to Maggie's house to look for information. Maggie, Man, Dragon (whom Chun has handcuffed to Ho), Uncle Bill (Bill Tung, who has a small part in virtually every Jackie movie), and finally Chun arrive in sequence. Each faction keeps moving around the small house, trying to avoid each other.

Dragon finally captures the spies, but Chun appears again and handcuffs himself to Dragon to transport him back to the station. Suddenly the pirates, who have been pursuing Dragon throughout the movie, show up to kill him. They chase the handcuffed pair into a hotel, where Dragon must fight them off—still cuffed to Chun—in a remarkable display of martial arts slapstick.

And then . . . there's a big battle. In the final showdown, it's Chun and the evil spies against Dragon and the revolutionaries—with the pirates trying to figure out just who to support. At one point, Dragon is dropped into a giant industrial mortar and must dodge a rhythmic steam-operated pestle.

Male or female, short or tall, Jackie Chan beats them all. Some of his assorted antagonists: Johnny Lo Hwei-kong in *Drunken Master II* and the high-heeled vixens from *Armour of God*.

Everybody takes chase . . . over roofs, through a birdhouse, up and down staircases, and eventually atop a giant ceremonial scaffolding, which Chan uses to restage Buster Keaton's famous falling-house gag—standing immobile as an enormous wall falls about him. But even this doesn't top Dragon's innovative impromptu chemical weapon—a mouthful of chewed-up chili peppers that he spits into the eyes of his adversaries! As the outtakes show, Jackie was not content to fake the scene, but stuffed a fistful of *real* red-hot chilies in his mouth!

—AK

Wheels on Meals

1984
Starring Jackie Chan, Sammo Hung Kam-bo, Yuen Biao, Maria Delores Forner, Benny "The Jet" Urquidez, Richard Ng, John Sham, Herb Edelman
Directed by Sammo Hung Kam-bo

Shot in Barcelona, *Wheels on Meals* features Jackie Chan and Yuen Biao as Thomas and David, a pair of expatriate Chinese entrepreneurs. They serve fried rice and burgers out of a tricked-out yellow van known as Everybody's Kitchen ("cocina para todos!"). That's more Spanish than you'll need to enjoy this action-comedy, in which everybody speaks fluent fist and cars and skateboards fly.

Sammo Hung is Moby, a hardworking guy who takes over a private eye business because his boss (a cameo by Herb Edelman) is fleeing Alfonso the loan shark. Moby's first client is a mysterious stranger who hires him to locate the grown child of a woman named Gloria. Gloria is dating David's father, who's in the loony bin but "getting better." Her child is Sylvia (former Miss Spain Maria Delores Forner), whom David and Thomas immediately dub "Princess."

But Sylvia is involved in the unregal career of pay-for-play. Our heroes—ga-ga over this *gwailo* courtesan—hide her from an irate client she's grifted. She repays them by stealing their money! Unfazed, David and Thomas play *Pygmalion*, and Sylvia promises to turn over a new leaf. The unlikely trio goes to work pushing spring rolls and soft drinks.

When well-dressed nasties appear and kidnap their waitress, the wheeler-mealers jump in their van and chase after them. The extended chase sequence features some spectacular rolling crashes and culminates in another one of those heart-in-the-throat Jackie Chan moments: the van flies over traffic—and into a truckload of fruit boxes. Fortunately, the stuntmen lazily perched atop the boxes are quick to leap off.

Well, it turns out that Sylvia is the illegitimate daughter of a nobleman. She stands to inherit plenty of pesetas, and her evil uncle Mondale is out to put her away. David and Thomas join forces with Moby, and the trio storms a medieval castle to spring Sylvia from Mondale's clutches.

The endgame includes an extended one-on-one match between Thomas and American martial artist Benny Urquidez. The action is so furious that one of Urquidez' kicks extinguishes an entire candelabra without toppling it over. When Benny topples over himself, Thomas delivers a kick that stands him back upright!

Yet, right in the middle of this bruising punch-up, Thomas decides to "treat it as a training session," and slumps on a chair to take a breather. He repeatedly gets up, strikes a pose, then relaxes—shifting between nonchalance and taut-bowstring readiness as Benny broils with impatience. The fight ends with Urquidez hanging out of a busted window, pleading *"no más,"* à la Roberto Duran. Unfortunately, no outtakes accompany the closing credits.

Hong Kong Noir

ilm noir got its start in Hollywood during the 40s and early 50s. A specific mix of hard-boiled narrative, dark and dramatic lighting, and a pessimistic outlook on the fate of humankind, Hollywood noir was a shadowy world of desperate criminals, treacherous McGimps, and perfidious lovers, all wrapped up together in that bleak blanket called fate.

With 1997—and the return of Hong Kong to the People's Republic of China—looming large on the horizon, the development of Hong Kong's own brand of film noir was a natural. Not surprisingly, HK noir hit its stride right after the Tiananmen Square massacre in 1989, reflecting the panicky fear of life with a brutal new landlord.

Like the Hollywood offerings, Hong Kong noir is gloomy and

127

cynical. But as with everything Hong Kong borrows from Hollywood, HK filmmakers have taken noir and made it uniquely their own. Hong Kong noir is both darker and more colorful, bleaker and more humorous. Bad things happen, and they can happen to anybody. If a villain holds a gun to a child's head, there's a fifty-fifty chance that the kid gets plugged. These films are brutal masterpieces, with not-so-happy endings in which the hero usually ends up feeding the worms.

As Tears Go By

1988
Starring Andy Lau Tak-wah, Maggie Cheung Man-yuk, Jacky Cheung Hak-yow
Directed by Wong Kar-wai

In Mongkok's clotted streets, a romance blooms, a rivalry rages, and a classic is born. Wong Kar-wai's smeary, brooding, vibrantly photographed *As Tears Go By* is a *Romeo and Juliet* for the MTV generation. Moving effortlessly from hushed, lush seductions to blood-drenched beatings, Wong's baroque take on the generic trappings of HK's youth-gang cinema blends longing, loss, and the impact of hot lead on tender flesh into an ultrastylish swirl of fluorescent realism and perspiring tragedy.

Ha-tau (Andy Lau) is a struggling "big brother" (low-level lieutenant in HK's triads) whose responsibility for the hot-headed little brother Fly (Jacky Cheung) threatens to ruin his chances of big-time success in the underworld. Fly's pathological behavior has already resulted in a mountain of unpaid debts; his refusal to "give face" to the other big brothers in the neighborhood has made him the target of a series of increasingly vicious beatings. Forever cleaning up after Fly's indiscretions, Ha-tau has begun to tire of assuaging (and sometimes mangling) his charge's understandably aggrieved enemies. Still, he cannot conceive of letting Fly suffer the consequences on his own and is eventually faced with sharing his friend's inevitable (and well-earned) fate.

In the meantime, Ha-tau—having just lost the girlfriend he's sent to have an abortion (or, as he puts it, a "stomach cleaning")—begins to fall for his beautiful cousin, Ah-ngor (Maggie Cheung). The throbbing scenes of desire between the kissing cousins—Ah-ngor spends a restless few days in the pastel melancholy of Ha-tau's underlit apartment—keep being interrupted by the violent fallout of Ha-tau and Fly's gang life. Wong makes the most of this dialectic—romance promise/reality's bite—in a mannered but nonmoralizing bid to equate urban and domestic violence.

There are few HK films that so successfully expose the underbelly of triad glamour without lapsing into cheap melodrama or tiresome "naturalism." Despite being a self-conscious reworking of Martin Scorsese's *Mean Streets*, *As Tears Go By* undercuts the macho swagger of its inspiration by emphasizing Ah-ngor's emotional yearnings and clearly condemning Ha-tau's loutish brutality to women. While the film's smudgy, expressionistic visual effects, sudden camera movements, and unexpected angles are closer to the art-film lexicon than the HK mainstream, it remains as an engrossing and extraordinarily stylish thriller (despite occasional lapses into sans-subtitle ambiguity). That *ATGB* also transcends those limitations and faces up to senseless brutality rather than merely endorsing and reinforcing it suggests that Wong Kar-wai may be one of the few HK directors more interested in making films *about* violence than simply making violent films.

—CS

Chungking Express

1994
Starring Tony Leung Chiu-wai, Brigitte Lin Chin-hsia, Faye Wong, Takeshi Kaneshiro
Directed by Wong Kar-wai

Chungking Express has the relentless energy and inexplicable grace of a perfectly crafted pop song: its giddy rhythms and infectious melodies linger long, circling around memories of forgotten lovers and ill-fated romances, teasing at emotions you'd long ago misplaced. Passions cross, pursuits dead-end, and romances disconnect in this bright, buoyantly atypical HK art film.

CKExp was shot in Hong Kong's Chungking Mansions—an enormous, rambling highrise teeming with grotty *Rough Guide* backpacker's hostels and filthy *vindaloo* joints. Its on-the-fly aesthetic (is there a single tripod-mounted shot in the entire film?) captures the antic authenticity of HK's bustling streetlife, putting its fast-forward

realism in the service of a fresh arrangement of rambunctious ideas and gorgeous images (thanks to director Wong Kar-wai's recurrent cameraman, the brilliant Australian, Christopher Doyle). Not that there isn't a plot. In fact, there are two.

In the film's first half, HK plainclothes cop number 223 (Takeshi Kaneshiro) spends his free time pining for his ex-girlfriend, May, who dumped him on April Fool's Day. One night, while pursuing a fleeing crook, number 223 brushes past a woman in a blonde wig (Brigitte Lin); fifty-six hours later, after consuming thirty cans of pineapples (May's favorite fruit) marked "sell by May 1," the heart-wrecked cop enters a bar, vomits the pineapples, and determines to fall in love with the next woman he sees.

Enter the woman in the blonde wig, who's just been burned in a drug deal involving Indian smugglers and a British money man. The two spend the night together in a hotel room: number 223 watching old movies on television while the mysterious blonde stranger sleeps soundly on the bed. The next morning, number 223 leaves to go jogging and, just as he abandons his beeper (and his pining for May), he receives a "Happy Birthday" page from the blonde-wigged woman. But he never sees her again.

Plot-half number two commences with number 223 stopping by an all-night fast food joint called Midnight Express. The owner suggests he try dating a new counter-girl, Faye (Faye Wong). Number 223 mistakes the tall, leggy, short-haired Faye for a boy . . . then promptly disappears from the movie.

Brigitte Lin and Takeshi Kaneshiro in a pensive moment from Wong Kar-wai's *Chungking Express*.

Six hours later, Faye falls in love with uniformed policeman number 663 (Tony Leung), who stops by every evening to pick up a Caesar salad for his girlfriend, an airline hostess. When the hostess takes wing, she leaves a letter for number 663 at Midnight Express, along with his keys. Fay intercepts the letter, learns number 663's address, and begins visiting his apartment while he's out: rearranging things, cleaning up, falling in love with the trappings of his life. Eventually number 663, who's prone to romanticizing everyday objects himself, catches Faye in his flat and finally asks her for a date. But she stands him up, then leaves HK for California.

One year later, Faye—now an airline hostess—returns to find number 663 resigned from the force and running the Midnight Express. He asks her to write him a boarding pass. Destination: wherever she wants to take him.

It is easy to see why *CKExp* was chosen as the first U.S. release from the Quentin Tarentino–managed distribution company, Rolling Thunder. While a plot synopsis barely begins to convey the assortment of visual riffs (mirrored images, smudgy chases, loopy body language) and thematic resonance, it is a film filled with possibility and energy and a sense that, though the clock is ticking, time is forever expanding, and that—1997 notwithstanding—the future isn't running out.

—CS

The First Time Is the Last Time

1989
Starring Carrie Ng Kar-lai, Andy Lau Tak-wah, Season Ma
Directed by Raymond Leung

A women's prison movie is supposed to satisfy certain criteria. Hoary clichés include sadistic prison doctors, cruel and sexually repressed female wardens, lusting lesbian inmates, and lots of gratuitous nudity.

TFTITLT, on the other hand, is one of those unexpected, female-driven dramas in which women and their relationships with each other are actually explored. The loser fathers and boyfriends who mess up their lives are also portrayed, adding depth and texture.

Season Ma plays a naive moll who is caught playing dope mule for her cheap-punk-triad boyfriend and sentenced to six months in the slams.

Her cellblock is run by He-Man, a six-foot hellion who extorts cash, chicken, and cigarettes from her fellow jailbirds. The guards use He-Man as corrupt muscle to keep the other prisoners in line.

The matronly, pregnant 5354 (inmates are numbers here) takes the "new fish" under her wing. Nonetheless, He-Man assaults the new inmate in the shower. In the process, though, she annoys the only inmate who scares both the guards *and* He-Man—Crazy Bitch (Carrie Ng, in fine form). Crazy Bitch thumps He-Man senseless, not out of a sense of outrage, but just because she's annoyed at having the showering process disrupted. Order is restored, and the inmates are returned to their cells. When a grateful 7144 (our new fish) reaches out to Crazy Bitch in friendship, she finds only a burned-out shell of a woman, huddled on the cell floor, chain-smoking her self-detested life away.

In flashback, we learn why Crazy Bitch (known as Winnie before her incarceration) is no fuzzy puppy. Sold to a brothel at nine by her heroin-addicted father, she drifted through a crud-injecting, pimp-dependent existence until snaring a handsome gangster/sugar daddy named Yung (Andy Lau). After a gang fight, the two consummate matters in a leaky industrial men's room—Winnie wiping the hot blood from Yung's *Kwan Ti* tattoos—and fall into that desperate sort of love at which the socially marginalized are so adept. Yung proves his love by forcing her to kick the junk, holding her all night while she shivers and shakes from withdrawal.

As Winnie's story unfolds, it becomes clear

HEX ERRORS

that she and 7144 share a secret of which neither are fully aware. Yung was greased by a group of hoods, and Winnie exacted revenge with a pistol, blowing the killers away for taking the only thing that offered her any hope—the guy she loved. The thugs were members of the same gang to which 7144's boyfriend belongs.

When 7144's scum-sucking beau comes to visit, he tells the bewildered young thing of her new friend's past transgressions. He further convinces her to perform a jailhouse assassination on Winnie. The attempted hit—and its consequences for 7144, a wayward teen a long way from home—leads *TFTITLT* to its shocking conclusion.

Gangs

1988
Starring Ho Pui Tung, Ma Hwa Ting, Tsi Wai Kit
Directed by Lawrence Ah Mon

Gangs examines the misadventures of a bunch of unpleasant juvenile delinquents—in particular, the teenaged tribulations of Big K. Big K belongs to the Sung Hing gang, an innocuous-looking band who extort money from local businesses. Other members of the group include Big K's brother, Little K; a cool and amoral toughie known as Coma; and an undersized psychopath called Little Demon. The gang is under the control of a charismatic thug named Wen, who works for Uncle Sing, a local triad boss.

After a brutal fight with their rivals—in which Wen and two others are killed—the gang goes into hiding. The stress of the situation takes its toll on the fugitives, and the gang soon flies apart. Coma is captured by the police after Uncle Sing rats on him. Big K's girlfriend—Lard Cake—is kidnapped and raped by a rival gang. Coma's girlfriend Kitty becomes a whore. Little Demon is drugged and thrown into the sea.

There is little comic relief in *Gangs*, and every scene is played

World Video & Supply

The adjudicated youth from Lawrence Ah Mon's film *Gangs* know, "Juvenile delinquency transcends ethnic differences."

for its grimness. "Cruelty's the name of the game," says one gang member while watching his buddies pour kerosene on a rat and ignite it.

The stars of *Gangs* are not the usual, well-known assortment of HK actors. The kids in this film look and act like real teenagers. The

CALL GIRL 92   1992

Female-centric film starring Veronica Yip, Carrie Ng, and Cecilia Yip as nightclub hostesses willing to go for "midnight snacks" with customers for a fee. Some jerk brings his nerdy wife (Sharla Cheung Man) in for a drink so he can show off. One of his friends comments, "your wife is more obedient than my dog." Wrong! When he serves her with divorce papers, she takes up school chum Carrie Ng's offer of a hostess job. She's shy with the customers, preferring the caresses of Ms. Ng. As entertaining as all this is, the show is stolen by the marvelous Cecilia Yip, who plays her alkie hooker like a genuine raging, outta-control gin-disposal unit, rather than the romanticized tipplers so often found in films.

fight scenes are chaotic, haphazard, and refreshingly free of any martial arts pretense. The kids charge at each other, shouting and swinging pipes. They run away and taunt each other; they cover their heads and scream.

The way these kids talk to each other is as important as what they say. This is the Cantonese of the streets, with its singsong roughness and drawled word endings. Like director Lawrence Ah Mon's other underworld peek—*Queen of Temple Street*—*Gangs* is uniquely natural and all the more depressing for it.

—JM

My Heart Is That Eternal Rose

1989
Starring Kenny Bee, Joey Wong Jo-yin, Tony Leung Chiu Wai, Chan Wai Man, Gordon Liu Chia-hui, Ng Man-tat
Directed by Patrick Tam Kar-ming

Veering wildly from the rainy, jet-black streets of downtown HK to the withering heat of the colony's rural islands, Patrick Tam's deeply romantic thriller has something for everyone: swimsuited honeys and heavy artillery, leering cretins and luscious ladies, disco and heartbreak.

Rick (matinee heartthrob Kenny Bee) is a hunky, stand-up guy in love with Lap (luminescent Joey Wong), the daughter of his affable, aging

鍾鎮濤 梁朝偉 王祖賢
陳惠敏 劉家輝 吳孟達 關海山 金諾 黃智禮主演
導演・譚家明

boss, Uncle Cheung. Uncle Cheung—now retired from the triads and managing the beachside bar where Rick bilks the locals with his barroom tricks—is called upon by crimelord Shing for one last favor: help smuggle Shing's son across the border from mainland China into Hong Kong's New Territories. Reluctantly, Uncle agrees, and (foolishly) contacts Tang (Ng Man-tat), a corrupt police detective, to assist him in the plot. Rick comes along as Uncle's driver.

When Tang realizes—midway through the caper—that the arrogant punk they're smuggling is a crimelord's son, he immediately plots to ransom the kid for a higher price. In a scene that's staged under the rotten jaundice of a relentless sun, Tang viciously beats the boy, then comes unglued, shoots the kid dead, and takes aim at Uncle. Rick rushes in, tussles with Tang, and plugs him. As Tang's lumpy corpse sails through the air, Rick and Uncle roar from the scene. Later that night, when Uncle is taken hostage by Boss Shing, Lap agrees to become rival boss Shen's (Chan Wai Man) concubine in exchange for negotiating her father's release. Despite

her love for Rick, Lap hides her agreement from him, and insists that he depart for the Philippines to escape retribution.

Six years pass. Lap has become Shen's prize possession—entertaining his business associates with her beauty and drinking abilities—while

King Rat's rat king. Tails hopelessly intertwined, Boss Shen (center) and his minions, Lap (left) and Liu (right), are skewered upon their true loyalties in *My Heart Is That Eternal Rose*. (From the lobby card.)

FALLEN ANGELS   1995

An ostensible sequel to *Chungking Express*, Wong Kar-wai's *Fallen Angels* mashes characters and situations from all of the director's previous films into an unending warp of wide-angle imagery, manic montage, and (Woo-inspired) hip-hop violence. Singing sensation Leon Lai wanders through the proceedings in a dullard's daze as an all-business hit man looking to get out of the life while Michelle Reis—Lai's "agent"—twists her fishnets into a knot longing for a less businesslike relationship with the by-the-book killer.

Takeshi Kaneshiro—who has apparently become Wong's all-purpose alter ago—turns up as the film's obligatory wistful misfit. This time, he plays a mute ex-con ("#223 was the number I had in jail," he confesses; it was also his Chungking badge number) who serves as the film's narrator. Goofy and romantic, *Fallen Angels* may be the best off-the-cuff art-flick out of HK in ages, even if it fails to push the already ultrastylish Wong into new and more challenging waters.

continued on next page

FLIRTING   1987

Steamy Kowloon is the backdrop to this eccentric, erotic love story. Director Lee Tai Hang constantly thrusts his characters into close, sticky proximity, and the humid look of summertime Hong Kong is guaranteed to make you crank up your air conditioner.

Puerile hothead Tsai (Alex Man) grows weary of contracting the clap at Mongkok "yellow boxes" and goes to Thailand to purchase a bride. He returns to his sweatbox flat (and its panoramic views of the Kai Tak Airport runway) with his new "locally born Overseas Chinese" bride, played by gorgeous Japanese ingenue Yuko Aoki.

His lifelong buddy Hsi also shares the flat and becomes sexually obsessed with the couple, boring a peephole in the paper-thin walls. The trapped bride gravitates toward Hsi—not because he's such a great guy but because Tsai is such a beer-swilling, philandering jerk. No one is innocent, and it all ends in unsurprising tragic splendor, leaving the characters to work out their "desire issues" in the next lifetime.

continued on page 138

Uncle Cheung has become a sodden ale-wisp. Tormented by Shen's underlings—especially the verminous Liu (Gordon Liu)—Lap can only take comfort in her friendship with one of Shen's minions, Chung (Tony Leung), who shares her grief after her father is killed while drunkenly crossing the street. Shen, meanwhile, has hired a hit man to rub out an associate who's about to turn stoolie. The hit man just happens to be Rick, who just happens to run into Lap immediately after he makes the hit. Romance re-ignites—and the lead begins to fly.

Director Tam, along with cinematographer Christopher Doyle, keeps the proceedings energized with bottle-rocket pacing, sudden shoot-outs, thwarted rapes, and a convenient bag of automatic weapons stashed in a gym locker.

And while there's no stinting on the body count, Tam takes time out for a variety of picturesque diversions: a stolen kiss; the kidnapping of a feisty, toothless granny; a thug with a preposterous toupee; and the sound of chirruping crickets that drown out the clamor of a noonday killing. You want slow-motion slaughter? You've got it. But it's the little touches—like the ill-fated brute who dies for wearing red slacks with white shoes—that endure.

—CS

On the Run

1987
Starring Patricia Ha, Yuen Biao, Yuen Wah
Directed by Alfred Cheung Hin-Ling

There is no better example of Hong Kong noir than *On the Run*. *OTR* tells the story of Ah Chui (Patricia Ha), a lady assassin of calm and skill. As the film opens, the liquid-nitrogen-cool hit woman steps into a restaurant and shoots Lo Huan, a female narcotics officer in the Hong Kong Police department.

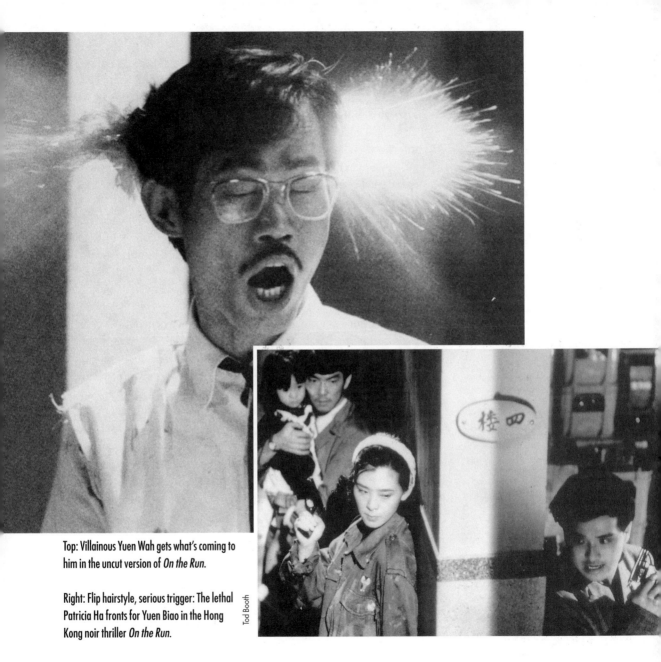

Top: Villainous Yuen Wah gets what's coming to him in the uncut version of *On the Run*.

Right: Flip hairstyle, serious trigger: The lethal Patricia Ha fronts for Yuen Biao in the Hong Kong noir thriller *On the Run*.

Tod Booth

HER VENGEANCE   1989

The terrific Pauline Wong stars in the HK remake of the "can you take this?" vengeance classic *I Spit on Your Grave*. Wong plays the manager of a Macau nightclub who disses the wrong group of thugs and gets attacked and raped in a blue-lit graveyard. They leave her with a virulent, untreatable case of venereal disease and an elaborate revenge scheme involving Lam Ching Ying, who plays the wheelchair-bound, double-amputee owner of Wanchai's San Francisco Club. Although this film is not for the faint of heart, the Rube Goldbergesque splatter finale is spectacular; Wong and Lam fight the miscreants with crossbows, noose contraptions, dangling nets of fishhooks, sharpened plumbing pipes, and a wok full of boiling oil!

THE INCORRUPTIBLE   1993

Ray Lui, a 1950s RHKP (Royal Hong Kong Police) triadbuster, and his spouse take on mobsters both on the streets and within the ranks of his own police department. Waise Lee is wondrously sleazy as a by-the-book gangster,

Lo Huan was married to Hsiang Ming (Yuen Biao), a policeman working in the political department of the Hong Kong Police, an office similar to U.S. Internal Affairs departments. The two were separated, but Hsiang needed his wife's help to emigrate to Canada. The hit, it turns out, was paid for by the villainous Superintendent Lu, head of the homicide department. The bullet-riddled policewoman had been having an affair with Lu but, when she threatened to blow the whistle on Lu's heroin smuggling, he had her killed.

Hsiang manages to capture the hit woman before Lu and his men catch up with her, and discovers that he has more to fear from the police than he does from his wife's murderer. Soon, both Hsiang and Ah Chui are running for their lives while Superintendent Lu uses the full resource of the police department to track them down.

Ah Chui—with her Jackie O hairspray-hardened flip—is played to perfection by Patricia Ha. Ha gives an evocative, emotional performance as a character who—paradoxically—never once betrays her emotions. She also wields a Walther PPK pistol like an artist's red paintbrush.

On the Run was made at a time when fear in Hong Kong over the impending takeover of the colony by the People's Republic was at a fever pitch. The film is as much about that paranoia as anything. Even Lu's heroin smuggling is motivated by his desire to get enough money to emigrate. When Hsiang Ming first encounters his wife's killer, he does not rage at the assassin because she killed the woman he loved—he's angry because she has eliminated his means of getting out of Hong Kong!

On the Run is more than just good Hong Kong noir, it is good film noir. The film is shot in a dramatic, nihilistic style with deep shadows and strong lighting. The romance is so understated it never seems forced or unbelievable. And in spite of a tortuously complicated plot, we never lose track of what's going on or why.

—JM

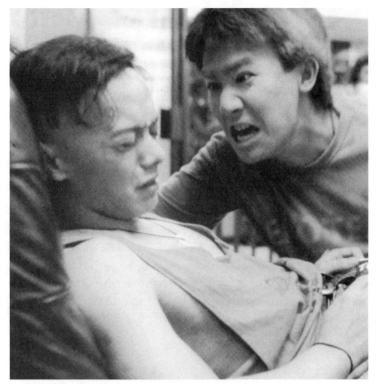

Dummkopf bank robbers Boney (Wong Pan) and Ah Sai (Tony Leung) start feeling the heat in *People's Hero*.

People's Hero

1988
Starring Ti Lung, Tony Leung Chiu-wai, Tony Leung Kar-fai, Wong Pan
Directed by Derek Yee Tung-shing

A small bank. Almost closing time. Two dangerously incompetent bank robbers. Hundreds of police surrounding the building. Wait a minute . . . it's *Dog Day Afternoon*! Nope. This is indeed a Hollywood-inspired almost-remake, but it's definitely no rip-off. In fact,

and Carrie Ng is even better as his sultry, opera-gloved, torch-singer moll. Simon Yam also appears as a turncoat triad member. Stolid and solid period piece; Hong Kong's answer to *The Untouchables*.

WOMEN'S PRISON   1988

Patricia Ha (the ultracool hit woman from *On the Run*) looks marvelous in her wedding dress. But hubby-to-be Simon Yam is in hock to the loan sharks, and her nuptials are disrupted when she ends up whacking one with a plaster statue for his rude behavior. Six months in the calaboose begin with a handcuffing to tuff gal Carol "Do Do" Cheng. Do Do has a feud going with the hideous Fatty over who gets to run this particular joint . . . you can see where this is going.

At present, Hong Kong is a British Crown Colony; a vestige of empire. It was once said that "the sun never sets on the British Empire," but HK's sunset occurs at 12:01 A.M. on July 1, 1997, when the colony will be turned over to the People's Republic of China.

The 1841 Treaty of Nanking—a result of Britain's victory in the Opium Wars—ceded Hong Kong to the Brits "in perpetuity." However, both parties signed a ninety-nine-year lease for the New Territories—the northern part of HK—in 1898. In 1984, then–Prime Minister Margaret Thatcher signed the Sino-British Joint Declaration with China, which declared that all of Hong Kong would become a Special Administrative Region of China (SAR) in 1997. In 1988, a Basic Law Agreement (a constitution of sorts) guaranteed that the SAR would retain Hong Kong's socio-economic and legal structure for at least fifty years after 1997.

It seemed an excellent solution,

despite its mongrel pedigree, *People's Hero* is a standout thriller. Directed by former actor Derek Yee, *PH* hinges on character and relationships rather than gunplay and wirework.

The film quickly establishes its own identity after the initial *Dog Day* set-up. The two bank robbers, Ah Sai (Tony Leung Chiu-wai) and Boney (Wong Pan), are no more than kids hoping for a quick score. Just as they're about to give themselves up to the surrounding cops, Ah Sai suddenly finds himself staring down the barrel of a gun wielded by one of the "hostages." This is Sunny Koo (Ti Lung), a most-wanted-list cop-killer who was going to rob the bank to finance his getaway to the Philippines. And these two pipsqueaks beat him to it.

Sunny is as cool as they come, though, and makes the most of a bad situation. Before long, he's arranged with the cops to bring in an old nemesis to assist with negotiations: detective Chan (Tony Leung). Sunny convinces Chan to have a van delivered for his getaway and arranges for his convict girlfriend to accompany him on his escape. Everyone settles in—nervously—to wait for the arrival of the van.

Things don't stay settled for long. Sunny—up 'til now charming and generous—suddenly decides he has to kill one of the hostages to make a point with the cops. He lets the horror-stricken bank customers perform a death lottery with an elimination round of Rock Paper Scissors. As possible victims are singled out, Sunny—conscience showing—rejects them for one reason or another. This scene alone is worth the price of admission—a perfect balance of comedy curdling into horror and teetering on the edge of absurdity the whole time.

The movie never veers from that horror/absurdity fulcrum. The human drama inside the bank is as riveting as the thriller elements that trapped them there. Every character is sharply and economically drawn. A terrific cast of mostly young actors provides the perfect touch of verisimilitude.

But best of all is the towering performance of Ti Lung as

Sunny Koo. He will always be remembered as one of the great Shaw Brothers kung fu stars of the 70s, but his performances in such 1980s films as *People's Hero* and *A Better Tomorrow* are at once graceful and commanding. Recently he has settled into "stern patriarch" roles, mostly in period movies like Jackie Chan's *Drunken Master II*. But *People's Hero* is the role of a lifetime.

—TB

Queen of Temple Street

1990
Starring Sylvia Chang, Rain Lau Yuk-tsui, Alice Lau, Lo Lieh
Directed by Lawrence Ah Mon

Tough love among the hard-bitten. *QOTS* focuses on a mother-daughter relationship between a middle-aged female pimp and her juvenile delinquent hooker daughter. Actress-director Sylvia Chang turns in her finest performance as "Big Sis" Wah, and teen phenom Rain Lau burns up the screen as Yan, the lip-curling, chain-smoking tart who sprang from her loins. Even subtitled, the dialogue is deft and cynical, and the relationship between the two women is explored with depth and compassion.

Big Sis stands, pimping, on Pak Hoi Street near the touristy Temple Street Market, muttering the mantra: "Young girls, young girls." "How many positions?" asks a potential john. "As many as there's in a coffin."

Upstairs, cramped red-lit cubicles brim with murky water basins, and drawers bulge with condoms by the dozen and half-squeezed K-Y tubes. *Pretty Woman* this ain't as Wah works her girls—Candy (Alice Lau), Octopussy, Big Mouth, and Swallow—through thirty tricks or so a night. Bored, aging harlots with punchcard-clock privates, they all carry dope habits, gambling addictions, or worthless boyfriends on their working backs.

until the Tiananmen Square massacre of 1989, which fueled widespread distrust of the authorities in Beijing. Later that same year, Britain announced that it would provide the "right of abode" to only fifty thousand HK passport holders, a fraction of the colony's six million residents. This provoked a panic among Hong Kong's residents. Many of those who could afford to left the colony to secure passports and citizenship from other countries (Canada and Australia being favored destination.). Some have now returned . . . with an additional passport as a security blanket.

As HK moves slowly and inexorably toward the People's Republic of China, the major hongs (trading companies), which form the financial backbone of the colony, have allied with PRC firms. Much of the partnering between the soon-to-be-former colony and the enormous political/financial entity poised to absorb it is based on ethnic ties. Triad crime syndicates also have roots on both sides of the border, and will likely be as big a factor after 1997 as they are today. As for nonethnic

continued on next page

Chinese caught in the mix—like the thousands of ethnic Indian HK passport holders who know no other home—their fate is uncertain.

The enormous changes that will arrive in 1997 are bound to affect people involved in the media, including film. John Woo and Ringo Lam have already moved to Hollywood. Director Ronny Yu (*The Bride With White Hair*) has taken up residence in Australia, and others may soon follow. Canadian cities like Toronto and Vancouver host satellite HK production communities.

On the other hand, cooperation between HK and the PRC after 1997 offers different opportunities. In fact, major HK/China productions have already been shot in Beijing and Shanghai, where cast-of-thousands-style epics are still affordable.

When Wah learns that her estranged daughter Yan is working as a nightclub hostess (several strata above the coffin-joys), she seeks her out. These two tangle hard.

Yan is a kid trying to be all grown up, with Marlboro, Louis Vuitton, and gangster-daddy accessories; her mom wants to tell her about Trojan and Ramses and the importance of regular gynie exams. Wah obviously loves the sneering little hellcat, but sees an eerie earlier version of herself—future mistakes dead ahead. As Yan brags of her fast life and taunts her mother with accusations of unmaternal behavior, Wah tells of her own hard-learned lessons of street-life abrasion.

Yan is not enthralled by her mother's company, but needs Big Sis's maternal charm (and underworld connections) to get back the quick-buck nudie pix she shot. Big Sis confronts the pornographers, matter-of-factly calls in triad muscle, and has heads cracked, then backs off when the negatives are returned.

Wah has her hands full running the brothel and caring for two sons from a second marriage (with Shu, a former cop now running a *mahjongg* dive and gambling away the boys' allowances). When she finds that Yan has signed on with an escort agency, Wah realizes that a young pretty face will attract more than a fortyish ex-hostess-mom could ever offer, and resigns herself to the loss. But Yan is popped by the vice squad—caught with a grandfatherly type at a no-tell motel—and calls Mom to bail her out.

Paths crossed again, the younger and the older scrap like terriers. Yan wants something from Mom that her nihilistic sex/love/money worldview can never deliver: an audience with the father she's never met. But when the kid finally comes face-to-face with the thieving Elvis (Lo Lieh), the deflation is palpable. "Disappointing, isn't it? Daddy didn't turn out like Paul Newman," consoles Wah as Yan cries a river on the ride home. *QOTS* closes with the two having reached a grudging respect as a pregnant Yan marries her not-too-scummy beau, perpetuating the familiar familial tradition.

Anita Mui displays long-gone Hong Kong elegance in Stanley Kwan's *Rouge*.

Rouge

1989
Starring Leslie Cheung Kwok-wing, Anita Mui Yim-fong, Kenny Bee, Emily Chu
Directed by Stanley Kwan

Rouge begins in 1934, a *Romeo and Juliet* tale of two lovers from different worlds. The man, Chen-Pang (Leslie Cheung), is the son of a rich landowner and stands to inherit his family's for-

tune. The woman, Fleur (Anita Mui), is a courtesan at a highbrow brothel. When Chen-Pang's parents turn down the couple's request to marry, the lovers decide to commit suicide together rather than live apart.

Suddenly the scene changes, and it's 1987. Fleur has returned from hell to find Chen-Pang and to find out why he didn't join her in the netherworld. It's important to note here that hell in Hong Kong films rarely conforms to the Western concept of the word; it is merely a misty after-life without the joyous connotations of heaven. Fleur meets a yuppie named Yuan Ting (Kenny Bee), who works at the newspaper where she places an ad to find Chen-Pang. When Fleur follows Yuan Ting home, he believes that she is merely crazy. Once he realizes that she is dead and overcomes his initial fright, Yuan and his wife (Emily Chu) offer to let her stay at their apartment until after the ad appears in the newspaper. Through a series of flashbacks, we learn the details of the love affair between Fleur and Chen-Pang.

A sadness over what Hong Kong has become pervades *Rouge*. There is a subtle anticommercialism here, lamenting the effects of Western civilization on Hong Kong. Shots of the Chinese theaters and markets from Fleur's time dissolve into shots of the 7-Elevens and shopping malls that have replace them. Fleur looks at the Coca-Cola that Yuan offers her with a mixture of curiosity and disdain.

Rouge moves at a langorous pace, with a haunting, sad mood uninterrupted by shock, gore, or slapstick. It is not a slam-bang action film, but it is beautiful, different, and great.

—JM

Ringo Lam

8

irector Ringo Lam (Lam Ling Tung) began his career with Hong Kong Television in the mid-seventies, where he first met the rising star Chow Yun Fat. Lam then went to Canada to study film at York University in Toronto. After returning to HK, he made a series of journeyman films, but his career didn't really take off until the breakthrough *City on Fire,* for which he was awarded Best Director at the 1987 HK Film Awards.

Ringo Lam is best known for his gritty portraits of HK crime figures. In stories set on both sides of prison bars, he explores the intricacies of the nearly feudal loyalties that exist between his characters. He first dealt with this theme in *City on Fire*, the first installment in Lam's "Fire" series, which continued with 1987's *Prison on Fire* and 1988's *School on Fire*. Lam's most infamous treatment of the

Ringo Lam at work.

subject came with 1992's *Full Contact*, an over-the-top crime drama.

Like many other talented directors, Lam has a stable of actors he returns to time and again. Lam's marquee actor of choice is Chow Yun Fat, whose charm, power, and versatility grace Lam's best work. His staple villain is the lantern-jawed Roy Cheung, Hong Kong's answer to Charles Napier. Griddle-faced Tommy Wong is often cast as the "second cop" or the "not-so-bad triad villain." More than any other HK director, Lam has realistically dramatized the activities of the triads while undercutting their celluloid glamorization. He also lets you see a lot of bitchin' triad tattoos.

Ringo Lam's film soundtracks are head and shoulders above the HK norm. Listen for the end-of-Empire bagpipe codas of *School on Fire* or the Cantorocking themes of Filipina diva Maria Cordero in *City on Fire*. Best of the lot is the wall of sound Lam constructs for *Full Contact*—a perfect complement to that film's visual mayhem.

Burning Paradise

1994
Starring Willie Chi Kwai, Carman Lee, K. K. Wong
Directed by Ringo Lam

Ringo Lam departs from his usual modus operandi of contemporary crime thrillers for this riveting period martial arts movie. *BP* features popular martial arts character Fong Sai-yuk, portrayed here as young, headstrong, and heroic, with a dearth of internal crises. Perhaps to compensate for his lead character's blandness, Lam drenches the movie with a brooding, sinister haze that makes this a grim—but worthwhile—martial arts movie.

Set during the Ching Dynasty, when rebellious Shaolin monks and students were being hunted down by the Manchurian government, *BP* opens with Fong Sai-yuk (Willie Chi) and his *sifu* pursued through the desert by Manchu soldiers, one of whom wields a bizarre weapon that can slice a horse's head off at a distance. The pair escape to an abandoned hut occupied by a runaway prostitute named Tou Tou (Carman Lee), who reluctantly shares the space. The next morning, the hut is blasted into oblivion by surrounding Manchu soldiers, and Fong can only watch in agony as his *sifu*—a disabled monk—is slain.

The two captives are transported to the Red Lotus Temple. The temple's mundane exterior belies a horrible underground prison where hordes of Shaolin students are caged and used as slave labor. In one scene, a new arrival foolishly protests his captivity, but when he's let out of his cage to test his mettle in a duel, spikes shoot up from the walkway beneath his feet.

Lording over all is the powerful Kung (K. K. Wong), an aged dictator with an insane bloodlust. "I want to enjoy life, even if it is inhuman," he snarls while clutching the head of a woman he has decapitated with his bare hands.

Ringo Lam places much of the action within the temple's claustrophobic confines, where lethal booby traps seem to be hid-

continued on next page

HEX ERRORS

NO BRAG...

More fractured English subtitles from your favorite Hong Kong movies (see chapter 3 for a full explanation).

I got knife-scars more than the number of your leg's hair!
—*As Tears Go By*

I'm a police of discipline.
—*Angel Enforcers*

You know I'm a roughie
—*Flirting*

I'm a sneaker.
—*Brave Young Girls*

I love hearing lascivious screaming.
—*Romance of the Vampires*

My nickname is "Iron Spade" spade the rubbish
—*Rich and Famous*

I only know how to shoot. I can't even write.
—*Gunmen*

...JUST FACT

Her ass . . . got the Symbol of the God of Death
—*Passionate Killing in the Dream*

Poodle Head attacked us
—*Doctor Vampire*

This is a hospital, not a charity.
—*Devil Cat*

An enurotic chick who have a bomb in her hand made us take our clothes off.
—*Dangerous Encounters of the First Kind*

The reproductive organ was bursted by bullet
—*Naked Killer*

African vampires don't go for Chinese women
—*Armour of God II: Operation Condor*

These corpses are young and active
—*Kung Fu Zombie*

Also, blind, cripple, bitchy and crazy ones are provided. All standard charge.
—*Romance of the Vampires*

den behind every wall, and rotting bodies are piled up knee-high in the dungeon. Time is marked by the decaying flesh of a buried corpse's uprooted arms.

Revisionist? A throwback to 70s gore-loving Shaw Brothers director Chang Cheh? Yeah, but this is still a martial arts movie, and its gloomy passages are counterbalanced by a number of exciting duels, including a pair between Fong and his friend Hung Hey-kwan, another famous martial artist from the annals of Chinese history. The finale finds Fong and Hung facing off against Kung, who uses his "Unlimited Stance" to fire deadly paint drops like bullets, but he croaks anyway.

—RAA

Odd Templars in the Red Lotus Temple. From *Burning Paradise.*

City on Fire

1987

Starring Chow Yun Fat, Danny Lee Sau-yin, Carrie Ng Kar-lai, Sun Yueh, Roy Cheung Yiu-yeung

Directed by Ringo Lam

City on Fire opens with classic noir sax blowing solo over the crowded, murky streets of Kowloon. An undercover cop is knifed in an outdoor market and left to die. Hangdog Inspector Lau (Sun Yeuh) surveys the chalk-outlined scene, then sends for new undercover cop Ko Chow (Chow Yun Fat, who won a Hong Kong Film Awards Best Actor award for his performance). Chow is in a local nightclub trying to patch up a spat with his spitfire girlfriend, Hung (Carrie Ng). A flurry of cops rush in and drag him out in handcuffs for the meeting with his boss, Lau. Despite being a cop, Chow's loyalties run to both sides of the legal ledger. He shies from Lau's request to infiltrate the criminal gang that iced the first undercover officer: "I fulfill my duties? But I betray friends!"

Lee Fu (Danny Lee) and his men are in the process of robbing the Forever Jewelry store when several beat cops who are chasing street hawkers stumble onto the scene. Despite violent bickering among his masked crew, Fu refuses to abandon anybody and leads his men out in a downpour of lead, tagging the backup cops who get in his way. The post-heist street is strewn with charred police car husks, and the veteran Inspector Lau is relieved of command by the young stuffed-shirt RHKP officer, John (Roy Cheung). Loyalty clearly runs deeper in the ranks of the mobsters as a hooched-up Inspector Lau (puking barely warmed cognac into a toilet) explains later to Chow: "Those who should die don't, those [who] shouldn't, do."

Chow takes the undercover assignment and infiltrates Fu's operation by funneling handguns to the gangster. But he soon finds himself in trouble with John's men, who are convinced that Chow really is dealing arms. Meanwhile, he's having difficulty explaining

Chinese ghosts bask in macho spirit
—*Rouge*

Her tongue is longer than yours!
—*A Chinese Ghost Story*

Much . . . cloud pass through me!
—*Master Wong vs. Master Wong*

He is executed to death just now.
—*Last Hero in China*

You were Mr. Pimp on Hookers Street 18 years ago
—*Wheels on Meals*

There's a vampire downstairs, sir.
—*Haunted Cop Shop 2*

He is the most stupid swordsman in the world of martial arts.
—*Holy Weapon*

Brother, my pants are coming out
—*Armour of God*

Then pop, he's gone.
—*The Big Heat*

Sir, your eyebrows are shaved!
—*Iron Monkey*

Snake Boy has told me everything
—*Holy Flame of the Martial World*

Danny Lee (right) can't hear Chow Yun Fat's duplicitous heart beat, but the audience can, during this tense moment from *City on Fire*.

underscored by a schlocky version of the Christmas carol "Joy to the World." But as the cops close in, Fu's boss suspects that the bleeding Chow is working undercover.

Shouts and accusations are exchanged. Guns are pointed at one another's heads. Denouement, as cop/criminal covers are blown, then blown away in a storm of slugs from within and without the gangster hideout.

City on Fire garnered additional attention when Quentin Tarantino's *Reservoir Dogs* was released in 1992 and invoked comparisons with the earlier Ringo Lam film. While elements of *City on Fire* were certainly worked into the fabric of *Reservoir Dogs*, especially elements of the third act, we're talking apples and oranges here. What's more important is that both films are excellent modern crime dramas that explore the complex dynamic of cops who have gone so deep undercover that their loyalties twist.

to Hung why he can't commit to marriage just now. While John and Lau argue over whether or not to use him as a pawn, Chow is accepted as a partner in the gang's next robbery.

As his bond with Fu deepens, Chow discovers that Hung (who fled the country with a wealthy Canadian guy) is waiting for him in San Francisco while the yawning chasm of the heist awaits him. It goes down, it goes wrong, and Chow takes a slug in the breadbasket while protecting Fu. The crooks motor to their hideout,

Prison on Fire

1987
Starring Chow Yun Fat, Tony Leung Kar-fai, Roy Cheung Yiu-yeung, Tommy Wong Kwong-leung, Nam Yin
Directed by Ringo Lam

Prison stories are often told from the perspective of the "new fish," an innocent who is tossed into a hellhole filled with bullying, predatory gangs but protected by a sympathetic old hand.

What sets Ringo Lam's *Prison on Fire* apart is its austere look and the gritty scripting by first-time screenwriter Nam Yin, who seems to have some, shall we say, inside knowledge of the subject. Coming on the heels of his triumph in *A Better Tomorrow*, *POF* helped cement Chow Yun Fat's reputation, and the film did gangbusters at the box office.

Advertising designer Lo Ka Yiu (Tony Leung) harasses some punks trying to rip off his father's shop and accidentally pushes one into the path of an oncoming bus. Three years for manslaughter.

Our new fish has his belongings bagged, his hair buzzed, and his orifices plumbed by a fierce-looking Sikh doctor. Assigned to the infirmary, he soon meets the wiseacre Ching (Chow Yun Fat), a positive thinker who knows how to work the prison rules and tweak the people in charge just far enough. Yiu looks like a gangly, somewhat retarded schoolboy in prison drag. He's driven to tears by the bullying of the prison's non-Sikh doctor, and forced to scrub the communal toilet. While he's there, Ching arrives to answer an urgent call, and ends up delivering some badly needed advice to the weeping, despairing Yiu. Chow's pontificating on the pot is funny enough, but he finishes both dump *and* lecture with a sprightly, "Take care, there's a better tomorrow!"

Ching is in Yiu's corner, but a dustup in the prison yard reveals the dark undercurrents of penal power systems. Baddie number one, a monster named Madly (Shing Fui-on), is punched out of the picture, leaving a struggle between unpleasant Mick (Nam Yin), not so bad Bill (Tommy Wong), and downright evil prison official Scarface (Roy Cheung). Mick and Scarface are in cahoots and conspire against the upright, naive Yiu for their own ends.

After Yiu's girlfriend deserts HK in favor of overseas study, he stands up to Mick in the prison laundry. The resulting fight leaves him at the edge of mad despair, with a two-foot triangular chunk of broken glass gripped tightly in his bleeding hand. Mick is transferred as a result of the violence, and time passes in relative calm.

The lull implodes a few months later, when Mick is locked back in with the terrified Yiu. A prisoner fast calls for solidarity, but when it's broken, various triad factions are pitted against each other. The fracas evolves into a death struggle between Mick and Ching. When Scarface tries to break it up, Ching goes animal-wild and thrashes him soundly, biting his ear off in the process! Yiu gets sprung on time while Ching goes smilingly back in stir, awaiting his "better tomorrow."

Prison on Fire 2

1987
Starring Chow Yun Fat, Wan Yeung Ming, Elvis Tsui Kam-kong, Tommy Wong Kwong-leung, Yu Li
Directed by Ringo Lam

With the success of 1987's *Prison on Fire*, a sequel was a shoo-in. Chow Yun Fat reprises his role as wiseacre inmate Ah Ching—lampooning

SONGS, BANGS, AND SWOOSHES

Hong Kong films are visually stunning, but there's more to them than meets the eye. The art of sound in Hong Kong cinema has come a long way from the dull thuds of the old chopsockies. When done right, the music and sound effects heighten the fantastic spirit of HK's visual component.

MUSIC

Cantonese pop songs are, as a rule, the most sappy-dippy-wishy-washy tunes on Earth. So we don't know why normally sane sophisticates get hooked on them. As a stand-alone, the stuff is sickly sweet and awful; when it appears in movies, though, something clicks.

Well, they are catchy. The martial theme of Tsui Hark's *Once Upon a Time in China* movies (if you've seen *OUATIC*, you're humming it now) is a traditional Chinese military song indelibly linked with the character Wong Fei-hong (see chapter 4 for more Fei-hong info). Instrumental versions turn up in many other movies about Wong Fei-hong, including Jackie Chan's original *Drunken Master*.

We also like the rousing "Hero of Heroes" in the *Swordsman* movies as well as the themes from *A Chinese Ghost Story* (sung by Leslie Cheung), *A Better Tomorrow*, *A Terracotta Warrior*, and *Heroic Trio*. You'll soon have your own favorites.

CDs or tapes are generally only available in Chinatown shops. But there is some good product worth the trip, like the soundtracks to *Green Snake*, *Once Upon a Time in China*, and *Swordsman II*. For those with no nearby Chinatown, Mute Records in England has released Michael Gibb's intense *Hard-Boiled* soundtrack, with trigger-happy tracks like "Gun Arsenal," "Body Count," and "Hospital Frenzy."

A surprising number of the more famous movie stars also have singing careers. In fact, Jacky Cheung is referred to as the "King of Cantopop"; the "Princes"— Andy Lau, Leon Lai, and Aaron Kwok—are also all instantly recognized by HK film fans. Sally Yeh and Anita Mui are both pop stars (Yeh's memorable songs from *The Killer* are on her album *Face to Face*).

Chow Yun Fat also sings, but cheerily admits that he is "lousy, lousy," so he donates all proceeds to charity. Even Jackie Chan sings the theme songs of many of his movies.

DUBBING

Hong Kong movies are routinely shot "MOS" (meaning "without sound"), which saves on production costs. Dialogue is then recorded in both Cantonese and Mandarin dialects. Some actors—

like Chow Yun Fat—dub both versions themselves; others have a stable of "voice-doubles" and don't do *any* dubbing.

SOUND EFFECTS

Audio effects in movies are like seasonings in food; you may not notice them when they're there, but you sure miss them if they're gone.

There are lots of fistfights in Hong Kong movies, so there are lots of fistfight sound effects. Moviemakers (and video game makers, for that matter) the world over add big crunching sounds every time their fighters make contact. But in Hong Kong, sound editors made a practice of adding something *before* the actual impact as well. Hong Kong movies are full of fluttering robes and swooshing hands and feet that sound like low-flying planes.

Coupled with inept fight choreography, the sounds are ridiculous (see chapter 11, "Kung Fu Theater"). But when done well, they really do turn up the heat. Jet Li's deadly "No-Shadow Kick" in *OUATIC* wouldn't be half as much fun if you didn't hear him thrashing through the air on his way to the target.

The master of the sound effect is John Woo. He has been known to assign specific gunshot sound effects to each of his major characters, so that when someone fires, you know who it is even if he's out of the frame. Woo also likes to emphasize other sounds that weapons make; the loading of a gun often makes as much noise as firing it. During *The Killer*, Danny Lee is chasing a gunman and suddenly finds himself face-to-face with the criminal on a packed tram. The abrupt silence Woo inserts is stunning; then when Lee cocks his gun, it's the loudest thing in the world.

A good Hong Kong movie should sound just as exciting as it looks, with as many bangs, swooshes, and songs as possible. Not to mention the odd moment of silence before all hell breaks loose.

—LEH

prison authority, scrawling motivational messages on the underside of prison stools, and even re-enacting his pontificating-during-a-poo scene.

As in the original, upright folks in a Hong Kong prison are trapped between rival factions and a sadistic, power-mad warden. In *POF2*, the usual local triads face another gang: a contingent of inmates from mainland China who loathe the "Hongkies." The mainland Chinese are kept in a separate cell, away from the HK contingent.

The leader of the mainlanders is a decent enough fellow named Big Dragon. But he runs afoul of Warden Zau (Elvis Tsui), who is fond of breaking the limbs of would-be escapees. A side-line business in the joint is betting on how long fugitives will remain free and on which limbs will be ruptured upon recapture. Zau cares little for the HK/mainland schism; he's an equal-opportunity sadist.

Zau uses the cover of a minor riot to smash Big Dragon's knee with a club, then humiliates Ching and denies him leave to visit his ailing son, who's been placed in an orphanage. Ching has to escape just so he can pay the tyke a visit! He surrenders and returns to the slammer.

The villainous official gets his sycophant Skull to stab Ching while he's in the shower, but it's the tattooed Snake who tastes the shiv instead. Zau fingers Big Dragon for the murder, but the mainlander crashes a dump truck through the prison fence and leaps from a cliff into the sea. Ching joins him in the leap to freedom, and the duo slog through the wilderness surrounding the prison, looking for a way out. They're reduced to eating snakes and a bunch of little green apples, which prompt the aforementioned excretory soliloquy.

Dragon convinces Ching to grab his son and flee to the mainland, but they're soon recaptured. Seeking revenge, Warden Zau and Skull toss Ching into the communal cell with vengeful mainlanders. And then . . . there's a big battle.

No one remains unbloodied, but Ching emerges in a patchable state, which is more than can be said for Zau! The warden goes loco and attacks his own subordinates, before taking a toothbrush-shiv in the eye from Ah Ching and expiring. Ching survives to beam over improving report cards from his son and dream of an unbarred future. With no *POF3* on the horizon, perhaps he made it to his "better tomorrow."

School on Fire

1988
Starring Fennie Yuen Kit-ying, Lee Lai-yui, Lau Chun-yan, Roy Cheung Yiu-yeung, Lam Ching Ying, Tommy Wong Kwong-leung
Directed by Ringo Lam

Lam's final installment in the "Fire" series, this is the darkest (and goriest) of the lot. As in the previous installments, innocents are placed in harm's way. This time though, it seems as though no escape or redemption is possible.

The setting is a middle school in crowded

Kowloon, overlooking the Kai Tak Airport runway. No stereotypical brainy Asian students here; our cast of characters are ne'er-do-wells and wanna-get-bys trapped in a web of triad-sponsored violence, drugs, and prostitution.

Schoolgirl Chu Yuen-fong (Fennie Yuen) is inseparable from her best bud, Kwok Siu-chun (Lau Chun-yan), a flunking-out teeny-bopper whose most precious possession is her call-girl pager.

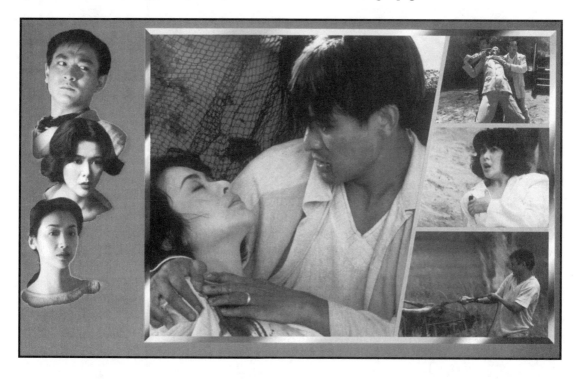

The Adventurers (1995). Despite its title, this Ringo Lam offering is a straightforward revenge drama. That is, as straightforward as an emotionally charged Hong Kong actioner with hokey conspiracy and romance-laced subplots driving several dazzling action sequences can be.

Beginning on the killing fields of Cambodia, renegade CIA agent Ray Lui and his band of mercenaries surprise and kill a family. Hidden from the mayhem, watching helplessly as Mom gets machine-gunned in the face at close range, is the young son who grows up to be handsome Andy Lau.

Twenty years and one survived assassination attempt later, Andy's character, Yan, adopts the pseudonym of Mandy and goes to San Francisco as a CIA-hired killer in order to exact retribution. Once there, he's aided and abetted in his quest by Rosamund Kwan as Ray's bitter concubine. Slaughter in San Francisco ensues.　　　　　　　　　　—MH

When Chu witnesses a fellow student being jumped by triad thugs, then killed by a passing van, she is warned against fingering the attackers by classmate George Chow, a triad-world bottom-feeder. Her father seeks the assistance of his old triad boss Sing, whose rival is young turk Brother Smart (Roy Cheung, at his villainous peak).

In this predatory world, the police are a nuisance at best. But Chu's teacher Wan and cop Hoi (Lam Ching Ying) talk her into squealing. When Brother Smart finds out about it, he literally scares the pants off the terrified schoolgirl, forcing her to strip to her skivvies as his goons jeer. Brother Smart then obliges her to recompense the HK$30,000 lawyer's fee for the assassin's defense. Paying off this debt—by renting her tender young body—sets Chu on the wrong path, a road that leads her and those around her (including her beau, the incorrigible punk Little Scar) to ruination and/or death. And yes, at one point we get a close-up of one of the school's PA speakers announcing, "Attention students, the school is on fire."

Set among two-dollar noodle shacks, concrete block flats bristling with television antennae, and crowded cramped classrooms, *School on Fire* looks and feels as bleak as its story. Cops and triads—opposing forces who both make offerings to Kwan Ti, the red-faced God of War—seem to follow predestined patterns of mutually assured destruction. HK's schools can't be *this* bad, but the relentless dirge of *School on Fire* makes you wonder.

Wild Search

1990
Starring Chow Yun Fat, Cherie Chung Chor-hung, Paul Chiang, Roy Cheung Yiu-yeung, Tommy Wong Kwong-leung, Ku Feng
Directed by Ringo Lam

Those expecting a rollicking bulletfest à la *Full Contact* from this Ringo Lam–Chow Yun Fat collaboration will be disappointed. But it's still a good example of Lam's prime strength as a director, developing strong characters and exploring their often surprising relationships. *Wild Search* is a crime-action film starring Chow as a hard-bitten RHKP officer, but it's also a romantic drama that sets its believable characters in a framework of powerful criminals opposed by hardworking cops.

Chow Yun Fat—whose character is named Mew Mew (go figure)—is slugging hooch out of a hip bottle while he waits for an informant to arrive. The snitch puts him onto an arms deal taking place in a vacant apartment: a pair of gat-peddlers named Elaine and Bullet are doing business with some Japanese gangsters. Chow and company bust in, and Elaine is killed in the shoot-out, leaving behind her button-cute daughter Ka-Ka.

Mew Mew and fellow cop Tommy Wong look up Elaine's address and set off to look for clues. They end up deep in the rural New Territories, the northern part of Hong Kong where the pace is closer to Chinese village life than the chrome and steel breakneck of central HK. Elaine's address is a simple farmhouse occupied

Rural tranquility is rent asunder by the intrusion of the irked Bullet (Roy Cheung), in Ringo Lam's *Wild Search*. Cheung's understated menace is a staple of many of Lam's films.

by her sister Cher (Cherie Chung) and her grumpy old dad (Ku Feng).

Mew Mew enlists Cher's help in tracing the trail of arms, which leads to Ka-Ka's natural father, Hung (Paul Chiang). The man is a horrible, cokeheaded gangster who's also a pillar of society. Mew Mew, never short on nerve, pays a visit to Hung at his office and requests a meeting with him and Cher to discuss Ka-Ka's future.

Hung sends a flunky instead, with a check for HK$100,000.

Insulted, Mew Mew crashes a high-society function with Cher in tow and pressures Hung for a cool million to support the illegitimate fruits of the scumbag's love labor. Hung's goombahs jump Mew Mew in the carpark, where the paparazzi photograph the aftermath: a bloody Mew Mew hauling Hung out of his white Rolls-

Royce at gunpoint. The ensuing scandal threatens to drive Mew Mew out of the police force.

As the personal histories of Mew Mew and Cher (obviously, they're made for each other) are slowly revealed, crusty old Grandpa also starts softening his attitude toward the illegitimate Ka-Ka. The only fly in the ointment is the vengeful Vietnamese villain Bullet (played with square-jawed greasy psychosis by Roy Cheung), who just can't stop chasing that cop. Fear not, this is not *School on Fire*. Happy ending ahoy.

Off the Wall

For one reason or another, almost everything in this book could be categorized as "off-the-wall." Maniac skulls fire death plasma lugies from their eye sockets, beautiful women brain each other with lug wrenches, and have-it-coming advertising executives are cursed with meter-stick boners right before the big underwear model presentation to the client. Being off-the-wall qualifies an HK film for further study and contemplation.

Thus, being labeled off-the-wall in this book means something significantly outside the realm of garden-variety weirdness—a four-sigma event, an outlier floating far from the line that best fits the other dots. These febrile flicks cause tectonic cracks in the worldview. Sudden shifts from serious highbrow to bawdy lowbrow furrow the brow, leaving the viewer giggly, whirly-headed,

HEX ERRORS

WHAT TH'?

More fractured English subtitles from your favorite Hong Kong movies (see chapter 3 for a full explanation).

I'm not Jesus Christ, I'm Bunny
—*Double Trouble*

We've got a bitle progress, since we found her head
—*The Gory Murder*

And these are toes chopped down by spacemen
—*The Seventh Curse*

Suck the coffin mushroom now
—*The Ultimate Vampire*

You always use violence. I should've ordered glutinous rice chicken
—*Pedicab Driver*

I give you a dish and berrior if you tell me now
—*City Cops*

Be a tearn and don't bite at each other.
—*Operation Pink Squad*

and amazed. When Chow Yun Fat plays a gambling king who gets a whack on the head and turns into an idiot gibbering for chocolate, that's just plain weird. But when that chocoholic defective turns out to *remain* the World's Greatest Gambler, that's off-the-wall.

Erotic Ghost Story II

1991
Starring Anthony Wong Chau-sang, May Law, Lui Siu Yip, cameo by Amy Yip
Directed by Lam Ngai Kai

More stylish and weird than its predecessor, *EGS2* features Anthony Wong as Wu Tung, who runs around his cave in white-face wearing little more than big plastic shoulder-boards, growling a lot, like some refugee from a KISS-revival band. He's growling because he's an underground demon. He's growling so that the village above him gets the hint: have a monthly lottery among the young ladies (to choose a playmate for him), or he'll put the hurt on everyone. But who knows why his demon concubine dances around naked, dripping molten wax from a candle into her mouth?

The village seems resigned to the system, and has their naked sorceress chant over each month's lithe tithe, who is oiled up, put on a sedan chair, and then left in the woods at the mouth of Wu Tung's cave, where she's transported beneath to party.

In between sacrifices, village life is pretty much normal, and lovely Yu-Yin (May Law) falls in love with the grinning beefcake fisherman Shan-kan (Lui Siu Yip). But wouldn't you know it, Yu-yin's number comes up at the very next lottery. Shan-kan is one of her sedan chair bearers, but when he sees that she's smuggled along a knife to fight with, he decides to help out with his big double-bitted battle-axe.

Mr. Big Demon gets wounded in the brief fight, and must

DeeeeTROIT! Are you ready ta parrrrrteee?!?! KISS-like Anthony Wong stars in *Erotic Ghost Story II.*

retreat down to his fortress of solitude, where, naked, he locks himself up to his neck in a giant spikey ball—evil's reducing cabinet. Back in town, Yu-yin and Shan-kan are given a hero's welcome.

The demon's concubine, looking like a glam-rock groupie, wants revenge, and appears on Earth where she finds Shan-kan's friends, a lusty rural couple. The concubine seduces the wife while the husband sits in front of a cluster of bananas, smoking a cigar. Then the trio get after it on a precarious jungle gym made of bamboo poles as goofy disco-reggae plays and Lawrence Welk bubbles float.

The demon wench kills the husband, then takes the wife back to the Pit. Back underground, the demon is feeling better and, to celebrate, he fornicates with the wife, magically cleaving her in two across the torso. While he sexually enjoys the lower half, ten feet away the upper half complains about a lack of satisfaction!

A big fool, with a gun, go to war. Surrendered and turned to a cake.
–*Haunted Cop Shop 2*

Ok! I'll Bastare, show your guts!
—*Transmigration Romance*

Flora, though I died, King of Hell said I didn't deserve it
—*My Better Half*

Suddenly my worm are all healed off
–*Aloha Little Vampire Story*

Designing is very brain-consuming.
—*Devil Cat*

God! I've got bruise. Insert!
—*Saviour of the Soul*

I'll give birth to a stuff for you in 10 months, OK?
—*Perfect Couples*

And you thought. I'm gabby bag
—*Dragons Forever*

I can't only jump to dead if you force me on
—*A Serious Shock: Yes Madam '92*

Explode at 11 o'clock sharp
—*Bury Me High*

continued on next page

Help! Please call my space phone
—*Armour of God*

Blonde chick, target for emigration.
—*The Big Heat*

Watch out, the road is very
   sweaty
—*Aloha Little Vampire Story*

To keep looking at the signal
   baboons make my eyes tired.
—*Angel Enforcers*

These are special tonic and 5-
   Toisoned Kid's urine
—*One Eyebrow Priest*

Pierce his face loci
—*Legend of the Liquid Sword*

Shan-kan, Yu-yin, and Shan-kan's Frazetta-model sister take it on the lam. They seek the wisdom of a dwarf monk, but the demon and his concubine catch up with them. The dwarf monk turns himself into a roly-poly bolide, but is still no match for his opponent.

Fortunately, Yu-yin is a dead ringer for the demon's lost love of long ago, Hsiao-yen. In fact, Hsiao-yen's essence was put into Yu-yin's pregnant mother, so the resemblance is more causal than casual. That old devil moons for Yu-yin and prevents his jealous concubine from strangling her. He does take Shan-kan back to his cave, where—naked and encased in a block of ice—Shan-kan has to watch Wu Tung get it on with half of his friend's wife.

Yu-yin and Shan-kan's sister sneak in to effect a rescue. As Yu-yin melts the block of ice by pressing her naked body against it, Shan-kan's sister fights with Mr. Big D, in a scene that recalls an airbrushed van panel. The two combatants then plunge into a stalagmite pool and have fierce underwater sex. Shan-kan is released, has sex with Yu-yin, then fights with the demon. The demon's phallic tail is chopped off and spews greens slime from its stump.

Finally, after all this, Yu-yin's birthmark is activated and Hsiao-yen appears from it in ghostly matte. Hsiao-yen's spirit joins with Wu Tung, and they perish together in purple flames.

There's a lot of good nudity in *EGS2*, a lot of sex, a lot of supernatural hoo-ha, colorful sets, and spinning dwarf monks. It's hard finding a subtitled version on video, but what the hell.

Note: Amy Yip appears only briefly, and under a shapeless robe as a Buddhist nun!

Fantasy Mission Force

1984

Starring Brigitte Lin Chin-hsia, Jackie Chan, Adam Cheng Siu-chau, Jimmy Wang Yu, Shin Bu Lia, Fang Jung, Sun Yueh, Chang Ling
Directed by Chu Yen Ping

Fantasy Mission Force is utterly ridiculous—but never boring—in that special kind of psychotronic way. There is an admirably consistent tone of lunacy throughout: Jerry Lewis remakes *The Dirty Dozen* high on laughing gas.

Just a footnote in Jackie Chan's extraordinary career, *FMF* is notable for being the most bizarre film he ever appeared in. Chan is paired with female action great Chang Ling as a pair of bumbling thieves who intermittently weave in and out of this film's mad, mad, mad, mad narrative.

Brigitte Lin stars as Lily, the one female member of an oddball commando squad. They're been promised big bucks by top mercenary Jimmy Wang Yu to rescue a multinational group of generals (including Abraham Lincoln) taken hostage by the Japanese—who are in the process of invading Canada. Lily's gadabout husband, who looks like an Elvis-imitator imitator, is recruited for the squad, but she won't let him tomcat and tags along. Her weapon of choice is a slimline bazooka, which she first uses to inexplicably blow up her own home.

Our goofy band of misfit adventurers, accompanied by a soundtrack that runs from bagpipes to bluegrass to honky-tonk piano in the space of a minute, are first captured by a village full of leopard-skin-wearing Amazons under the command of some debonair James Bond character (Adam Cheng). The Amazons kill Wang Yu on the fly, then humiliate our guys by making them wear sandwich boards on which are painted the bodies of provocative lingerie models.

Lily et al. escape from, then detonate the Amazon village, only to spend the night in a haunted house fully stocked with stiffs.

CENTIPEDE HORROR   1988

Sensitive drama concerning a young girl and her pet centipede Ling-Ling. Wrong! Opening credits alone are enough to give one the screaming meemies as large vigorous centipedes writhe toward the camera. Despite the novelty of a few reanimated chicken skeletons, this sorcerer vs. sorcerer flick is a bit on the dull side *until* the juddering heroine starts heaving forth cornucopious amounts of the hideous, wiggling invertebrates!

THE DRAGON FROM RUSSIA 1990

Director Clarence Ford (Fok Yiu-leung) makes films noted for their wonderful visual style and nonlinear plotting. Sometimes, frankly, it's hard to tell just what the hell is going on. But Clarence

continued on next page

has a pleasant habit of putting Carrie Ng in his movies, and that's not all bad.

This one involves the relationship between Sam Hui and Maggie Cheung, ethnic Manchurians who grew up together in Russia. Sam develops amnesia and is kidnapped by the 800 Dragons organization, who tattoo him and turn him into a masked assassin named Freeman. He then embarks on a series of lurid, brutal hits, but when Maggie's number comes up, his memory starts to return. This stylish silliness is a fully entertaining ninety minutes, rumored to be a personal favorite of Boris "Liter of Parliament" Yeltsin.

EROTIC GHOST STORY   1990

A tale of three sisters discovering their sensuality amid a backdrop of witches, triple-headed sex-fiends, and other erotic ephemera. Fluttering silk robes, ethereal sets, and architectural hairstyles adorn the licentiousness. Alternatively silly and steamy, the film marked the debut of buxotic Amy Yip, she of sweet face and outrageous norks.

When one commando answers the call of nature, the bathroom walls sprout rows of bloody arms, all offering him toilet paper.

We are treated to a wealth of inane costumes throughout. A crybaby commando wears a chrome-plated Prussian helmet. UN forces drill in kilts and blue tam-o'-shanters. Bad guys wear conquistador outfits.

When the fantasy mission force finally arrives at Japanese HQ, the enemy forces have all been slaughtered. Who's got those world leaders? Why, double-crossing Nazi Wang Yu, who faked his own death! His army of *Road Warrior*–style goons surf toward our force atop beswatikaed seventies-era Detroit automobiles, firing automatic weapons as they approach.

As a sad harmonica version of "Camptown Races" plays, frantic gunfire drops our heroes one by one, until only Wang Yu and Jackie Chan remain alive. Their martial arts showdown amidst the old clunkers is good stuff (though Chan gets no help from the timid world leaders). Chan wins, gets the money, and all the Nazis and Japanese are dead. The end.

God of Gamblers

1989
Starring Chow Yun Fat, Andy Lau Tak-wah, Joey Wong Jo-yin, Sharla Cheung Man
Michiko Nishiwaki
Directed by Wong Jing

Ko Chun—the world's greatest gambler—faces off against a pretender to the throne. *Mahjongg* tiles are thrown face down on green felt and shuffled; the two combatants fence furiously with wooden sticks over the anonymous game pieces. Ko Chun (Chow Yun Fat) picks out the correct tiles unseen, and wins the round with a perfect hand. His opponent, Wong, sends his assistant—a beautiful Japanese woman (Michiko Nishiwaki)—to assay the second round. Michiko slips off her kimono, revealing an exquisite dragon tattoo, then picks up the dice cup and throws six ones—a perfect low score. Ko applauds her effort, then asks for a heavier shaker. He's brought a steel martini shaker, chucks in his six dice and rattles it furiously before banging it on the table. The result? Five ones and a die smashed to pieces! The awestruck Wong exclaims, "You are really God!"

His defeated rival then asks for Ko's help to destroy a clever and corrupt gambler named Chan. Before the intended meeting with Chan can take place, though, Ko suffers a blow to the head that reduces him to the mental level of a four-year-old!

Ko's accident is the result of a booby trap set by Knife (Andy Lau), a bottom-feeder tough guy, that was meant for someone else. Knife, his girlfriend Jane (Joey Wong), and his buddy Crawl are unaware that it's the God of Gamblers they've turned into a mental midget, but they decide to nurse him back to health. Knife soon discovers that, in spite of his retarded mental state, Ko retains his amazing gambling skills—a plot device obviously borrowed from *Rain Man*. However, he won't touch a card until Knife bribes him with his favorite chocolate bars!

While Ko is away, Ko's cute girlfriend (Sharla Cheung) is killed, *then* raped by Ko's avaricious assistant, the villainous Yee. Yee learns where Ko is staying and goes to kill him. Rumors spread that the God of Gamblers is a fallen one. But Ko eventually regains his memory, outwits and outgambles the nasty Chan, and gets revenge on Yee.

God of Gamblers was an enormous hit in Hong Kong. In a place where money is seen as the only means of escaping both the dreariness of daily life and the impending takeover by China, the concept of an invincible gambler was an irresistible one. Several more films about gambling in Hong Kong followed its lead, including a comedy series starring *mo lei tau* ("no-brain") comedian Stephen Chow (see page 175) that is as popular as the original. *God of Gamblers* breathed new life into the old genre, the Hong Kong Gambling Movie.

GHOSTLY VIXEN   1990

Buxotic Amy Yip is Evil Girl, a ghost who must suck off one hundred virgin boys to gain an eternal body. When we first meet her in a Thai bar, she finds and finishes number ninety-eight. But before she can enjoy the afterglow, a rugged ghost hunter named Hui (Shing Fui-on) and his coin-operated sword chase her into a *mahjongg* tile bound for Hong Kong.

Cut to Hong Kong. Virgin junior executive Sau Yan just can't get laid. He takes one hooker to his apartment, and the power goes off. Trying to stay suave, Sau Yan brings out candlelight and champagne. The champagne cork pops his date in the eye and, when he tries to help, the candle sets her hair ablaze. Dousing her with the champagne, he tells her to wait in the bedroom. After drinking a sex charm, he follows her in, only to discover that the bedroom had been invaded by a pair of robbers who are armed and horny. Sau Yan offers them the services of his hooker, only to discover that they are gay.

He's having trouble getting laid because he's supernaturally

continued on next page

promised to his old home-village sweetheart, a spinster-in-training named Yumy. Sau Yan wants nothing to do with the frumpy Yumy. But she's a gamer and, armed with a couple of charms from her wizard father, heads off to the big city to get her man.

She arrives, catching Sau Yan with a second hooker's hair caught in his zipper. Pissed off, she uses the first charm to give him a leg-length penis which scares off his escort—then gets him into trouble at the next day's corporate presentation to a manufacturer of skimpy lingerie.

Disposing of ghost hunter Hui (he's a virgin, too) in a Hong Kong mental hospital, Evil Girl starts a seek-and-destroy sortie for Sau Yan, virgin boy number one hundred.

Yumy tries to save her guy by sleeping with him, but Sau Yan can't get it up, even when Yumy holds photos of supermodels over her face. So they must fight Evil Girl. Yumy dies, then comes back as a ghost and defeats the Yipster. A momentarily grateful Sau Yan marries Yumy in a ghost wedding but, after consummation, Yumy turns his member into a flower (to

Chow Yun Fat—always fun to watch—turns in an amazing performance, going from suave gamesman to childlike savant and back again. Andy Lau is appropriately buffoonish, and Joey Wong is as gorgeous as ever. The theme song is a rip-off of "Raindrops Keep Falling on My Head," the gambling sequences are spellbinding, and there's a nifty shoot-out. Director Wong Jing (who built his career upon the success of GOG) telegraphs every plot twist, but twenty bucks says you won't guess Ko Chun's secret trick at the end!

—JM

Robotrix

1991
Starring Amy Yip, David Wu, Chikako Aoyama, Hui Hsiao-dan, Billy Chow
Directed by Jamie Luk Kin-ming

In this entertaining, nonsensical flick, top-heavy androidettes battle a robotic villain with a penchant for carnal mayhem. *Robotrix* is a T and A flick (titanium and aluminum!)—robocore has never looked so good.

An oil sheik stages a robot competition in Hong Kong to garner competitive bids on his plan to build a "Robot Legion." Will-triumphant androids from Germany descend from the ceiling and strut their stuff. When an American scientist challenges the German product, the Teutonic titanium titan is pitted against the American entry. The Krautbot smashes the Yankbot's brain-wiring, and it goes berserk, attacking the crowd. But waiting in the wings is Eve R27, the product of lovely Japanese engineer Dr. Sara (Hui Hsiao-dan) and her assistant, the fetching Anna (Amy Yip). Eve—who looks like a cross between Maria from *Metropolis* and a Mighty Morphin Power Ranger—chains up the runaway robot as the crowd cheers.

Amy Yip and fellow jailbirds are shown the error of their criminal ways in *Jail House Eros* (aka *Haunted Jail House*).

keep him from straying), a spell that only she can reverse. Laughter and freeze-frame.

JAIL HOUSE EROS (*AKA* HAUNTED JAIL HOUSE)   1991

Women's prison. *Haunted* women's prison. The warden is a sadistic woman who forces the firehose on the unfortunate inmates—including the buxotic Amy Yip. Fortunately, the warden dies in a tragic accident. Unfortunately, she returns as a fierce ghost!

A trio of local goobers—who just want to romance the incarcerated crimekittens—pose as Taoist priests to get inside, but lack the right stuff for exorcism. So it's up to the Good Witch of the Cellblock (Loletta Lee) to whack the demon. Red-blooded males want to know how Amy Yip looks when shorn of makeup and wrapped in plain jaildresses. Terrific!

MY NEIGHBOURS ARE PHANTOMS 1990

Four thirties-era ghosts (two male and two female) escape from an old black-and-white photograph

continued on next page

and begin to slake their thirst for human blood. First slated for slaking is the household next door—police inspector Dragon and his two sisters, Yummie and Sandy. But good female ghost Siu-Sin, whose ashes are controlled by the evil boss ghost, falls for Dragon—even before his trophy-winning performance at the annual high society Dirty Joke Contest (it's for charity)—and tries to protect his clan from the fangs of her master.

Dragon's superstitious sisters are the first to suspect all is not right with the new neighbors. Fortunately, another cop moonlights as a Taoist priest and provides the necessary charms and holy water.

As Siu-Sin and her unwitting beau drive around in a giant paper Hell Car (see "Hell Bank Notes," page 104), Dragon's sisters, with help from his ex-fiancée (played by the buxotic Amy Yip), holy-rope the evil female. But they must hold her tethered motionless till the priest/cop gets there. The angry ghost unfurls a six-foot-long tongue that attacks the only thing within reach—the straining buttons of Amy Yip's tight blouse.

In the final fight, a fleeing Dragon slows down a cemetery's

But there's bad news for the sheik, who learns that his son has been kidnapped. The kidnappers delivered a videotape, which shows mad scientist Ryuichi Yamamoto committing seppuku (hara-kiri) before transferring his consciousness into an evil, powerful android (Billy Chow). He wants to convince the sheik to build an evil robot Legion. This psychobot spends his time using a Freudian power drill on the kidnappee, or running around HK in Billy Idol punk garb and murdering hookers. Transfer cracked-shell,

From *Robotrix*, a startling view of things to come. Chikako Aoyama costars as a policewoman killed in the line of duty who is brought back to life as a beautiful android. The only man not happy about it is fellow flatfoot and former lover, David Wu (inset).

evil-egghead brains into killer androids, and stuff like this is bound to happen.

The not-so-bright cops get the bright idea to use Anna as a prostitute-decoy to trap Yamamoto. Anna (who, naturally, turns out to be an android herself) is keen on the idea since she's curious about human sexuality. They pour the buxotic Cyber Yip into a red minidress, then set up a hidden camera in her room.

Voyeuristic video glimpses of her passion cause a hairy cop named Puppy to experience nosebleeds! He excuses himself, then puts on an absurd disguise and returns as a customer. The ruse fails, but soon there's a line around the block, and the police have to abandon the operation.

The cops then put informer Hui on Yamamoto's trail. Hui's killed, but the scientists remove his eyeballs, hook them up to their robotic supercomputer, and view the dead man's last image. The eyeballs finger the sheik's bodyguards as stooges for Yamamoto, who kills them anyway. Finally, the Yipster traps the man-made monster in a junkyard, tosses him (via electromagnet) into a car crusher, and terminates him.

Taxi Hunter

1993
Starring Anthony Wong Chau-sang, Ng Man-tat
Directed by Herman Yau Lai-to

In the 1950s, American International Pictures was notorious for the rapidity with which they brought topical themes into the theaters and drive-ins of America. Let a Russkie satellite blast into space, and three weeks later the kids would be heavy-pettin' in the balcony during *Rock 'n' Roll Sputnik*. Was AIP celebrating the sweet transience of AmeriPopCulture in those proverbial good ol' days?

uprooted tenants with *a cha* spell, but accidentally aims it at a mirror and unintentionally casts the spell on himself, too. The life-or-death chase continues in frantic slo-mo. He finally must confront the mean boss ghost inside the old photo (an inspiring act of courage for someone who's peed his pants twice already) to save Siu-Sin. He triumphs, but Siu Sin can't follow him to the temporal world.

Dirty jokes, bloodsucking, Amy Yip, and a doomed man/ghost love story—bring a date.

THE NOCTURNAL DEMON   1991

Comedy about a psychokiller cabby who inhales lighter fuel to put himself in the mood, then cuts out his victims' tongues. Yes, a *comedy* with requisite bubble-fart synth music, buttheaded cops, boob jokes, the works. *TND* stars Moon Lee as Wawa, a seventeen-year-old martial arts student from the mainland who sports a Louise Brooks bob. She thrashes the crazy hack (Yuen Wah) while wearing roller skates, then dons

continued on next page

rock-trash drag (and an Elvira wig!) to thump the psycho with her thigh-high leather boots. This flick runs to partly dorky, but Moon has the tenacity to render any inanity with a straight face.

OPERATION PINK SQUAD 2   1988

A bunch of female cops must pose as hookers to trap a counterfeiter. Unfortunately, their hideout is haunted by a rabid lady ghost. They chop this ghoul's head off with a shovel, which makes her

"You think I'm falling for that old 'There's a floating witch's head behind you!' bit?" A gangster played by Shing Fui-on is about to get what's coming to him in *Operation Pink Squad 2.*

Creating reams of rich appropriatable material to assist creatively bankrupt future generations? Nah, just trying to make a buck.

By contrast, present-day Hollywood inertia often results in inappropriate delays, so that a film like *Dave* (satirizing George Bush) wasn't released until everybody was already sick of Bill Clinton.

But many in the Hong Kong film industry hold fast to the AIP exploitation model: milk a newsworthy topic for box office cream. In 1993 (the year of *Dave*), HK taxi drivers came under fire for all sorts of rude behavior: cruising around with "Out of Service" notices that disappear at the wave of an HK$100 note, levying illegal surcharges in bad weather, and refusing to take people short distances. A sizable groundswell of ill will spiked up. Almost immediately, *Taxi Hunter* banged into the theaters, featuring Robert (Anthony Wong) as a meek-mannered businessman bedeviled by those horrid hacks.

Wong (visually styled like Michael Douglas in *Falling Down*) puts up with cabbie abuse and corruption until the Hong Kong taxi-drivin' mob causes the death of his pregnant wife. Crestfallen, Wong starts hitting the San Miguel hard, and eventually turns into a vigilante, taking out taxi drivers (whose transgressions range from rape to rudeness) with his "Barnetor" nine-millimeter automatic. As he alternates between meek accountant and crack-brain taxi-vigilante, Wong does a send-up of Robert De Niro in *Taxi Driver*, explaining to buddy (Ng Man-tat) that his serial killings are okay because "I only kill those blacksheeps!" No sympathy allowed for *Taxi Hunter*'s cabbies, who exude sneering greed and arrogance; the lone honest driver in the bunch, however, always gets a *big* hand from Hong Kong audiences!

市民俾錢仲要受氣
我要企出嚟主持公道

製作人 梁鴻華
導演 邱禮濤
聯合主演 黃秋生

的士
TAXI

的士
TAXI

于榮光
吳孟達
朱茵
黎海珊
聯合主演

"Ya talkin' ta ME?" In *Taxi Hunter*, the mild-mannered guy (Anthony Wong) that flips is the passenger, not the driver, and Hong Kong audiences rejoice.

really angry. Not only does the head go flying around trying to bite people in sensitive spots, but the headless body proves a fearsome foe as well! The local Taoist is summoned to shoot down the head with an array of red-on-yellow Buddhist toy helicopters, but she uses the radical "Blood Out" technique to best him. The cops' only hope is to invoke "the Elf." But which of the male characters possesses the prerequisite for Elfhood—virginity?

SAVIOUR OF THE SOUL   1992

Andy Lau and Anita Mui play star-crossed lovers hunted by master criminal Silver Fox (Aaron Kwok). Fox sucks purple smoke out of test tubes and uses his "Terrible Angel" stance to possess Anita; she can only be cured by the Pet Lady (Carina Lau), a haughty sorceress living in the Pet Palace. The camera angles and art direction of this fantasy-romance are styled after Japanese *animé*. Lots of wirework and fantastic action abound; Anita Mui plays a dual role as her own wisecracking sister.

continued on page 174

YOK DANS

Just like Hollywood, particularly 30s-era Hollywood—when guys like Bugsy Siegel and Mickey Cohen could be found on the set—Hong Kong has its share of scandal and sleaze. Also like 30s-era Hollywood, not very much of it filters out to the general public. Ask about a dead stuntman, or why one of the Colony's top young actors suddenly retired, and you run into a great wall. But the information that does get through is primo.

Let's start with Amy Yip, "the Jane Russell of Hong Kong." The buxotic Ms. Yip, star of such films as *Ghostly Vixen*, *Jail House Eros*, and *Sex & Zen* has had her 36-inch bust insured for a million dollars against damage or shrinkage.

In 1990, Yip made "And Elsewhere . . ." news around the world when an obsessed Bank of America executive was jailed for attempting to improperly transfer $2.4 million to her account. He told investigators that Yip was his girlfriend and that her constant demands for money drove him to it. Before committing his crime, the exec had first sold his home and moved his own mother into low-income housing to finance the relationship.

The diminutive *Yok Dan* ("flesh bomb") is also famous in Hong Kong as hostess for the adults-only video magazine *Le Club* and for having recorded a telephone message about her silk underwear that jammed telephone lines—earning the sponsors HK$8,000 a day.

In late 1992, concluding that the soft-porn business was being "taken over by beauty pageant contestants and starry-eyed newcomers," Yip turned to singing. But she was banned from performing in mainland China after being blacklisted for spreading "spiritual corruption."

Yip has been careful not to give everything away in her films; no full-frontal nudity, no nipples.

"When people have seen you completely naked, they are not curious about you anymore," she once advised.

With all this pent-up pinup curiosity, you can hardly blame the organized crime syndicates in Hong Kong—triads—for strongly suggesting that she make a more explicit film for one of their production companies.

Instead of surrendering her celluloid chastity, Yip went to the police for protection. "The harassment is continuing, and all I can do is delay giving a reply," she said.

The pressure on her was no idle threat. The triads have made a determined effort during the 90s, the final years of the island's British oversight, to take control of the local film industry. One actress was gang-raped, allegedly on the orders of a rebuffed triad producer, while many others have come forward to say that they have been threatened and black-

AND TRIADS

mailed to appear in triad-run productions.

In early 1992, armed men burst into the offices of a leading film company and stole two reels of *All's Well, Ends Well*, a major release due for distribution during the Chinese New Year holiday (imagine someone stealing Paramount's next Christmas offering).

Hundreds of stars and producers, including Amy Yip, then staged an unprecedented protest against triad interference. Marching with a banner reading "Show Business Against Violence" to the headquarters of the Royal Hong Kong Police, they demanded that action be taken against the gangs.

A few months later, Wong Long Wai, a film company owner and kung fu stuntman, was killed in a private hospital in Hong Kong while being treated for a strained elbow. A gunman simply walked into his bedroom and shot him in the head with a .38 revolver. Weeks later, producer Jimmy Choi Chi-ming stepped out of an elevator and into a hail of bullets fired by two men disguised as security guards.

"The gangsters are getting naughtier every day," concluded Chua Lam, another producer of kung fu movies.

STONE AGE WARRIORS 1990

Crunky jungle hijinks with Nina Li, Elaine Lui, and Fan Siu Wang (star of *The Story of Ricky*) adventuring in Indonesia. The best thing about this cracked actioner is the outtakes that roll under the closing credits. Witnessing what HK directors expect their talent to suffer through is scarier than any hopping-vampire picture. Watch as sex kitten Nina Li is first menaced by a quick and agile seven-foot Komodo dragon, then dragged insensible out of a raging river! See Elaine "Angel" Lui freak out *for real* when covered with huge jet-black scorpions, and spit out an enormous glob of chewed-up banana mush! Eccch!

The Wicked City

1992

Starring Leon Lai Ming, Jacky Cheung Hak-yow, Michelle Reis (Lee Kar-yan), Tatsuya Nakadai, Roy Cheung Yiu-yeung, Yuen Woo-ping, Carman Lee
Directed by Mak Kit-tai

An ambitious attempt to translate the flamboyant creativity of Japanese *animé* to live action cinema, the Tsui Hark–produced *The Wicked City* is a visually intriguing mixture of sci-fi and melodrama. The movie moves with comic book quickness, without much of that boring cinematic connective tissue. Scenes are short and often contain extreme angle-ons or forced perspective to give the movie its exciting graphic feel. *TWC* faithfully re-creates some

Davian International, Mike Leeder

Stalwart half-breed Ken Kai (Jacky Cheung) fights against full-blooded rapter Shudo's blebby entreaties in *The Wicked City*.

scenes from the similarly titled Japanese animated film (also known as *Supernatural Beast City*) and also draws inspiration from *Alien Nation* and *Blade Runner*.

The story opens with 1997 approaching rapidly. Hong Kong is in chaos due to an influx of havoc-wreaking otherworldly immigrants known as rapters. These shape-shifting aliens have infiltrated Earth's society by assuming human guise, and it's up to the government's Antirapter Bureau to track down and eliminate them. In the movie's nifty opening sequence, our hero, Antirapter Bureau agent Taki (Leon Lai), takes a beautiful prostitute up to his hotel room, then exposes her as a rapter. Once unmasked, she mutates into a murderous insect woman! Taki's half-human/half-rapter fellow agent, Ken Kai (Jacky Cheung), arrives in the nick of time to decapitate the sinister beast.

Back in Hong Kong, a powerful corporate head named Daishu (played by Japanese actor Tatsuya Nakadai) arrives for a gala birthday celebration, unaware that the Antirapter Bureau has caught on to his nonhuman lineage (Daishu's age, 150, was the tip-off). Taki infiltrates the party but is stopped in his tracks by the sight of Daishu's ravishing rapter girlfriend, Windy (Michelle Reis). Windy is a former flame whom Taki abandoned years ago, upon discovering her identity as an alien monster. Meanwhile, Daishu's birthday bash turns ugly as a fellow rapter accuses him of disseminating a deadly street drug called "Happiness," which is destroying the rapter community.

It turns out, Daishu is actually a wealthy pacifist polymorph seeking to foster peaceful relations with humans. It's his young turk son Shudo (Roy Cheung) who is facilitating his own takeover plans by secretly distributing the destructive drug.

The relationships between the main characters and their tragic potential are clear, if tangled. Taki still loves rapter Windy, who still kind of loves him but really loves fellow rapter Daishu. Half-breed Ken Kai is mistrusted by the Bureau chief and falls for fellow agent Orchid, who should not be trusted. And always horny Shudo is a

HONG KONG COMEDIES AND THEIR KING

In Stephen Chow's box-office smash, *Flirting Scholar*, a despotic Ming Dynasty ruler pits his prize poet against Chow (as the film's Flirting Scholar). The two poets recite in each other's faces, going at it like rap-assassins as onlookers cheer the beauty of their spontaneous verse. The match ends as one of Chow's stanzas—delivered in rhyming Cantonese at breakneck pace—causes the tyrant's poet to fall insensible to the ground, bleeding from the nostrils.

This is *mo lei tau* (approximate translation: "no-brain" or "non sequitur"), a uniquely Chinese brand of comedy pioneered by Stephen Chow Sing-chi. *Mo lei tau* is constrained by neither logic nor reality. Ancient martial arts wisdom coexists with high-tech wonders. Characters spon-

continued on next page

taneously acquire supernatural powers for brief scenes, only to lose them thereafter.

Stephen Chow films are wildly popular in Hong Kong. In 1992, the top four HK moneymakers were all Chow vehicles. Despite Hollywood competition in 93 and 94, he still claimed three of the top ten spots in each year. He is currently HK's highest-paid actor.

But for all this buildup, we don't recommend renting HK comedies unless you really want to. There are two reasons. First and foremost, there is the language barrier. Chow's comedy—with its rhyming puns and double entendres—is so heavily based on spoken Cantonese that it doesn't even translate well into Mandarin, let alone English. You face the same problem with any HK comedy that relies on wordplay. It's nobody's fault, but you just won't get it.

Second, there is a cultural gap. Knowledge of Chinese referents— folklore, literature, and cinema— is needed to understand the jokes. This is true of nearly any comedy composed for one audience and shown to another; when was the last time you split your sides at a Ritz Brothers retrospective?

Davian International, Mike Leeder

Va-va-va-voom. Hubba-hubba. Rrrowwwlll. Hot-cha. It's the woman who out-Mamied Van Doren. It's the most JPEGed starlet in the East. It's the one and only Yipster, as seen in *Erotic Ghost Story*.

powerful threat to life as we know it. Ultimately, Taki and Ken Kai must rely on each other in this crazy place. Tragic potential energy becomes tragic kinetic energy, and almost everyone dies during the big third-act showdown.

The Wicked City only hints at the graphic eroticism of its Japanese animation antecedent, preferring instead to cut loose with an unending series of increasingly bizarre special effects. This is gaudy visual spectacle at its inventive best (and occasionally at its campy worst). Members of the Antirapter Bureau run around in a group, using telekinesis to levitate Taki whenever he gets thrown out a high-rise window. Liquid rapters hide in cocktails, then explode the heads of anyone who drinks them. A flying killer clock chases our heroes, and a seven-foot female rapter transforms into a sexually mature pinball machine or a screaming motorcycle to be played or ridden by the movie's male characters.

—RAA

Chinese rental outlets have big comedy sections. Fortunately, HK comedies are easy to spot, and you rarely rent one by accident. Posters and video box art in which the stars are shown with large comic-book heads and tiny bodies are a dead giveaway. Titles like *Double Fattiness* and *Stooges in Tokyo* should also warn you off.

Yuen, Sammo, Yuen

10

T he exploits of Jackie Chan (see chapter 6) are well known; the cinematic efforts of his "brothers" less so. That's too bad, because many of these are on a par with HK's best and brightest.

Chan was one of many orphans raised at Hong Kong's Peking Opera school, where martial skills are taught with arduous single-mindedness. A group of children from this school, including Chan and the three men featured here—Yuen Biao, Sammo Hung, and Yuen Wah—toured as the Seven Little Fortunes. All seven ended up making action movies in some capacity. And each appears, mix and match, in the others' projects. Jackie repeatedly cast the Yuens and Sammo in his films until 1987's *Dragons Forever*, their last film as a group.

The film *Painted Faces* accurately depicts their singular upbringing and the rigorous training that turned these spiritual brothers into martial screen idols.

Yuen Biao

Yuen Biao, the junior member of the troupe, broke into film with a brash physical grace in *Dreadnaught* and *The Prodigal Son*. A cheeky chap with a grin full of crooked teeth, Yuen has played everything from hero to scalawag to bumpkin to flying-pigtail fighter. Like several other members of the Seven Little Fortunes, he adopted the surname "Yuen" as tribute to their *sifu* Yuen Chanyuan, who now lives in Southern California.

Sammo Hung Kam-bo

A seminal figure in the development of the modern action film and the senior member of the Seven Little Fortunes, Sammo Hung has served as actor, director, and/or action director on dozens of films. While Sammo's stocky build (earning him half of his nickname "Big Brother Big") and guileless moon face are not the usual leading man stuff, his martial arts skills are nonpareil.

Sammo also has a good touch with comedic roles, and often plays a lovable sap in ghost stories. His name comes from a popular cartoon character from his childhood, "Sam-mo" ("three hairs").

That guy with the evil grimace, Yuen Wah, mixes it up with Michelle Yeoh in *Police Story 3: Supercop*.

Rim Films

Yuen Wah

Known as the "Who *was* that guy?" guy. Never top-billed; incredulous audiences, nonetheless, want to know: Who was that guy with the cigar in *Dragons Forever*? That guy with the fan in *Eastern Condors*? That guy with the nerdy spectacles in *On the Run*? That guy with the electric-blue kung fu in *A Kid from Tibet*? While he looks like the last person you'd pick for the softball team, he is an amazingly talented martial artist who takes his opponents—and his audience—completely by surprise. *That guy* is HK cinema's number-one villain, the sunken-cheeked Yuen Wah.

Yuen Biao makes quick dispatch of some unworthy lurdan in *Eastern Condors*.

Eastern Condors

1987
Starring Sammo Hung Kam-bo, Yuen Biao, Yuen Wah, Lam Ching Ying, Joyce Godenzi, Dr. Haing S. Ngor, Dick Wei, Billy Lau, Corey Yuen Kwai, Yuen Woo-ping, Ng Ma, Melvin Wong
Directed by Sammo Hung Kam-bo

War spectacular with an all-star cast of HK regulars, and a ringer, Oscar-winner Dr. Haing S. Ngor (Best Supporting Actor, 1984). The action sequences are expert as the best in the business get to strut their martial stuff.

David Chute

HEX ERRORS

WARNINGS AND ADVICE

More fractured English subtitles from your favorite Hong Kong movies (see chapter 3 for a full explanation).

Don't bullshit, shovel.
—*Queen's High*

There's no way you can trust her. Her missile is gigantic.
—*I Love Maria*

With potbelly facing Heaven, he'll be Herculean!
—*Mr. Vampire Part III*

I'll fire aimlessly if you don't come out!
—*Pom Pom and Hot Hot*

Quiet or I'll blow your throat up.
—*On the Run*

The wolves will burst your tits this time!
—*Naked Killer*

Don't be misleaded by the Skinny. He is protected by Inner Air.
—*Last Hero in China*

Lieutenant Colonel Lam (Lam Ching Ying) is recruited to lead a Dirty Dozen–style suicide mission into 1976 Vietnam: a missile dump left behind by hightailing Yanks must be destroyed before it falls into the wrong hands. His squad is composed of ethnic Chinese criminals sprung from a New Jersey hoosegow.

Parachuting behind the lines, the camo-clad mercenaries hit the ground ready for action (though one—nicknamed "Stammer"—has a particularly hard time with the ripcord count). They immediately rendezvous with three female Cambodian patriots led by Joyce Godenzi (the future Mrs. Sammo). The guerrilla trio are a hard-bitten, battle-seasoned lot and, to throw a wrench into the proceedings, one is a double agent.

An unlikely ally is found in Rat Chieh (Yuen Biao), a local lad who peddles whiskey and cigs from a huge music-blaring motortrike, a sort of black-market Good Humor man. Yuen lives with his uncle, a harmless grinning simpleton, Yeung (Dr. Haing S. Ngor). The squadron brings both along to help scout the local terrain.

They're pursued by the Vietcong, who are led by a sanguine VC general (Ng Ma). Captured by the Cong, our heroes are confined in bamboo cages with water up to their waists. In a virtual *Deer Hunter* rip-off, they're forced to play Russian roulette to amuse their captors, but turn the tables and shoot their way out.

The Cong pursue them into the booby trap–infested jungle, where the martial arts skills of Yuen Biao and Tung Ming-hsin (Sammo) save the day. Sammo quick-strips palm leaves, hurling the stems like darts into necks. Yuen tosses a coconut in the air like a soccer ball and kicks it into the noggin of an onrushing Commie, braining him. It's fast, it's wild, and it ain't no Chuck Norris–style hairy-backed sleepwalking.

The female double agent is unmasked and terminated. Then a strange Commie commando commander (Yuen Wah) starts dogging their trail. A dour pantywaist wearing silk pajamas and wire-rimmed specs, he communicates in hiccups and cools himself with a dainty folding fan as he surveys the carnage in our heroes' wake. He only comes alive when he calls in the heavy artillery on the valiant squadron, who've lost a few through attrition and are guarding a strategic bridge. Sitting in the back of a jeep, the qualmish Congster shakes his pencil wrists in the air and hysterically screams, "FIIIIIRE!" as hell pours down on the bridge guardians.

The remaining heroes make it to the munitions dump—festooned with gleaming missiles—and set their time bombs. The Cong burst in, and the pitched end battle begins. After disposing of the brawny frontliners, Yuen and Sammo face only the scrawny Mr. Big. But instead of folding like a wet noodle, the bespectacled villain explodes into eccentrically fluid, masterful kung fu! He puts up a hell of a fight, but is nevertheless finally subdued, then dispatched by the old grenade-stuffed-in-the-mouth technique. Our heroes escape the exploding armory and live to fight another day.

Encounter of the Spooky Kind 2

1990
Starring Sammo Hung Kam-bo, Lam Ching Ying, Meng Hoi
Directed by Sammo Hung Kam-bo

Sammo and his beloved are on the lam and hole up in a haunted temple. Inside, a detestable ghoul couple molt their coffins to indulge in opium smoking and philandering with the quaking loving humans. Soon the four are daisy-chain bloodsucking. This is the opening dream sequence, but things don't get much better for Sammo when he wakes up.

He's the dirt-poor student of eternal *sifu* (Lam Ching Ying) and hopelessly in love with the innkeeper's daughter, Little Chu. However, the elder Chu is unimpressed with Sammo's prosaic uprightness, catering instead to wealthy Sze, a bejaded "toad lusting after the swan."

Well, I've got furious now!
—*A Kid from Tibet*

He wants to be the toppest fight, shit!
—*Thirteen Cold-Blooded Eagles*

Wait for death in 18 years
—*Holy Flame of the Martial World*

I'll tell the world your breasts are injected!
—*A Hearty Response*

Don't tell any that I have high anxiety or I'll beat you up!
—*Prison on Fire 2*

More than a horse's, shit!
—*Once a Thief*

Stick back your heads
—*Long Arm of the Law*

You have a gun, return him with the bullet!
—*People's Hero*

If the Iron Monkey dared come, he'd be in deep shit!
—*Iron Monkey*

I'm firing. Don't move.
—*Blood Ritual*

You bitch is going wilder and wilder.
—*Escape from Brothel*

continued on next page

Who gave you the nerve to get
    killed here?
—*Armour of God*

The 5 infants will creep out and kill
    people
—*Red Spell Spells Red*

That chap's damned, beat him!
—*On Parole*

Sock him unconscious
—*Armour of God II: Operation
    Condor*

Maniac! Be smart and release
    them, or I'll root out your clan
—*Holy Flame of the Martial
    World*

When an evil sorcerer transfers your soul to a piglet, there's only one way to get it back. Sammo inhales in *Encounter of the Spooky Kind 2*.

In a hysterical kung fu grudge match between Sze and Sammo, Sze is aided by his sorcerer—a fiendish personal trainer—who bewitches a pet monkey and transfers its abilities to his client. Lurking nearby, the sorcerer has the monkey do backflips and killer kicks, which in turn cause identical movements in Sze. When he notices the subterfuge, Sammo's fellow student (Meng Hoi) comes to the rescue and sics a German shepherd on the ape.

Sammo enlists the help of a virtuous female ghost in thwarting Sze, and convinces his one-track-mind *sifu* not to destroy her with his ghost-wrecking Taoist yo-yo. But just as *EOTSK2* seems destined to cute itself out, unique spooks start getting cranked up.

Sze's sorcerer animates a Mutt-and-Jeff pair of zombies by stuffing them with handfuls of live cockroaches. As a terrified Sammo fights them off, their heads split open and gallons of roaches boil over his naked torso. Sammo can't stand it, and his soul flees, butt-naked, only to be captured by Sze's sorcerer and fed to a piglet. Meanwhile, Sammo's body, capable only of uttering "scared, frightened" over and over in a zombie daze, is quickly occupied by the female ghost, who continues to fight the seemingly unstoppable sorcerer and his assault with leeches and ground-skull powder.

Sammo's soul returns, but Sze subdues Little Chu further with a frog-eggs charm, then sends him to chop up Sammo in the crepitorium.

All this proves too much for Sammo's long-suffering *sifu!* He constructs a Taoist altar around Sammo, then duels in cyberspace with the sorcerer, who astrally projects from his own witchin' pit—a stylish array of wacked-out furniture and red-painted cow skulls. The *sifu's* potent spells send the warlock over the edge. Suddenly bright purple with unruly white hair, the warlock binds up Sze, then hides innkeeper Chu's antidote in the hapless creep's innards.

The final spooky encounter pits *sifu* and his two students against the warlock, who marshals energy bolts, animated "bewitched corpses," and finally a great pair of creepy, sinuous snakefighters.

A Kid from Tibet

1991
Starring Yuen Biao, Michelle Reis (Lee Kar-yan), Yuen Wah, Nina Li Chi, Roy Chiao, Ng Ma
Directed by Yuen Biao

Yuen Biao's directorial debut opens with a shot of the historic Potala Monastery in Tibet. The camera lingers over the prayer wheels, the hall of chanting monks, and the Himalayan landscape, before focusing on a crippled man painfully lurching up the Monastery's impressive 1,341 hillside steps. Fortunately, when he reaches the top, the Lama on duty is Wong La (Yuen Biao), who cures the man's leg with the cheerful flourish of a parlor magician.

Wong La has never been beyond the cloistered walls of the Monastery, but is directed by the head monk to journey to Hong Kong, along with an escort, Chiu Seng-neng (Michelle Reis). His job is to transport the cap of the magical Babu Gold Bottle, which was used to repel the evil "Black Section" many years ago, and reunite it with the bottle itself.

However, the HK Lama in charge of the bottle has been waylaid by a rogue priest (Yuen Wah) and his evil witch sister (Nina Li). Yuen is a titanic villain—that guy with the electric-blue kung fu who can shout his way through plate-glass windows. His evil goal—to install "Blackism" as the national religion of Tibet—inspires him to impersonate the Lama and trick the good guys into handing over the reunified relic.

Meanwhile, Wong La is tossed unprepared into HK's pace and techno-ambiance. Trench-coated villainess Nina Li coaxes Wong La into her hot red Porsche and rips into HK traffic. Her driving technique literally scares the piss out of him.

At a deserted construction site, Nina tries to seduce the bottle cap from Wong. She whips off her trench coat to reveal spandex kink-glory: black satin with steel accents. Wong's eyes bug out, but he resists her considerable charms.

Unmasked ("you've shown your cloven feet!") and angry, she pulls out her bull's pizzle and

Sammo directs his "little brother" Jackie Chan in *My Lucky Stars*.

Enter the Fat Dragon (1979). Starring and directed by Sammo Hung.

Encounters of the Spooky Kind (1980). Starring Sammo Hung. Action Direction by Sammo Hung and Yuen Biao.

The Dead and the Deadly (1982). Starring and Action Direction by Sammo Hung.

Prodigal Son (1983). Starring and directed by Sammo Hung.

Zu: Warriors of the Magic Mountain (1983). Starring Yuen Biao and Sammo Hung.

Righting Wrongs (1986) aka *Above the Law*. Starring and Action Direction by Yuen Biao.

Shanghai Express (1986) aka *Millionaire's Express*. Starring Sammo Hung, Yuen Biao, and Yuen Wah. Directed by Sammo Hung.

Spooky Spooky (1986). Directed and coproduced by Sammo Hung.

On the Run (1987). Starring Yuen Biao and Yuen Wah.

Painted Faces (1988). Starring Sammo Hung.

Portrait of a Nymph (1988). Starring Yuen Biao.

Eight Taels of Gold (1990). Starring Sammo Hung.

Pantyhose Hero (1990). Starring, directed, and produced by Sammo Hung.

Skinny Tiger and Fatty Dragon (1990). Starring Sammo Hung.

The Iceman Cometh (1991). Starring Yuen Biao and Yuen Wah.

Slickers vs. Killers (1992). Starring, directed, and produced by Sammo Hung.

Sword Stained With Royal Blood (1993). Starring Yuen Biao.

Kickboxer (1993) aka *Ghost Foot 7*. Starring Yuen Biao and Yuen Wah. Action Direction by Yuen Biao.

attempts to take by whip what wiles could not wrest. The duel begins. An animated pile of fifty-five-gallon oil drums loosens Wong's grip, and the cap falls on a live electrical grid. Nina grabs for it anyway—frying her hand—then escapes through a wall of flame.

Wong returns to Chiu Seng-neng's modern HK apartment for a series of rube-in-the-city gags, some of which (like building a fire on the floor instead of turning on the heat) fall flat. As an exasperated Seng-neng says, "This is not super-natural power, but super-stupid power."

Finally, Wong arrives at his prearranged rendezvous with the bottle Lama, not expecting a trap. When the deception is realized, the stage is set for a final Yuen Biao/Yuen Wah showdown—two gifted martial artists flailing upon one another with fists, feet, spiritual boxing, and a pair of large and unusual swords.

Painted Faces

1988
Starring Sammo Hung Kam-bo, Lam Ching Ying, Ching Pei-Pei, John Sham, Ng Ma
Directed by Alex Law

A gentle mother walks her seven-year-old son to his new school. There the boy signs on for ten years, never to go home again. The schoolmaster will keep any money the boy earns and, if the boy

Roll call at the school of hard knocks. From *Painted Faces*.

BIZARRO NAMES

Chinese people aren't born with English names, but they often adopt them for business reasons. Sometimes they are everyday Western handles like Michael or Linda. But sometimes a Chinese person (with little use for the English language) will adopt a moniker that defies comprehension, like the sales engineer for an HK trucking company who adopted the name Hitler Wong. Here are some of our favorite names used by actors and production people.

Tomato Chan: Cinematographer, *Tiger Cage*

Noodle Cheng: Teenybop Idol, *Why Wild Girls, Boys Are Easy*

Curry Lau: Action Director, *The Ultimate Vampire*

Elvis Tsui: Actor, *Sex & Zen, Deadful Melody, Prison on Fire II*

Ridley Tsui: Director, *No Regret, No Return*

Casanova Wong: Actor, *Master Strikes, Shaolin Plot*

is killed while in the school, it's just too bad. No, this isn't Charles Dickens's London. It's the Peking Opera school in the Hong Kong of the 1950s.

Painted Faces is based on the early lives of Jackie Chan (here called Big Nose), Sammo Hung, and Yuen Biao, and their troupe called the Seven Little Fortunes. Sammo Hung himself stars as his real-life teacher, Master Yuen Chan-yuan. Master Yuen trains these dirt-poor kids in kung fu, acting, and opera, in exchange for the money made at their performances. The students learn their acrobatic acting skills under iron rule, twelve to fifteen hours a day, lorded over with the constant threat of being beaten by the Master and by each other.

The kids' first performance is a disaster. Big Nose catches a pair of pants on his spear and carries them onstage. Sammo flips right off the stage into the audience. Another performer falls sound asleep, missing his cue and prompting the curtain drop.

The Master is furious—not just at the bad timing, but because they didn't look out for each other. These kids, whose biological families couldn't support them, now belong to a group as close-knit as any combat patrol, where each member is responsible to and for his "brothers."

"It takes three years to train a scholar and ten years to train an actor," Master Yuen tells the tailor who shares the building with them. But the tailor is not impressed. He wants his son, a mousy kid in glasses, to be a professional. The tailor has a point. As hard as the Fortunes train, and as skilled as they become, times are getting harder for them. Hong Kong is modernizing. It's now the 60s, and the introduction of motion pictures has changed the audience's tastes.

Teen stars of traditional stage, the boys still want to listen to the Beatles. They meet some girls through a Cantonese opera troupe (led by the elegant Ching Pei-Pei), but the girls are more impressed by the tailor's son, who plays the guitar.

When the theater where they perform becomes the home of a

strip show, the boys audition for extra roles at the movie studio. Even though no-talent directors and smarmy assistants mistreat Opera alums, Master Yuen feels that it's the only chance he can give them. Some Fortunes are chosen and the rest rejected, and their solidarity is shattered.

Painted Faces features no kung fu fights, sex, or guns—just a group of acrobatic bald-headed kids and their Master. It's about change and pain, and a shared experience that goes beyond friendship. It is also about the culture and ferment that shaped the creators of current Hong Kong movies.

—KAT

Peacock King

1988

Starring Yuen Biao, Hiroshi Makami, Pauline Wong Siu-fung, Gloria Yip, Narumi Yasuda, Eddie Ko, Gordon Liu Chia-hui

Directed by Nam Nai Choi

Man's depravity has undermined justice, again, and the Four Holes to Hell are opening up. It's up to a pair of hardened Buddhist youngsters to repel the "Unholy Trinity"—Hell King, Hell's Agent, and the cute-yet-destructive Hell Virgin.

Peacock King opens at an archaeological dig in Nepal, where the first hell hole busts open. Rushing to the surface are Ashura the Hell Virgin (Gloria Yip) and Witch Raga, Hell's Agent (spidery-do'ed Pauline Wong). Ashura's eyes turn into mirrored orbs as she hurls fireballs.

The opening of the hell hole, along with disasters in China and Bangladesh, foretells of future destruction. So Tibetan *sifu* Ku Fong (Eddie Ko) sends his pupil Peacock (Yuen Biao) to intercept Ashura and calm the waters. At Japan's Koyasan monastery, another *sifu* similarly directs Lucky Fruit (Hiroshi Makami). Both holy men

Even weirder are some of the nicknames applied to favorite performers. Many are based on facial attributes.

Comedic actor Richard Ng (*My Luck Stars, Magnificent Warriors*) is known as Shoehorn for his prominent chin. Taiwanese lovely Brigitte Lin is also known as The Cheekbones. Singer Sandy Lam has the eccentric moniker Blur Pig's Eyes. Also popular are handles based on status: Stephen Chow is known as Godfather Chow, Jet Li is Boss Li, and heavy-set Sammo Hung is Big Brother Big.

Our favorite nickname belongs to character actor Shing Fui-on—the James Coburn of Hong Kong—who's affectionately known as Big Sillyhead.

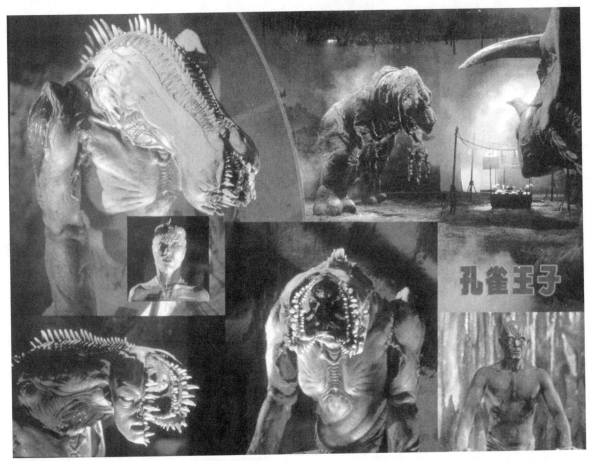

See, we're not makin' this up. Some of the monsters in *Peacock King*.

head for the second hell hole, which has opened inside Toyko's fashionable Odakyu department store.

En route, Peacock gets distracted while walking past a discarded burger container on the sidewalk. As the bemused monk looks on, a gaggle of cute l'il stop-motion animated creodonts vacate the styrofoam pod. One hides up the pant leg of a passing salaryman while another is eaten by a passing dog!

Lucky Fruit gets to the department store first, where skeptical Miss Okada (Narumi Yasuda) is too busy setting up Odakyu's next in-store exhibition—a bunch of huge dinosaur models—to be bothered by his warnings. Then the voodoo starts, and of course the dinos get into the act. A huge claw bursts into the ladies dressing room, but just as it seems poised to rip Lucky Fruit and Miss Okada to Jurassic shreds, Peacock comes whirling in right through the offending appendage. Peacock leaps atop a rogue reptile, riding it like a bucking bronco while Lucky Fruit attacks with spinning steel and explodes the mutants. Miss Okada is a believer.

Third hell-hole: Hong Kong. Hell Virgin Ashura turns up at an amusement park and, bored, speeds up all the rides, causing people to go flying off. Peacock scolds her but promises to keep her amused, recognizing the child within. Witch Raga is not so kind; she drags Ashura to a sewer hideout and vengefully upbraids her while snacking on fresh flesh plucked from a hapless, screaming victim.

The two monks (trailed by tabloid photographers) track down Raga, but she transforms herself into a biomechanoid monster with a vertical, multitoothed set of jaws. Setting the silver-eyed Ashura on the monks, she eats a few startled paparazzi and gallops off.

Ashura is subdued, having suffered serious internal injuries from Raga's fury. The monks take her to Tibet for the *sifu* cure. There, Peacock and Lucky Fruit learn that they're separated-at-birth twins (with unique horoscopes), who must use their yang power to stop the Hell King. Lucky Fruit's *sifu* also arrives as does Kubira (Gordon Liu), a freelance assassin. They've all gathered for the opening of the fourth and final hole.

(Cue lighting.) The sun is eclipsed. Ladies and gentlemen, Hell King is coming. His opening act, the biomechamonsterwitch, drops by the monastery to chomp a monk or two before our heroes can decapitate her. Hell King is a fanged giant who looks like he clomped out of a Ray Harryhausen *Sinbad* movie. He balls up Kubira into a disposable wad, but Peacock and Lucky Fruit combine their yang powers and triumph. Hell King goes down and the Earth survives, so that man's depravity can continue unchecked.

Righting Wrongs

1986
Starring Yuen Biao, Cynthia Rothrock, Melvin Wong, Karen Shepherd, Ng Ma, Fan Siu Wang
Directed by Corey Yuen Kwai

Righting Wrongs is a bleaker version of Hollywood's *The Star Chamber*. Fortunately, the courtroom scenes are kept to a minimum, and action prevails. Directed by another of the Seven Little Fortunes, Corey Yuen Kwai, the film is a skill showcase for Yuen Biao and American martial artiste Cynthia "Blonde Fury" Rothrock.

Biao plays a frustrated Hong Kong prosecutor whose caseload is complicated when scumbag defendants blow up the apartment of his witnesses' families. These guys play so dirty that even the judge privately recommends vigilante-style execution for the creeps. Biao takes the hint, cat-burgles his way into a bad guy's office, and strangles him.

Rothrock plays an HK detective called Shih Li-Yi (go figure), whom we meet as she emerges victorious in a *mahjongg* parlor fracas. She performs a great bit of martial shtick by hand- and footcuffing four guys together—using only a chair and one pair of cuffs. Tough as nails, she tells her underlings, "Book them for attempted murder, dope pushing, assaulting, kidnapping, and [slapping one] they look disgusting!"

Meanwhile, Biao is assaulted by underworld thugs in a hair-raising scene in a parking garage. He jumps on top of a moving car and, as it hurtles toward another vehicle, rolls down the hood, falling just under crashing front ends. Undaunted, he sets out to finish another scofflaw, but a turncoat cop, played by Melvin Wong, just beats him to it. Shih catches Biao with the stiff and after a tussle, he handcuffs her to a balcony and escapes. The juris-imprudent judge provides Biao with an alibi, but Shih is bulldog-determined to muzzle the loose cannon.

Wong starts executing anyone, good or bad, who might have found out about his bad-egg ways. After murdering a fellow officer, Wong earns a heartfelt hiss from the audience when he duplicitously comforts the deceased's sobbing father.

Bodies are piling up when an icy *gwailo* assassin, played by Karen Shepherd, tangles with Shih. In the movie's best fight scene (coupla white babes flailing with feet, fists, and fashion accessories), the two go up and down bamboo scaffolding and escalators with the graceful intensity that only HK films can achieve. Shih triumphs here but is not so lucky in a final throat-versus-hand-drill encounter with supervillain Wong.

Vigilante Biao finally fingers the renegade cop but, as Wong points out, "We're both killers." No man is above the law, as *Righting Wrongs*'s surprise finale illustrates—but only after we choke on our hearts as Biao dangles at several thousand feet from an airplane-slung rope!

Unpolished Fists

11

Martial arts are centuries old and have changed the course of Chinese history (ever wonder how the Boxer Rebellion got its name?). They are a pan-Asian phenomenon, with many competing schools and philosophies. But even a cursory examination of the martial arts is beyond the scope of this book.

Which is fine. We are not judging *wushu* competitions or arguing whether or not Bruce Lee would kick Jet Li's ass. Some fans complain if they suspect that wirework provides pretend lift to a flying kick; our feeling is that if it makes for a more exciting movie scene and you can't see the wire, what's the problem? Suspension of disbelief is a simple matter in the rapid and eccentric HK film universe. Certainly, no one expects Clint Eastwood or Chow Yun Fat to load their guns with real bullets or complains that Joey Wong isn't *really* flying through those trees!

"Action" used to mean martial arts action almost exclusively, until the "new wave" swept HK in the mid-eighties. Directors like John Woo and Taylor Wong started packing their films with hyperbolic gunplay—a populist move—and the ability to handle a Beretta or AK-47 became as important as well-tuned drunken monkey technique. After all, it was the Chinese who invented gunpowder . . . for the purposes of entertainment.

The Assassin

1993
Starring Zhang Fengyi, Benny Mok Siu-chung, Rosamund Kwan Chi-lam
Directed by Billy Chung Siu-hung

Despite the film's poster art, which makes it look like a classic Shaw Brothers swordfest, *The Assassin*, which stars Zhang Fengyi (fresh from *Farewell, My Concubine*) as a man in the killing business, is much closer in spirit to Clint Eastwood's *Unforgiven*. But broadswords replace six-guns in this violent tale of Ming Dynasty–era power struggles.

Zhang plays Tong Po Ka, a guy planning an idyllic life as a rural florist with his sweetheart Yiu (Rosamund Kwan). But corrupt officials, led by the odious Eunuch Mi, take him into custody and toss him in a dungeon. In a hard-wincing scene, he receives the "Eye Closing Penalty": his eyelids are sewn shut as rivulets of blood course down his cheeks.

He and seven other similarly penalized captives are led into an arena. Their stitches are opened, and big bowls of rough food are served. As the starving men wolf down the swill, instructions to a Darwinian showdown are read. They are to fight to the death, with the lone victor to serve as apprentice to Sung Chung, the senior killer.

The seven other unfortunates slaughter each other as Tong gulps down as much as he can while keeping an eye on the carnage; he then dispatches the runner-up! In this regrettable situation, our hero finds nobility in simple survival.

His victory earns him an audience with the equally odious Eunuch Ngai, who indulges in the sort of multiconcubined kink that only the absolutely power-corrupted (and the partners who love them) find appealing. When it gets down to short strokes, Ngai has to rely on fetishistic cylinders to do his dirty work, but for a eunuch, he does okay. The creepy, white-haired eunuch (appropriately) renames our hero Tong Chop, and puts him to work cutting necks.

"I kill to survive," says the Chopster, who is just playing out the string. Nevertheless, he attracts a worshipful, nihilistic young disciple, Wong Kau (Benny Mok, topped with a heavy-metal fright wig). Tong takes him to a hill of bones, which he sets afire—to "breathe the air of hell"—and Wong's in buddy-heaven. But on the next hit, Tong Chop spots his former lover Yiu in the crowd and stays his hand, forcing Wong to finish the job.

Tong decides to abandon his bloody career and hides out on the farm of old-flame-with-new-family Yiu, but is (of course) dragged back into the killing field by those who appreciate his sword work. Final showdowns with the young turk Wong and Eunuch Ngai are assured.

The sword duels in *The Assassin* are big and brawny, and the wintry landscape is used to stunning effect by cinematographer Zhao Fei, who shot Chinese director Zhang Yimou's *Raise the Red Lantern*. Blood flies freely, and Eunuch Ngai's killing techniques (the sort of rip 'em apart methods favored by gorehounds and video game devotees) earned the film an adults-only Category III rating.

The Big Heat

1988
Starring Waise Lee Chi-hung, Kuo Chui, Matthew Wong, Lo King Wah, Paul Chu Kong, Stuart Ong, Joey Wong Jo-yin
Directed by Andrew Kam and Johnny To Kei-fung

A wild ride through the soulless world of gotta-get-out-before-97 HK criminals. This film is visually rich, well cast, and exceptionally brutal. For openers, the first scene depicts a power drill boring through the center of a human hand!

The hand-drilling, it turns out, is just a dream. John Wong (Waise Lee) is a cop who's suffering from some sort of Police Special Repetitive Stress Injury—his right hand freezes on him during gunfights. Squeezing off too many rounds?

His doctor suggests retirement but, when his partner Skinny Tse is torched in Malaysia, he puts everything on hold (including his forthcoming marriage) until he cracks the case.

Wong and his men inspect the evidence: Tse's crispy corpse, a shipping schedule, and a series of blackmail-bait photos showing the wealthy and powerful Mr. Ho (Stuart Ong) in the sweaty embraces of a male hustler. Wong's men find that they are under surveillance themselves ("I thought only cops tailed people, how come *we're* being tailed?"). Compatriot Kam (Kuo Chui) goes to question the hustler; too late, since the punk is in the process of being executed. When Wong and Kam confront the tailing creeps, weapons are unholstered, and the screen ignites in a furious chase that ends with one of the miscreants splattered across passing autos on various freeway levels.

The cops pose as blackmailers to force Ho to divulge the name of his crime boss. Ho slashes his wrists in anguish, but Wong chases him to the hospital and browbeats him into giving up Ching Han (Paul Chu), a scurrilous Malaysian who forces Ho to smuggle a mysterious substance in milk-powder cans. The hospital is crawling with Han's assassins, and a shoot-out drags nurse Ada (Joey Wong) into the fray and marks the end of Ho.

Ching Han, sensing he's been found out, meets with Wong's group and slips them a wad of bank notes, which the cops toss gleefully in the air! When Wong has his fiancée Maggie analyze the stuff found in the milk-powder cans (it turns out to be raw coca), Han has her killed as well. The scoundrel then transfers a large sum of

HEX ERRORS

COMPLAINT DEPARTMENT

More fractured English subtitles from your favorite Hong Kong movies (see chapter 3 for a full explanation).

Lucky Fruit, the dried corpse is horrible!
—*Peacock King*

I am damn unsatisfied to be killed in this way.
—*Holy Weapon*

I have been scared shitless too much lately.
—*Final Victory*

Please don't point your gun at my client's head.
—*Satin Steel*

Youngster, your brain is useless, I guess
—*A Kid from Tibet*

You're crazy mad-nutcase.
—*Royal Warriors*

It's hard for me to tolerate such bitch
—*Raped by an Angel*

money into Wong's account, which causes him to be brought up on corruption charges. Han just wants to get rich and get the hell out of Hong Kong, working in tandem with the Russian villain Mr. Molotov (!) to smuggle contraband.

Naturally, Han's comeuppance comes in ultraviolent fashion as his car is pancaked by a commandeered garbage truck. But his death doesn't end matters. A turncoat cop—who'd helped Han smuggle—appears and points a shotgun at Wong as he lies bloodied on the ground. Our hero's hand has frozen up on him again; what to do? Thinking quickly, he hooks Maggie's chain necklace around the trigger and fires a shot directly into the pumpgun's magazine. The remaining shotgun shells explode and pepper the rogue cop like a cartoon character.

A tender kung fu moment in *Fong Sai Yuk*. Valiant Fong Sai Yuk (Jet Li) locks legs with the tough-as-nails Siu Lee Wan (Sibelle Hu).

Fong Sai Yuk

1993
Starring Jet Li, Josephine Siao Fong Fong, Michelle Reis (Lee Kar-yan), Sibelle Hu Hui-ching, Paul Chu Kong, Zhao Wen Zhou, Chen Sung Yung, Adam Cheng Siu-chau
Directed by Corey Yuen Kwai

Jet Li stars as another mythological character from China's past—not Wong Fei-hong this time, but Fong Sai Yuk. While the martial arts skills (and moral righteousness) of these two heroes are comparable, Fong Sai Yuk is the more playful of the two. If Fei-hong is the Fred Astaire of mythic martial figures, Sai Yuk is the Gene Kelly.

FSY is a martial arts showcase for Jet Li but, even more, its comic touches recall HK costume farces of the past. Sai Yuk's mother is played by a delightful comedienne named Josephine Siao. She and Fong the elder (Paul Chu) run a fabric shop in Canton. A former bandit named Tiger Lu (Chen Sung Yung) tries to go legit with his wealth and sponsors a martial arts competition, offering his daughter's hand in marriage as the prize. The objective is simple: climb a wooden tower guarded by Lu's wife, Siu Lee Wan (Sibelle Hu), and you win.

Sai Yuk's pals tell him that the daughter, Ting Ting (Michelle Reis), is a real knockout, so he boyishly enters the contest. Fellow contestants bite the dust as Lu's capable wife hurls them off the tower. Fong Sai Yuk and Siu Lee Wan's battle extends to the crowd as they duel while standing on people's heads (touch the ground and you lose). It's comical—the martial arts equivalent of chicken-fighting! Although Ting Ting is the apple of Sai Yuk's eye, she's fled the scene and been replaced by Lu's maid; when the maid's homely face is revealed, Sai Yuk loses on purpose and retreats.

This does not sit well with his mother, who dons male garb and goes to fight, posing as Fong's brother to avenge the family honor. She wins, of course, earning the undying love of Siu Lee Wan in the process! The two families are bonded as Lu demands a warm body for betrothal, and Sai Yuk ends up marrying his beloved, willy-nilly.

Miss, a couple of basters are following me
—*Tiger on Beat*

I hate the scissy type. Looking so pale like a ghost
—*Run Lover Run*

That may disarray my intestines
—*Eastern Condors*

Can't I sleep? You're dictator, it's not yet 1997!
—*My Better Half*

Damn it, what a maniac!
—*Seeding of a Ghost*

You never change, you fight even when dead
—*A Chinese Ghost Story*

Boss, Zhao is ridiculous.
—*Angel Enforcers*

Fatty, you with your thick face have hurt my instep
—*Pedicab Driver*

Why do you always have to bring me the blood of drunks?
—*Doctor Vampire*

BLOODSTAINED TRADEWINDS 1990

Death-a-minute thriller about two childhood friends (Waise Lee and Alex Fong) with ideological differences over their duties to their HK criminal organization. When a Japanese crime boss seeks to expand his HK operations, the hills come alive with the sound of gunfire. There's so much bloodshed in this flick that the misty red image conjured up by the title makes sense.

BURY ME HIGH   1990

Feng shui freaks will rejoice at this action film, which celebrates the geographical divination abilities of both the protagonist and antagonist. Wisely (Chin Kar Lok) is a Los Angeles computer hacker with powers of geomancy and an IQ of 200. He must travel to Indochina to sort out some ancestral burial problems (which are causing his inoperable brain tumor!).

Things get further complicated when it's revealed that Sai Yuk's father is a secret member of the rebellious Red Flower Society, an organization dedicated to the overthrow of the corrupt Manchu Dynasty. The main Red Flowerbuster, Governor Oryeetor (Zhao Wen Zhou), pays a visit and tries to separate a list of RF members from the rebels. Sai Yuk squares off in an extended pole-fighting sequence with the governor, which ends in a draw.

The Manchu forces capture his father, though, and force a showdown in Execution Square. The rematch pits the governor and Sai Yuk in a delirious under-the-boardwalk kickfight.

Gunmen

1990
Starring Tony Leung Kar-fai, Adam Cheng Siu-chau, Carrie Ng Kar-lai, Elizabeth Lee Mei-fung, Elvis Tsui Kam-kong, Waise Lee Chi-hung, Mark Cheng Hau-nam, David Lai
Directed by Kirk Wong Chi-keung

Kirk Wong's films are notable for their oblique approaches to crime drama. Wong is a subtler, more enigmatic director than John Woo or Tsui Hark, yet his films do not wither for lack of action. Like Ringo Lam, Wong seems more concerned with characters' relationships with one another, and provides us with sincere moments of tenderness amid the carnage.

Gunmen is a period piece set in Shanghai in the turbulent 30s. Ding Chun-bee (Tong Leung) plays a Shanghai cop torn between his duties and his family, dutiful wife Chu-chiao (Carrie Ng) and young daughter Sze-Sze. Things are further complicated by the lovely urchin-turned-courtesan Mona Fong (Elizabeth Lee), who acts as Ding's informant and Chu-chiao's counterfoil.

Ding is determined to bust an opium-smuggling syndicate operating in Shanghai, but he loses face among his fellow cops when one of his tips fails to yield a collar. The cops, who dress in

Mo-kei (Jet Li) leaps over scores of soldiers clashing in the desert in *Kung Fu Cult Master*.

That guy Yuen Wah has the plum role of an Indochinese military leader who is using geomancy to create a despotic dystopia. Los Angeles businesswoman Moon Lee and Indochine Sibelle Hu model stunning evening wear at social functions, but later change into more sensible outfits to kick butt. Lots of sound and fury, plenty of tanks, land mines, heavy artillery, and other war surplus, plus evil Yuen Wah has a Blofeld-style hydraulic *feng shui* divination diorama that rises out of the floor at the touch of a secret button!

KUNG FU CULT MASTER   1994

With a plot metronome set to prestissimo and a cast of thousands, you can't tell the players without a program in this enjoyable old-style ride. Fortunately, a program of sorts is provided on the video box.

Jet Li stars as Mo-kei, a young hero who learns the Great Solar Stance to seek revenge upon a long list of Evil Sect masters, like Master No-mercy, who caused his parents to commit suicide when he was a child. Li's companion in this quest is the spunky Siu Chiu

continued on next page

(Chingmy Yau), but the sparks truly fly when he matches wits and crosses swords with the enticing but treacherous Chao-Min.

The movie has some great warring-hordes sequences, with huge armies doing battle in the middle of nowhere, flapping banners, mirrored shields that turn into waves of flying beheado-blades, and buried booby traps that swallow horses and men. Of course, everyone in the film knows how to fight.

IRON MONKEY   1993

A straight-ahead martial arts remake of the 1970s kung fu film of the same name. Yu Rong Guang plays Iron Monkey, a Robin Hood–type with a day job as the local herb doctor. The corrupt Ching Dynasty officials are powerful foes, but Iron Monkey enlists the help of Wong Kei-ying (Donnie Yen) and his son Wong Fei-hong. Curiously, the part of the young folk hero Wong Fei-hong is played by Jean Wang, a preteen *girl* with exquisite martial skills.

Davian International, Mike Leeder

Hammer lock and hammer drop. Ding Bee (Tony Leung, left) is one of the Gunmen.

long, fleece-lined coats and stylin' hats, get a better tip and are soon staked out outside the gang's headquarters.

Inside, Haye (Adam Cheng) is squabbling over profits with flunkies when a fracas erupts. Haye hoses his opponents with gasoline and sets them afire; they fight and shout at each other while on fire, faces clearly visible amid the flames. The cops bust in, and Ding shoots Haye's boss Uncle Liang. Haye reciprocates by killing Ding's boss Captain Kiang. The cop swears revenge against the gangster as an ill wind blows the bloodstained sheet off Kiang's still-warm corpse.

Ding receives more grief in the form of a hardass new superintendent (Elvis Tsui) who's sent by French bureaucrats to root out police corruption. He becomes involved in a footchase on Shanghai's crowded streets and is thrashed by a group of rickshaw drivers who resent the crooked beat cops. The drivers, though, turn out to be old army buddies Kwong, Ching, and Fan (Mark Cheng, Waise Lee, and David Lai)! Ding wastes no time signing them up as fellow gunmen. Things move rapidly toward their grinding, violent conclusion.

The finale of *Gunmen* is reminiscent of an epic western. Rickshaws, huge trucks, and mounted combatants clash. Everyone is shot repeatedly. Finally, the frightening Haye is terminated by Ding's daughter Sze-Sze, who picks up a .38 and plugs the thug! A happy ending for all, except for the "scarlet woman" Mona Fong, who ratchets up a few notches in the reincarnation sweepstakes.

Legacy of Rage

1986
Starring Brandon Lee, Michael Wong Man-tuk, Regina Kent, Chan Wai Man, Meng Hoi, Kuk Fung, Shing Fui-on, Ku Feng
Directed by Ronny Yu

The late Brandon Lee (Bruce Lee's son) left precious little cinematic legacy. *Legacy of Rage*—made for Dickson Poon's D&B studios in 1986—displays Brandon more favorably than his Hollywood snorers *Showdown in Little Tokyo, Rapid Fire*, and *The Crow*. With his good looks, muscular fame, and glowering "freeze 'em" stare, one wonders what Lee might have accomplished had he been as prolific as most Hong Kong action stars.

In *Legacy of Rage*, an early effort by *Bride With White Hair* director Ronny Yu, Brandon is a working stiff holding down two jobs: junkyard crane operator and nightclub waiter. He dreams of buying a motorbike and having a happy home life with his girlfriend, fellow nightclub employee May (Regina Kent). His inexplicable friendship with dope dealer Michael Wong, however, leads him to ruin. Michael lusts after May and, when Brandon turns down a lucrative drug-merchandising offer, Wong sets him up as the patsy for the murder of a rival drug lord.

LAST HERO IN CHINA   1993

This time, Wong Fei-hong (Jet Li) needs a bigger kung fu school for all his eager young students. His assistants scout out a nice building in Canton but, when Wong arrives, he finds it's right next door to the local brothel! The Boxer Society causes more problems for Wong, and he must fight them in a martial-arts competition. The Boxers send out a dozen of their fighters at once, each wearing a section of a huge centipede costume, with a head that spouts flame. Wong dons a chicken-beak helmet and iron claws, then vanquishes the centipede with chicken kung fu!

SEVEN WARRIORS   1989

Akira Kurosawa's classic film *The Seven Samurai* was remade by Hollywood in the early 60s under the title *The Magnificent Seven*. Decades later, here comes the Hong Kong version. Set in modern times, it's inspired more by Sergio "Spaghetti Western" Leone than anyone else as Adam Cheng, Benny Mok, Ng Ma, Jacky Cheung, Tony Leung Chiu-wai, Sammo Hung, et al. mix it up.

continued on next page

THE TAI CHI MASTER 1993

Jet Li and Chin Siu Ho play fellow students in a Shaolin Temple, but Chin's aggressive ambitions get him expelled. Jet also leaves, to help his friend in the outside world. They meet Michelle Yeoh, who's leading a rebellion against the evil and powerful Eunuch Jin. Jet joins the rebels while the ambitious Chin joins the eunuch's forces. The two former friends scrap with broadswords, and Jet suffers a subsequent loss of memory, turning into a kung fu idiot savant. But while he's convalescing, Jet invents the new and powerful Tai Chi style—the perfect tool to defeat Chin's Iron Palm technique.

TIGER CAGE 1990

Jacky Cheung and Donnie Yen are cops busting dope-slinging thugs in typical two-fisted Hong Kong fashion. In a departure from her usual comedy roles, Carol "Do Do" Cheng plays a policewoman whose fiancé was murdered by the joy-powder merchants.

When Donnie finds that fellow cop Ng Man-tat is on the payroll of the local drug dealers, he

Lawyers and corrupt policemen conspire to frame Brandon for manslaughter, and he ends up with an eight-year sentence. Meanwhile, Michael's violent sexual advances toward May convince her to flee to the South American country of "Basil" with a benevolent sugar daddy who admires her cancan dancing. Brandon befriends Four-Eyes (Meng Hoi), a bespectacled fellow inmate, and burns with vengeful lust over Michael's betrayal.

Eight years pass, and Michael has evolved into a repugnant, cocaine-honkin' Hong Kong godfather, when he crosses Brandon's path once again. He kidnaps May and her son (Brandon's, unbeknownst to him) and sets his thugs on May's elderly sugar daddy. They rapidly turn him into worm food. Brandon escapes the hit, evading his pursuers by hiding out in a chicken coop, but the feathers really fly when he assaults Michael's fortified gangster hideout with his old prison buddy Four-Eyes, whose gunrunning business conveniently provides the necessary hardware.

Brandon's screen presence, and his chemistry with Michael Wong, make you wish they had had the chance to team up as heroes just once. The final gun battle—obviously influenced by Brian DePalma's *Scarface*—is humorously apocalyptic, but Brandon's duels with veteran heavy Shing Fui-on and Michael Wong are taut and gory. The bittersweet ending reunites Brandon with his son; unfortunately, the real-life Lee legacy was not so generous.

Long Arm of the Law

1984
Starring David Lam Wai, Wong Yan Tat, Wong Kin, Yeung Ming
Directed by Johnny Mak

This seminal film foreshadowed the violent realism of later efforts by Ringo Lam, John Woo, and Kirk Wong. Based on a series of HK robberies committed by mainland Chinese, the story could have leaped from the pages of the *South China Morning Post*. The neon-flamed Christmas ambiance of Hong Kong has never looked meaner.

HK crook Tung (David Lam) takes the train up to mainland China to rendezvous with his ex-army buddies. Together they plan a forty-eight-hour junket to Hong Kong, with a jewelry heist as the centerpiece. The men are attracted by the money he offers, but they complain that there's not enough time to visit the massage parlors ("not even enough time for shopping!").

Trouble starts as they climb the fence separating HK from China: one of the gang is ripped apart by German shepherds. As they case the joint prior to the job, they're intercepted by beat cops, forced to shoot it out on crowded Kowloon streets, and escape in a commandeered taxi.

Tung decides to wait three days and try the caper again. While the troops are not criminally engaged, they're busy enjoying themselves with nightclub hostesses. One of the bumpkin-punks, Rooster (Wong Yan Tat), latches onto a haughty strumpet, waves a wad of cash, and demands satisfaction. She suggests he watch TV unless he has HK $10,000. "I'll give you ten, where do you want it?" yells Rooster as he pulls out his .45! Wearing a ridiculous paper foil crown on his head, he makes her crawl at gunpoint. Gentlemen they are not.

The fence, Tai (Yeung Ming), boss of the Crimson Kid video arcade, is not pleased when Tung shows up without the goods, but he offers a little side employment: rubbing out a corpulent creep named Fatso. The gang executes the hit, and Fatso swan-songs onto a shopping-mall ice rink. As Tung's men glimpse Fatso's handcuffs gleaming through bloody crushed ice, they realize that Tai has conned them into murdering an undercover policeman. Furious, Tung has the crime boss tied inside an automobile, douses it with gasoline, and sets it afire. As Tai screams from within the burning car, Tung has the flames extinguished and takes up the dialogue again. Hard-core negotiation! Tai rats him out anyway.

becomes enraged and bursts a bag of cocaine in Ng's face, powdering it white. Police supervisor Simon Yam arrives on the scene, but he's dirty, too, and sprays Donnie's blood across the whitened face of the disgraced (but alive) Ng. When Jacky finally unravels the mess, the fur and bullets fly. A dark violent tale of double crosses, loyalty, and revenge.

KUNG FU THEATER,

Flowing robes and topknot hairstyles. Plot? Characters? Nah, combat! Combat accompanied by sound effects collages of fresh fish slapped on concrete and bare-derrière gym-towel snaps. Poorly dubbed into English, a never-changing stable of hammy voice-overs delivered dialogue like "Chan, you're too arrogant, see? So we're going to have to chop off your wife's arms" (*The Crippled Avengers*). You've seen 'em on late-night TV or in the "martial arts" section at Blockbuster.

Film critic David Chute refers to them as "But Still" movies, after the oft-used phrase, which helps sync English dialogue to longer-duration Chinese mouth movements: "*But still*, you killed my master. I'm going to have to use my Berserk Piglet style on you." We call them "Right Then" movies for the same reason. For the past twenty-five years, "Right Then" movies have been the purview of insomniac TV addicts and inner-city kids catching a double-feature at the local grindhouse.

Chopsockies—the generic term for these types of motion pictures—are ripe for satire, and they've been parodied by American comedians since their stateside introduction in the early 70s. Whether in *Kentucky Fried Movie* (1973) or *Wayne's World 2* (1993), the jokes are the same. Chopsockies have become a part of the pop culture lexicon, helped along by spinoffs like the *Kung Fu* TV series and Carl Douglas's 1974 Top 40 hit "Kung Fu Fighting."

But still, the problem is that this poorly translated reduction of Chinese culture and history remains the paradigm of Asian cinema for many Westerners. Chopsocky snaps an easy-to-handle clown mask on HK cinema and, by extension, Asian cinema. When HK movie fans who've been attracted by the likes of John Woo, Jackie Chan, or Tsui Hark mention their interest, they're often met with an incredulous "What, you like *those* movies?" Old stereotypes die hard.

Right then, we should point out that there are more than a few gems among the thousands of gut-bucket chopsocky flicks cranked out in the 70s. The films are in Blockbuster for a reason—people continue to rent them. We list our all-time favorites in the Shaw Brothers section, since most were produced by Shaw Studios. But the name that leaps to mind—somersaulting over a banquet table in the process—is Bruce Lee.

What Elvis Presley was to rock 'n' roll, Bruce Lee was to celluloid kung fu. Bruce got his start on the American small screen playing sidekick Kato in *The Green Hornet*. He was subsequently discovered by Golden Harvest boss Raymond Chow; his first film, *The Big Boss*, was a smash hit. Although Lee made only a handful of films (including *Fist of Fury*,

OR THE OBLIGATORY BRUCE LEE PIECE

Enter the Dragon, and *Game of Death),* he possessed a charisma and sexuality that defined a proud underdog masculinity. His intense, angular face and astounding physique were legendary in Hollywood as well as in HK, and his fame helped launch the film careers of Americans like Chuck Norris and Jim Kelly. Moreover, Lee's warm-up suit/gradient-sunglasses look acquired a certain celebrity chic.

It was only after Bruce's mysterious death in 1973 at age thirty-three that he became a cottage industry. Bruce Lee imitators like Bruce Li, Bruce Le, and Dragon Lee came boiling out of the woodwork as producers frantically milked the legend. Betty Ting Pei, the woman who was with Bruce when he died, starred as herself in a fictional sexploiter she also wrote called *Bruce Lee: His Last Days, His Last Nights.*

Bruce's son Brandon followed in his father's footsteps, only to die in

Seven-foot two-inch basketball legend Kareem Abdul-Jabbar toe jams on Bruce Lee in *Game of Death.*

an accident on the set of *The Crow.* Finally, *Dragon: The Bruce Lee Story,* a bio-pic done chopsocky style and starring Jason Scott Lee (no relation) as the Brucester was released in 1993. For those seeking to pay homage, we suggest visiting Bruce Lee's

star on the Hollywood Walk of Fame (in front of Mann's Chinese Theater, natch) or his grave in Seattle's Lakeview Cemetery, on the northern slope of Capitol Hill, where he and Brandon are buried next to each other.

WHO ARE THOSE WHITE GUYS?

The most unsung action heroes in HK cinema are the legions of anonymous *gwailo* fighters who appear briefly, usually just to do some bit of evil before croaking in short order. Who are they? Well, we don't know.

We've identified a few who pop up more than once, like Karen Shepherd, who fought with Cynthia Rothrock in *Righting Wrongs*. Or Louis Roth, who plays a buffoonish police captain oblivious to the sexual Cantonese puns of his HK charges in *Naked Killer* ("You don't know 'bird'?" "No, I don't know 'bird.'"), and to whom Chow Yun Fat asks the audience-pleasing question in *A Better Tomorrow 2*, "You don't like my rice?"

But mostly these unidentified backup players are referred to as just "that bearded guy Cynthia Khan trounces in *In the Line of Duty 3*" or "the bearded guy

As you might guess, when it finally happens, the heist goes badly. The gang barely gets away and, when they go to fence the stuff, they confront a battalion of enraged cops. In the shoot-out, Tai is riddled by both sides, and Tung's man Blockhead (Wong Kin) takes a few slugs. Blockhead's only chance is an underground doctor in Kowloon's infamous Walled City, a solid city block, which is off-limits to regular HK cops (see Glossary). But the doc's wife finks on them, and a battalion of SWAT-types invade. The ensuing shoot-out, waged in the claustrophobic alleys of the Walled City, cements *LAOTL*'s reputation among fans of bleak HK gangster killcake.

Rock 'n' Roll Cop

1994
Starring Anthony Wong Chau-sang, Wu Hsin-kuo, Carrie Ng Kar-lai, Yu Rong Guang
Directed by Kirk Wong Chi-keung

Pairing up a flamboyant Hong Kong cop with a stuffy mainland China counterpart is a familiar plot device of latter-day HK action movies. As a reaction to HK's impending reunification with China, these escapist films offer anxiety-ridden audiences a glimmer of hope. The mismatched law enforcers constantly knock heads before eventually realizing that cooperation holds the key to their success. Used to good effect in Jackie Chan's *Police Story 3: Supercop*, this formula is successfully reworked in *Rock 'n' Roll Cop*, a riveting mix of melodrama and action.

Anthony Wong plays an unorthodox Hong Kong cop named Hung. Tracking a murderous gang of robbers from HK to Shenzhen in mainland China, Hung receives the reluctant cooperation of mainland authorities, because the same gang is responsible for the brutal killing of a mainland officer. Hung forms an alliance with police captain Wang Kung (Wu Hsin-kuo, who portrayed the naive scholar in *Green Snake*). Despite a difference of opinion on how the investigation should proceed, the pair are soon hot on the trail of the outlaw gang, using a lover of one of the gang members, Hou-yee (Carrie Ng), as an unwitting accomplice. Things become complicated when it's revealed that before Carrie became a gangster's moll she was Wang Kung's girl.

Rock 'n' Roll Cop is quick to exploit the rift between HK and the mainland, while in the end it offers a halfhearted appeal for cooperation between the two sides. As directed by Kirk Wong, however, the film downplays political messages in favor of soap-opera-style heartache punctuated by bursts of jarring violence. Wong weaves his way through the plot with an aggressive directing style, playing up the tense theatrics to a fever pitch. It works well here, especially in a scene in which the HK cop and his mainland counterpart must frantically wheel the critically wounded Carrie Ng to a hospital on a makeshift gurney.

Rock 'n' Roll Cop is another of Kirk Wong's enjoyably gritty police procedurals. Filled with vivid portraits of cops teetering on the edge, it showcases his talents at the top of his game.

—RAA

Tiger on Beat

1988
Starring Chow Yun Fat, Conan Lee, Nina Li Chi, Gordon Liu Chia-hui, Tsui Siu-keung
Directed by Liu Chia-liang (Lau Kar-leung)

Veteran HK actor/director Liu Chia-liang made *Tiger on Beat* as Chow Yun Fat was achieving fame for his roles in crime dramas like *A Better Tomorrow* and *City on Fire*. Francis Li, Chow's character in *TOB*, is introduced with a hard-rocking theme song by HK power diva Maria Cordero. The polar opposite of his twin-Beretta/high-fashion slayin' persona in *ABT*, he's decked out in

Chow Yun Fat bayonets in *Tiger on Beat*." However, a list of some of these people appeared in the closing credits of *In the Line of Duty 4* and, with the goal of honoring these unsung heroes, we reproduce it below:

- Stephan Berick
- Blaine Camoureux
- Tim Hyland
- Eddie Maher
- David Petersen
- Ray Pachette
- John Salvitti

"But Stihl!" Some of the Legendary Weapons of China: Gordon Liu and Conan Lee grind and spew in *Tiger on Beat*.

being smuggled in hollow surfboards by Tsui Siu-keung and his gang of creepy *gwailos*, headed by ultrabad guy Gordon Liu.

Eye-popping aerobics instructor Marydonna (Nina Li) gets roped into carrying dope for her bad-egg brother. The brother expires as a result of his nefarious activities, inspiring Marydonna to spill the beans. Francis and Michael bust the big dope deal but, despite a hair-raising car chase scene (with stuntmen clinging to the hoods of flying subcompacts), the baddies escape. They vengefully kidnap Francis's sister, who must be rescued from a warehouse full of heavily armed thugs.

a ridiculous leather visor, driving a gussied-up Renault Le Car; a clueless Chow Yun Fat wannabe.

Gobbling a spray-painted-to-the-plate ham-and-eggs breakfast (chased with a tumbler full of *Rocky*-style raw eggs, slugged down in one stomach-churning take) at one of Hong Kong's innumerable plastic fast-fooderies, our hero suffers the indignity of being taken hostage in an armed robbery. Fellow undercover cop Michael Cho (played by muscley Conan Lee) rescues him, but not before Francis has pissed his pants in terror and passed out on the floor. Afterward, Michael is assigned as Francis's partner. The pair begin work on a dope-smuggling case; poppy powder is

In battle, Chow's character is about as far from the *A Better Tomorrow* Gucci/Armani slo-mo firepower-dude as you can get, hyperactively improvising weapons from dime-store items (like the around-the-corner shotgun). Despite Chow's heroics, it's the balletic martial arts fight between the crazed Gordon Liu and Conan Lee that provides the film's kicker. Did we mention that it's performed with chainsaws? Not those puny weekend-warrior cord-o'-wood-for-the-fireplace jobs, but big honkin', heavy-timber, wood/flesh rippers. The combatants go at it, sparkin' and spewin' blue smoke as they run around the warehouse trying to dismember one another. This gory Armageddon duet consistently scores on Top Ten Endbattle Lists among HK film aficionados.

Shaw Brothers

ounded by Sir Run Run Shaw, the son of a wealthy Shanghai textile factory owner, and his three brothers, Shaw Brothers built a postwar celluloid empire that included production, distribution, and exhibition across Asia.

Despite competition from Golden Harvest (whose boss, Raymond Chow, discovered both Bruce Lee and Jackie Chan), the name Shaw Brothers was synonymous with Hong Kong films for decades.

Run Run was knighted by the British government and founded Shaw University in Hong Kong while his brother Runme supervised their Singapore operations. In the mid-eighties, SB suddenly abandoned film production and founded HK-TVB, now Hong Kong's major supplier of televised soap operas.

The Shaw studios were a feudal operation. Stars often lived in

ATTACK OF THE GOD OF JOY
1983

A Peking Opera troupe disembowels an upright but annoying actor. Revenge comes quickly when the actor's ghost uses his old guts like a Hindu rope trick, strangling his assassins while blood spurts from his wound. He's aided in further mischief by a berserker baby doll, the "God of Joy," who is born *Alien*-like from a bystander's belly. A big supernatural battle explodes as fire-breathing spirits of ancient Opera characters fight with the flying baby doll. Total vengeance. Director? Our pal, Chang Cheh.

THE CHINATOWN KID   1977

After getting in trouble with local gangs in Hong Kong, a young man (Alexander Fu Sheng) flees to San Francisco, where the same gangs are still causing problems. He becomes part of one gang, then eventually decides to play them against each other to clean up the town. All sorts of moral

dormitories, were paid pittances, and had no say over which directors or costars they'd like to work with. The Shaw stable included such actors as Gordon Liu Chia-hui (*Tiger on Beat, Peacock King*), Ti Lung (*A Better Tomorrow 1* and *2*), David Chiang (*Once Upon a Time in China 2*), Lo Lieh (*Police Story 3: Supercop*), and Kuo Chui (*Hard-Boiled*), all of whom are still making movies today.

On the directorial side, the SB studio was split along Mandarin- and Cantonese-speaking lines. The Mandarin side was headed by a director named Chang Cheh, who was influenced by the Japanese gangster films of the 60s, especially the work of director Seijun Suzuki (*Detective Bureau 23: Go to Hell, Bastard!*). Chang was a roughie at heart, and even musical dramas like *The Singing Thief* (1969) contained brutal fight scenes in which combatants pounded, skewered, and burned one another.

Chang's blood-soaked *One Armed Swordsman* (1967) featured Jimmy Wang Yu as a differently abled death machine, and the box-office receipts piled up higher than the bodies. Chang Cheh made over one hundred odd and imaginatively gory films, such as *Five Deadly Venoms, Human Lanterns*, and *Attack of the God of Joy*, before packing it in sometime during the mid-eighties.

Shaw's Cantonese-speaking side was headed by an actor/director named Liu Chia-liang (also known as Lau Kar-leung). Liu was an old-school martial artist whose kung fu lineage stretched back to the real Wong Fei-hong (see page 78-79). Liu began his Shaw career choreographing action for Chang Cheh before making his directorial debut in 1975. Liu injected new life into tired kung fu plots and remains active today, appearing in Sammo Hung's excellent *Pedicab Driver* (1988) and directing Jackie Chan's *Drunken Master II* (1994).

These two directors were but part of the Shaw machine that made hundreds—no, *thousands*—of films. Here are a few of the good ones.

Challenge of the Ninja, *aka* Shaolin Challenges Ninja, Heroes of the East

1979
Starring Gordon Liu Chia-hui, Yuko Mizuno, Shoji Kurata
Directed by Liu Chia-liang (Lau Kar-Leung)

Director Liu Chia-liang built his Shaw Brothers career with groundbreaking, creative kung fu films, revitalizing a genre that many people thought moribund. The underlying philosophy of *COTN* is quite different from that of the usual Shaw mayhem. For starters, it is an action-packed kung fu film in which no one dies. Compared to Chang Cheh's bloodbaths like *Super Ninjas* and *One Armed Swordsman*, where a combatant will lay waste to a hundred men in a single scene, Liu's *Challenge* is a radical change of pace.

More importantly, the film challenges ethnic and national stereotypes. The Chinese and Japanese have always been at odds, and the Japanese occupation of China during World War II didn't help matters. Japanese are the staple villains in dozens of kung fu films, and they are—predictably enough—ruthless, bloodthirsty killers. In *COTN,* however, we get something starkly different. Gordon Liu plays Ho Tao, a Chinese man who weds a Japanese

DIRTY HO   1979

A kung fu *Melvin and Howard, DH* features a wiseass street kid protecting a prince in disguise, who then gets left in the dust. Gordon Liu Chia-hui plays the wine-tasting prince who has slipped out of the palace for some R and R, and Jimmy Wang Yu plays Dirty Ho, a jewel thief he picks up on the way. The prince must fight his way back into the palace in time for the naming of the new emperor. One of the first kung fu movies to feature introspection and character development, along with the requisite collisions of fists and skulls.

continued on next page

A classic tale of feet and fists from the Shaw Brothers factory: Gordon Liu in *Dirty Ho.* Did you know that the same Shaw Brothers lot on which many movies like *Dirty Ho* were filmed was recently used as the set for the video game *Supreme Warrior,* designed to capture the furious feel of a high-speed kung fu movie? "For added authenticity, players can toggle between both an English and Cantonese sound track."

EIGHT DIAGRAM POLE FIGHTER 1983

Savage tale of bloodlust and double crosses. The mood is bleak, angry, and depressing. It didn't help that one of Shaw's favorite sons, Alexander Fu Sheng, was killed in a car accident during filming. The spectacular final battle has Gordon Liu Chia-hui and Kara Hui Ying-hung taking on a gang of villains in a room filled with a pyramid made of coffins. A battalion of monks show up to "defang the wolves," a painful sequence in which the monks use poles—or their bare hands—to rip out entire sets of villain teeth!

FLYING GUILLOTINE   1976

The emperor is getting paranoid and orders a loyal subject to invent an undefeatable weapon. The result is the terrible flying guillotine, a sort of a hatbox attached to a rope. Thrown like a Frisbee, it settles on a person's head then, with a tug on the rope swiftly slices it off! The device is yanked back and the newly shorn corpse drops to the ground. The infernal Flying G also appeared in *Master of the Flying Guillotine.*

woman, Kun Tse (Yuko Mizuno). Even during the wedding there are signs of cultural clashes, but it's not until the honeymoon that the fried rice really hits the fan. The couple spend their waking hours fighting and arguing over which martial arts styles are superior, Japanese or Chinese. Never have hurled chopsticks and rice bowls carried such deadly intent!

Liu triumphs in every match until his wife uses the elliptical art of *ninjitsu* to best him. Liu, however, is far from impressed by what he calls the "art of dirty tricks." Sensing irreconcilable martial differences, his wife leaves him and returns to Japan. Liu, realizing how much he loves his wife, makes a rather lame attempt to win her back by writing a letter of apology. The letter is interpreted by her brothers, all skilled Japanese martial artists, as a challenge. Needless to say, they accept.

In the ensuing skirmish, neither nationality proves more valiant than the other. When one of the Japanese offers his sword handle-first to Liu as a sign of respect, Liu slaps it away, ignorant of what the gesture means. In *COTN*, the real villains are ignorance of another culture, a lack of understanding, and an unwillingness to learn or accept new ideas or part with old traditions.

Fortunately, this message is delivered amid a flurry of exquisitely staged king fu fights. By the film's close, Liu and his adversaries have come to respect, admire, and even like one another, and the couple reunites with enhanced understanding.

—KWA

Crippled Avengers

1978
Starring Kuo Chui, Chiang Sheng, Lo Mang, Sun Chien, Lu Feng, Chen Kuan-tai
Directed by Chang Cheh

Director Chang Cheh's *Five Deadly Venoms* was based on a simple premise: five guys with virulent martial arts skills rip the bejesus out of their opponents and one another. The film proved popular, and Cheh decided to use the *Venoms* cast in an even weirder sequel: *Crippled Avengers*. The five actors (leader Kuo Chui, Chiang "Cutie Pie" Sheng, block-faced Lo Mang, high-kicking Sun Chien, and sneaky Lu Feng) are horribly crippled at the outset. But rather than demanding wheelchair ramps or Braille versions of *Dream of the Red Chamber*, our heroes develop crackerjack kung fu styles based on their physical challenges.

A nobleman (Chen Kuan-tai) is driven mad when his family is butchered and his son's arms are chopped off by ruthless enemies. After outfitting his son with mechanical arms that can elongate and fire darts, the nobleman becomes a vengeful thug. But rather than developing a thoughtful, comprehensive plan of revenge, he simply goes around mutilating anyone who displeases him. A trinket salesman (Kuo Chui) makes the mistake of pointing out his son's armless condition: "He has no arms." "But you have no eyes." "What do you mean? I have eyes. I have . . . AAAH! AAAAAHH!"

The mad nobleman also chops off the feet of a passerby (Sun Chien) and deafens a hapless blacksmith (Lo Mang). But the most horrible torment is reserved for a martial arts hero who arrives to rid the village of this outta-control blue blood. He's turned into a mental midget by having a metal band slowly tightened around his skull!

The four afflicted ones join forces and seek out the newly retarded hero's *sifu*. They learn to communicate despite their disabilities, and develop special kung fu skills. For example, the guy with no feet is outfitted with deadly mechanical ones.

Their chance comes when a gala birthday party is thrown for the now-dissipated nobleman. Security is assured by the presence of every evil kung fu master in the kingdom. Undaunted, the gang of cripples heads off to avenge the loss of their cherished parts. In the furious endbattle, the band's retarded leader is mortally skewered by a volley of darts from the evil son's metal arms. Despite the loss of their mentor, the remaining crippled avengers complete their bloody task.

Fans of the underdog will love this drenched-in-scarlet eccen-

HOUSE OF TRAPS   1981

This was the final film featuring the complete "Venom" team working for Shaw Brothers. Our heroes brace their way through a booby-trapped pagoda to get the treasure inside. Naturally, the walls of the death-maze shoot spears and arrows, the floors grow spike-forests, and the staircase contains razor-sharp blades that slice off people's toes. It's no surprise that Chang Cheh was at the helm of this one.

ONE ARMED SWORDSMAN   1967

A supreme swordsman gets attacked, but is saved by his servant, who dies in his master's place. The swordsman takes the servant's son, Fong Kong (Jimmy Wang Yu) as his own, teaching him everything he knows. But the swordsman's daughter grows jealous of Fong and, in an attack she orchestrates, Fong's arm is lopped off. He retreats, studies diligently, and learns the one-armed sword technique, then returns and slaughters everyone. The first sword-hero film to feature extreme violence and brutality, which would become the staple of all martial arts films to follow.

continued on next page

THE SEVEN BROTHERS MEET DRACULA 1973

Britain's Hammer studios brought their brand of gothic horror to HK in this coproduction with Shaw Brothers, directed by Roy Ward Baker. Dracula assumes the identity of a Taoist priest and flees to China, where he resurrects an army of Chinese zombies. The fiend is pursued by Dr. Van Helsing (Peter Cushing), who is aided by Shaw stalwart David Chiang. The East-meets-West schism reaches its absurd zenith when

The wind howls, the ground trembles, and out of nowhere jogs an attacking monster in *The Seven Brothers Meet Dracula.* Semiotical types who study this Hammer-Shaw coproduction from 1973 would tell you that there's a great deal of relative power-structure information contained in the fact that all the Chinese brothers die, and none of the Englishmen do, while the Englishwoman who loves a Chinese man dies, and the Chinese woman who loves an Englishman doesn't. It would be interesting to see how many Brits would live through a contemporary remake.

tricity. Clearly, even having one's essential body parts hewn off does not disqualify one from martial arts hero status—or eventual victory. Although *Five Deadly Venoms* is the classic Venoms film, *Crippled Avengers* is a great (mechanical) kick.

Descendant of the Sun

1983
Starring Cherie Chung Chor-hung, Derek Yee Tung-shing, Ku Kun-chung, Lung Tin-cheung
Directed by Chu Yuan

One of the most beautifully photographed efforts from Shaw Brothers studios, *Descendant of the Sun* imbues an electric life to scenes from classic Chinese scroll paintings. Unfortunately, the only way to see it these days is on videotape or non-letterboxed laser disc. Fans of beauty Cherie Chung (*Peking Opera Blues, Once a*

Thief, Wild Search) will want to seek it out; this was her first major film.

Descendant is a fairy tale revolving around a pair of supernatural babies from "fairyland." Naturally, one is righteous and the other is evil. The good baby is discovered embedded inside a huge glowing obelisk and extracted by a kindly woodcutter, who raises him as his own. When the kid, Shih Sheng, turns eight, he displays some remarkable talents: causing peaches to sprout from dead branches, fires to start, and people to levitate. His foster parents wisely counsel him to keep his powers under wraps, and he grows into a strapping young man (Derek Yee) without incident.

When corrupt government officials start conscripting the villagers for labor, Shih Sheng thrashes them with his superpowers and takes refuge in a nearby palace. He's hassled by cheeky handmaidens Pao and Pei for inadvertently freeing their caged birds, but is rescued from a threat of beheading by the Princess (Cherie Chung). He magically recalls the coop-flown birdies, then charms the palace parrot into reciting the steamy folktale *Dream of the Red Chamber*!

This amusing stunt earns him a job at the palace as houseboy. Before beginning his new job, however, he visits the glowing obelisk for advice. The spirit therein tells him of the Evil Infant haunting the globe with a chip on his evil shoulder.

Meanwhile, the regent of the province decides to embark on a eugenics program, rounding up babies and eliminating the weak ones. Realizing that the Princess will never stand for such a program, he decides to terminate her, and sends a band of killers to the palace for just that purpose. Shih Sheng does a quick-change into a gold-and-white tunic to stomp the brigands while preserving his Clark Kent identity as palace gofer. The Princess goes gaga over the mystery superman.

Unfortunately, before love blooms, the evil regent releases the Evil Infant from its green-glowing sarcophagus, and it instantly becomes full grown. Trouble.

Cushing explains to Chiang that crucifixes are useless in China, and they must use statues of Buddha to repel the ghouls!

Also released as *Legend of the Seven Golden Vampires*.

SUPER NINJAS 1982

Another Chang Cheh dismemberer. A kung fu clan is decimated by a band of ninjas imported from Japan. The ninjas then destroy the people who imported them and set themselves up as rulers of the martial world. One scene has a man stabbed through the abdomen, and as he keeps on fighting, his intestines slowly seep out of his belly. He is killed when he accidentally steps on his own innards and trips. In the end, the heroes pull apart the lead villain with their bare hands.

HEX ERRORS

The unleashed Evil Infant does battle with Super Shih, with each transforming himself into giant feuding objects: shears vs. carpet, axe vs. tree. Finally, the evil one turns into a scuttling crab, and Shih becomes a monolithic rock column and falls over, cracking the crustacean. It looks bad for the bad guy, but he starts conjuring atop a giant *feng shui* mirror: "Come, every evil, to my aid." Earth and walls split as gleeful ghouls come pouring out to attack Shih! Finally, the bad guy is exploded, and virtue reigns again.

Five Deadly Venoms

1978
Starring Chiang Sheng, Sun Chien, Kuo Chui, Lo Mang, Lu Feng, Wei Pai, Ku Feng, Wang Lung Wei
Directed by Chang Cheh

Five Deadly Venoms was the first of a very successful series of Shaw Brothers movies, all starring the same five actors. A *Kung Fu Theater* favorite, it was seen on late-night American TV by millions of kids, many of whom made Venom masks out of grocery sacks and then ran around trying to Lizard and Toad one another. It's a wild story of greed, betrayal, and friendship.

The venerated *sifu* of the Poison Clan is dying, his last student at his side. Over the course of his life, he trained five other students, each in one of the five deadly forms—Snake, Centipede, Scorpion, Lizard, and Toad. Student number six, Yan Tieh (Chiang Sheng), a righteous man, is trained in all five Poison styles. *Sifu* makes Yan Tieh promise to seek out the others and kill those who are doing evil.

The catch is, he can't do it alone. Having learned a part of each style, he's master of none. To eliminate any of the other five, he must pair up with another Venom. Yan Tieh has one clue to help him find the other Venoms. *Sifu's* old partner has amassed a fortune

Toad (Lo Mang) is one of the quintet of toxic warriors poised for martial apocalypse in Chang Cheh's seminal *Five Deadly Venoms*. Its producer, Shaw Brothers, is a publicly traded company on the Hong Kong stock exchange, and films like *Five Deadly Venoms* are why firms like NBC (owned by General Electric) are now-and-then rumored to be strategic partners to help exploit its 800-film library. Mostly produced from 1950 to 1985, the library could be worth over $70 million. Why, back in 83, Star TV bought a 580—Hong Kong film library from Golden Harvest for $94 million.

with Poison skills and is now retired under an assumed name. *Sifu* rightfully believes that the other five Venoms will come out to claim the treasure.

All the Venoms converge, but they don't know who the *sifu*'s partner is. They don't even know one another, because each was trained separately, wearing masks. Toad, the nice-guy beefcake with iron skin (Lo Mang), finds Lizard (Kuo Chui), an honest cop, and they decide to "redeem" the clan by getting the treasure. Meanwhile Centipede (Lu Feng) and Snake (Wei Pai) find *sifu*'s partner first and slaughter his whole family. No treasure is found, and a local boy spots Centipede leaving the scene. But Snake is well con-

Let me make a mark on your chest.
No. I want to wear low-cuts.
—*God of Gamblers*

It'll be bad if we become top gigo-
los. We'll be tortured every
day.
—*Pom Pom and Hot Hot*

The tongue is so ugly.
Let's imagine it to be Tom Cruise
—*My Neighbors Are Phantoms*

Game of chess? What kind?
Strip beast game.
—*The Informer*

From their stammering reaction, it
seems to be complicated.
—*Malevolent Mate*

I won't dump the used napkins
anywhere too.
Not to let the vampires use them
as tea bags, right?
—*Eternal Evil of Asia*

So you really are fully bruised?
No bruises on the tongue, the
palm or the buttocks
—*Pedicab Driver*

Bring in some pops, Monkey
—*Long Arm of the Law*

continued on next page

A normal person wouldn't steal
   pituitaries.
That's reasonable.
—*Brain Theft*

Tell him a hill will collide into his
   car tonight
—*Queen of Temple Street*

Those two with tattoos are fanatics.
   They're descended from canni-
   bals. Don't provoke them.
—*Marianna*

Do you really have one eye?
You don't believe me: Here, take a
   look!
—*Night Caller*

nected and fixes it so that a bribed witness helps Centipede get acquitted while Toad is falsely accused, then drugged, tortured, and smothered. The judge is so crooked you're sure he's the Scorpion.

Lizard and Yan Tieh team up to find and kill Centipede and Snake. But when they rendezvous for revenge, they run into the virtuous Captain Ma (Sun Chien), who has quit the police force and agrees to help them waste the stray Venoms.

Snake knows he's about to buy the farm and waits for them, stretched out on a chaise longue in white satin and pearls. Lizard and Yan Tieh fight him and his partner Centipede while Captain Ma stands off to one side and refuses to fight. Snake finally confronts him, saying, "I know who you are, you're the Scorpion."

Ol' Ma gives an evil laugh, then rips out Centipede's guts. Yan Tieh and Lizard are invincible, though, and after disposing of Snake and the unmasked Scorpion, they take the treasure map from Scorpion and march off to do right. Yan Tieh wants revenge on the crooked judge, but Lizard says, "All judges are crooked, and the next one might be worse. You can't kill them all." Some things never change.

—KAT

Five Fingers of Death *aka* King Boxer

1972
Starring Lo Lieh, James Nam, Wang Ping, Tong Lin, Nangong Xun, Tian Fong, Gu Wenzhong
Directed by Cheng Chang Ho

Five Fingers of Death was the first kung fu movie to hit the American crossover market. Without the success of *FFOD* paving the way, even a Bruce Lee might not have received his due.

Five Fingers of Death features eye-gouging, disemboweling, and hands being pushed into burning sand; it's a carnival of carnage that's truly not over till it's *over*. No character is too minor to avoid getting nailed in some nasty way.

Lo Lieh plays Chow Chi-hao, a nice orphan kid who lives with his kung fu teacher, Sung Wu-yang (Gu Wenzhong). *Sifu* says that if Chow wins the upcoming kung fu tournament, he can marry his cute daughter Ying-Ying (Wang Ping).

Meanwhile, the *sifu* of a rival school, Meng San-yeh (Tian Fong), wants to bag the tournament's title himself. The problem is that his son (Tong Lin) is a no-talent gangster with a cigarette holder permanently attached to his sneering mouth. The solution? Hire some hoods and kill all your opponents before the contest. The gangster's son meets a head-butting heavy named Chan in the marketplace and brings him home. Dad hires a band of "Japanese" fighters (Chinese guys in black fright wigs), just in case.

Old Sung sends Chow to study with an old friend to sharpen up his skills. The current favorite at the new gym, Han Lung (Nangong Xun), gets jealous and crosses over to the evil team. They use him for a while, then poke out his eyes and throw him in the street; they kill Chow's old teacher; and they flatten Chow's hands, so he can't learn the Iron Palm technique (he does anyway). Some folks are just plain bad.

Evil Meng sends the Japanese assassins to ambush Chow on the way to the tournament, but wild man Chan has seen enough Japanese savagery, so he tips Chow off and ends up paying with his life. Chow makes it to the tournament

With his hands flattened by bad guys, there's no way Chow Chi-hao (Lo Lieh) can learn Iron Palm technique in time to win the big kung fu tournament. Or is there? From *Five Fingers of Death* (aka *King Boxer*).

just in time and wins. Sound like the end of the movie? No! Meng stabs Chow's new teacher out of spite and heads for home.

The blinded Han Lung, meanwhile, is hiding in Meng's school. When Meng and his son enter the darkened building, Han Lung blinds the son and then, with a girl singer giving stage directions ("Aim high!" "Straight ahead!"), he manages to fight the older Meng and gets him to accidentally kill his own son. Enraged, Meng kills them both. Chow arrives to late to save them. He corners Meng, who commits suicide. Sound like the end of the movie

Packed with wiggly action, *Holy Flame of the Martial World* bemuses, confuses, and delights as it slices through strata of supernatural shenanigans like a well-sharpened blade.

Profits from films like *Holy Flame* allowed Shaw Brothers to create Television Broadcast Ltd. (TVB), the world's biggest producer of Chinese programming.

This company makes 6,000 hours of television a year in Hong Kong and 2,000 hours a years in Taiwan, which it also broadcasts throughout Asia and on a smaller scale in North America and Europe. It has an English channel in Hong Kong, a joint venture arm in India, and plans to coproduce in Indonesia and Thailand.

In early 1995, international media group Pearsons acquired 10 percent of TVB from Shaw Brothers and the Shaw Foundation for about $160 million. Shaw Brothers still owns 23.5 percent.

When Hong Kong becomes a Special Administrative Region of China, TVB will become the most successful commercial TV station in the world's biggest market. Its local audience will grow from 6 million people to a potential 1.2 billion. And all thanks to movies like *Holy Flame of the Martial World.*

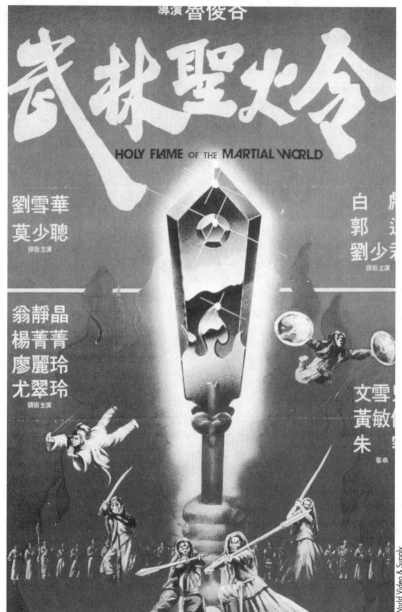

now? Wrong! The leader of the Japanese arrives, carrying the head of Chan for effect. Chow has to throw him through a brick wall *twice* before he dies. Only then can Chow walk off with his girl.

—KAT

Holy Flame of the Martial World

1983
Starring Benny Mok Siu-chung, Mary Jane Yung, Yang Ching-ching, Liu Lai-ling, Yau Chui-ling, Kuo Chui
Directed by Lu Chin Ku

As with most Shaw Brothers films, the only way you will ever see this film is on video: a square taken from the middle of a wide-screen picture, with subtitle edges cropped off port and starboard. And that's a damn shame, 'cause a movie this much fun oughta be shown big, to a packed house of families on an afternoon outing, kids screaming with delight until their shredded squid snack comes shooting out of their tiny nostrils.

Flame's mile-a-second pace may well bruise the viewer's skull. Combatants spend more time in the air than on the ground, somersaulting repeatedly over one another, clinking swords, or shooting energy gobs. Martial energies turn people bright blue, gold, or red, and can peel flesh, producing instantaneous skeletons. Despite the presence of the Snake King and the Bloodsucking Clan, the film is more goofy than scary—a Méliès matinee melee, if you will.

Led by the evil lady *sifu* Yi Tsing-yin, the Seven Clans waylay and kill an innocent couple who refuse to reveal the location of a potent kung fu weapon. Madam Yi and her cohort, Ku Pan-kuai, are about to do away with the couple's infant children when they are beset by *sifu* Yama Elder (Kuo Chui), who rocks the scene with his special martial arts skill, Ghostly Cries. The children are spared, and the boy, Yin Tien-chu, is reared by Yama Elder while the girl, Yi Tan-fang, is raised as a member of Madam Yi's O-Mei School of Virgin Swordplay.

Eighteen years later, Yin has grown into a strapping young man (Benny Mok) and is sent by Yama to retrieve the Holy Flame, a peculiar-edged weapon that his unfortunate parents had secreted in a cave. Yin must solve a (very) physical riddle involving an enormous *feng shui* mirror and torso-sized Chinese ideograms that spin and fly about the chamber. A huge drum splits, revealing a skeleton with a book in one claw and the Holy Flame in the other.

The weapon comes in handy when Tu Chuan-erh (Mary Jane Yung), the comely daughter of the local snakecatcher, is kidnapped by Lin, the evil leader of the Bloodsucking Clan, which is using virgins' blood to resurrect some pet monster. The sorcerer unfurls demons on painted scrolls, which come to life and fight furiously with Yin and his friend, Tuan, who torch the adversarial mutations. Lin then animates the monster, who is masked like a Mexican wrestler, speaks only English, and fights with superhuman strength. Only the Holy Flame can pierce and dissolve him!

Meanwhile, a lucky snakebite gives the snakecatcher's daughter's index finger the power to knock people senseless with energy bolts. It turns out there's another Holy Flame (the blue yin version of Yin's red yang one), which Yin and Yi eventually unite to blast the baddies into skeletal oblivion, leaving the theater aisles littered with little giggled-out bits of squid.

Human Lanterns

1982
Starring Lo Lieh, Chen Kuan-tai, Liu Yung, Sun Chien
Directed by Chang Cheh

A wonderfully gruesome tale of the mighty brought low by pride. Lo Lieh stars as Chao Chun Fang, lanternmaker by day, gibbering madman by night. When the spirit strikes him, he leaps around in a monkey suit and a skull mask, kidnapping beautiful women and stripping the bark off them for lantern material. Pride, jealousy, misunderstandings, and violence. Lives ruined, beautiful women flayed alive. Just another Chang Cheh thriller.

Chun Fang's clients are the prideful Lung Shuai (Liu Yung) and Tan Fu (Chen Kuan-tai). These two local big shots are rich, powerful, and insanely jealous of each other. They both want to rule the town, and each thinks that their ends justifies all possible means.

Lung is introduced to Chun Fang, the maker of Tan's beautiful lanterns, and recognizes him as an old rival in love whose face he once cut and scarred in a duel. Lung suggests that Chun Fang

"forget the past, get rich and famous," and contracts for the most beautiful lamps possible, no matter what it takes. What it takes, unbeknownst to him, are the hides off Lung's favorite courtesan, his wife, and Tan's sister.

When Tan's sister Yen Chu, the town beauty, disappears, Constable Pan (Sun Chien) thinks Lung has kidnapped her out of jealousy. Of course, she's actually in a basement being peeled by Chun Fang.

Tan suspects that it's Lung's doing and hires a killer to take him out. But the killer, Kuei (Lu Feng), is an old friend of the wacko lanternmaker, and while Kuei is fighting Lung, Chun Fang kidnaps his wife. When Kuei fails to kill Lung, Tan kills Kuei, using a fan with knives hidden inside.

Tan begins to see that this is getting out of control.

Tan's men take the dead Kuei out of town to dump the body. Chun Fang kills them just for fun, though, and hangs their heads in the town square. He then makes sure that Lung knows who hired Kuei in the first place. Tan realizes that both he and Lung are being set up.

Rumors start circulating about lamps made from human hides. Lung's suspicions lead him back to Chun Fang. Breaking into the old mill where Chun Fang works, he finds his flayed wife and sees three lovely lanterns. One has his wife's beauty mark prominently displayed on it. Tan arrives to ask Chun Fang, "Why me?" Chun Fang replies, "You're his rival. Now you both know that money and fame are hollow."

Fists and swords are put to work to end this

madman's mayhem but, in the struggle, the mill catches fire and collapses, leaving Chun Fang and Tan dead and Lung horribly burned. In the final scene, Lung realizes he's lost his wife, his health, and his looks. Constable Pan tells him "It's over. Forget it." Lung does just that, moving to a monastery to atone for his stupid pride.

—KAT

Legendary Weapons of China
aka 18 Legendary Weapons of China

1982
Starring Liu Chia-liang, Liu Chia-yung, Gordon Liu Chia-hui, Alexander Fu Sheng, Hsiao Ho, Kara Hui Ying-hung
Directed by Liu Chia-liang (Lau Kar-leung)

During the 1890s, with big chunks of China under foreign control, some kung fu societies tried to find a "spiritual" kung fu strong enough to stop bullets. In *LWOC*'s opening sequence, four martial art students stand before four marksmen, rifles aimed at their bared chests. Bang! They're still standing as a chanting Shaolin monk pastes yellow paper spells over the bullet holes.

Those watching the demonstration smile and nod; invulnerability to bullets has been attained! Then the quartet drops dead. The *sifus* sigh. Sooner or later they'll get it right, if they don't run out of disciples first.

Clearly, this is no way to treat one's students, and *sifu* Lei Kung (Liu Chia-liang) recognizes the futility of the situation. He disbands his school and drops out of sight, assuming a new existence as a woodcutter. The other *sifus* don't want the foreigners to learn of his skepticism; so they decide he must die.

Assassins are dispatched in the personages of Shaolin monk Ti Tan (Gordon Liu) and Tieh Hou (Hsiao Ho). As they head off in search of Lei Kung, they're shadowed by the monk's niece (Kara Hui, disguised as a man). They converge in Kwantung, where narrow alleyways form a maze as the assassins angle for info.

Because they all expect to find a bragging, swaggering Lei Kung (convincing the townspeople with a bewildering array of kung fu stunts), that's who they find. But it's not really Lei Kung; it's a con man (Alexander Fu Sheng) who's been hired to impersonate Lei Kung by his brother Lei Yung (Liu Chia-yung). Lei Yung is a shadowy hypnotist who uses voodoo to transform the phony Lei Kung into a kung fu kook. He hopes to draw out his brother and show him who's really the boss.

The monk's niece tracks down the real Lei Kung. She's become convinced that Lei Kung is right and the society must be disbanded. Lei Kung also befriends Tieh Hou, and when Tieh gets sick (from fighting the crazy con man in a cesspool, no less), he and the niece nurse him back to health.

Poor Tieh Hou. Every time he tries to get out of bed to kill Lei Kung, all he gets is hot soup and sympathy. Eventually, he's converted, but then there's the duplicitous Lei Yung to deal with. The last third of the film is combat—using all eighteen of your favorite weapons—between monk and magician.

In the end, "spiritual" kung fu is no match for actual martial arts skill. When the magician finally limps off, a shattered wreck, Lei Kung tells him, "Just say you killed me." Lei Kung couldn't care less about fame in the martial world, and this self-effacing *sifu* is a true martial arts hero.

—KAT

Mad Monkey Kung Fu

1979
Starring Liu Chia-lian, Liu Chia-yung, Gordon Liu Chia-hui, Alexander Fu Sheng, Hsiao Ho, Kara Hui Ying-hung
Directed by Liu Chia-liang (Lau Kar-leung)

Mad Monkey Kung Fu is squatting, screeching, rocket-fast madness. The heroes don't pose in robes; they dangle from the rafters, scratching and laughing like maniacs. *Mad Monkey Kung Fu* is a typical Shaw tale of remorse and revenge, but director Liu Chia-liang, who also stars, bends the brittle master/student/revenge story line into something with humor and even dignity.

Liu plays Chen Po, a traveling Peking Opera performer. After a successful stage performance as the Monkey King, he accepts an invitation from the evil, smirking local boss, Tuan (Lo Lieh). Chen has such a high opinion of himself that he doesn't even notice Tuan leering at his sister (Kara Hui). Proving that "the higher the monkey climb, the more he expose," Chen gets so drunk

he passes out. Tuan's evil wife, in exchange for her very own brothel, frames Chen for an imaginary rape. Adding injury to insult, Chen's sister is delivered to Tuan as a love-slave and Chen's hands are smashed flat with bamboo poles.

The broken Chen gets a monkey and sells candy on the street, his crippled hands wrapped in black bandages. He befriends a street kid, nicknamed Monkey (Hsiao Ho, one of director Liu's real-life students), who uses tricks to steal from the local extortionist dandies.

But when Chen can't ante up enough protection money, the evil grifters slam his monkey's head into a tree. Human Monkey replaces simian monkey, and the kids love it. Monkey convinces Chen to train him in monkey-style fighting, and incorporates his own antics into the style. Half-trained and half-cocked, Monkey takes on the cigarette-holder mob. With wild-style Monkey boxing, he literally ties them in knots. When one hood squats with his palms forward and starts projecting his *chi* energy, Monkey says, "That's old-fashioned. No one wants to see that anymore," then slaps him silly with his own shoes.

Monkey finds out that the man behind the protection racket is Tuan, but Tuan grabs him, then punches his head through the center of a table. Tuan's going to serve him up as "live monkey brains, a good winter dish." Chen's sister—still Tuan's concubine—is there and, not being a big fan of brains, "accidentally" rips the skirt off the boss's wife, creating havoc so Monkey can flee. Monkey escapes, but the girl is thrown off the balcony to her death.

Chen and Monkey go to the brothel for revenge. Chen can fight—but can't win—with his mangled mitts. Monkey forces Tuan's hands into a glass lamp. Looking at the bloody results, Monkey says, "Eye for an eye, right, master?"

Chen's not so sure. Restraint was the code he broke, which started this tragedy. But before he can stop it, Tuan's lying dead and Monkey's ready to finish off everyone else in the brothel. Chen just shakes his head. Together they walk away, Monkey still the disciple, Chen still the master.

—KAT

Seeding of a Ghost

1982
Starring Philip Kao, Tsui Siu-keung
Directed by Yang Chuan

Barmy Shaw sorcery 'n' revenge flick, which draws inspiration from slasher films, Z-grade Yankee sexplo, and John Carpenter's *The Thing*. The film's plot recalls Dada's "Exquisite Corpse," in which one person starts a story, then the next person continues it with only the last line to go on. It will find favor with the grindhouse/drive-in set whose idea of heaven is a dusk-to-dawn beastfest.

Chou (Philip Kao), a Hong Kong taxi driver, accidentally runs over a wandering sorcerer. Even though the sorcerer appears to have come through the accident unscathed, he puts a hex on Chou and his family. The taxi driver scoffs at the

Shaw Brothers has recently discussed plans to build a $100 million theme park at Nanshan, Shenzhen. Modeled on Universal City, the project would include a studio, a cinema theme park, and an amusement park on a 300-hectare site.

Shaw Brothers also expects to complete a $10 million "virtual reality" theme park in Singapore in 1997. We can only hope that both parks contain a *Mad Monkey Kung Fu* thrill ride.

curse . . . until things start going hideously wrong.

First his wife, Irene, runs off with a married man named Fang Ming. When Fang Ming refuses to marry her, she storms out of his car on a desolate road in the middle of the night, gets assaulted by a pair of teenage criminals, then accidentally plunges to her death.

The bereaved husband, remembering the curse, goes back to the sorcerer and asks for his help in avenging his wife's death. The sorcerer performs an ancient ritual known as the "seeding of a ghost," warning the husband of the grave consequences of this ritual. Irene's body is dug up (already looking as if it had been entombed for eighty years), and Chou's life energy is supernaturally drained into the corpse, fertilizing a killer-zombie baby ready to rock!

Up until this point, *Seeding of a Ghost* looks like any other Category III film from Hong Kong. We saw Irene in the shower while the cool jazz saxophone obbligato played in the background, the camera zooming in on her breasts. We saw Irene frolicking with her lover, running topless through the surf in slo-mo. And, of course, we saw Irene and Fang Ming making love to more saxophone jazz. Then the film turns nasty with a brutal rape scene reminiscent of a mid-sixties American sexploitation film.

Suddenly we are watching a different movie. Now *Seeding of a Ghost* becomes a crime drama, with police investigating the woman's death. A few scenes later, the film veers into the realm of the supernatural, with Buddhist priests battling the sorcerer for possession of another woman's body. Before the film is over, it has mutated into a low-budget monster movie when a *mahjongg* game gets interrupted by a placenta with teeth!

Seeding of a Ghost is a carnival ride that heads in one direction, then suddenly careens off at a right angle. Although Yang Chuan is billed as the director, the changes in the tone and plot are so sudden that it seems as if every fifteen minutes someone else took over the production. Reasoning is useless. Give up and enjoy it.

—JM

Over the Edge

ver-the-edge films aren't for kids, the overly sensitive, or the easily queased. Most of 'em aren't even for vegetarians. But that doesn't mean that they are cheapo road-show quickies, no matter how bad they sound. After all, try explaining the plot of *The Silence of the Lambs* to someone who hasn't seen the film. Then explain why you liked it, then why it won a truckload of Oscars. When Hannibal Lecter's necrophagic shenanigans struck gold in America, HK directors perked up their ears. The title of HK offering *Doctor Lamb* is no coincidence.

Hong Kong filmmakers are not the sort to shy away from a meaty story. Unlike *Silence*—which qualifies at Urban Legend Folklore—many of these films are based on fact. HK's cramped environs have created more than a few corpse-disposal problems for the colony's murderers, and the acid bath beckons. The *Sweeney*

MONDO

DOCUMENTARIES

The word *mondo* gets its modern meaning from a 1963 Italian documentary, *Mondo Cane* (literally "Dog's World," but translated as "Cruel World"). The film depicted unusual vignettes from all over the world: religious flagellation in Europe, shark-bitten fishermen in the South Seas, insect-based haute cuisine served in American restaurants. Some of the scenes were faked, but the film was a huge hit, and the theme song, "More," wormed its way into the pre-Beatles pop-instrumental lexicon. *Mondo Cane*'s success inspired so many imitators (*Mondo Bizarro, Mondo Pazzo, Mondo Mod,* etc., etc.) that the term "mondo" came to describe bizarre events or eccentric ways of looking at the world.

Hong Kong uses its proximity to many of the leading mondo-exporting nations to fashion modern documentaries along these lines. Most HK mondo concen-

Todd–like events depicted in *The Untold Story: Human Meat Roast Pork Buns* actually occurred. So, too, did the wartime atrocities depicted in the tough-to-take *Man Behind the Sun*. On the flip side, nothing in *Story of Ricky* has ever happened or ever *could*.

After popping one of these flicks in your VCR, close the drapes. Hide the Linda McCartney records. Hit Play. Now peek through your fingers.

Doctor Lamb

1993
Starring Simon Yam Tat-wah, Danny Lee Sau-yin, Kent Cheng
Directed by Danny Lee Sau-yin

"Give me some bowel-cake, please!" screams a frustrated youngster, from somewhere in the depths of Hong Kong's congested Mongkok district. So begins the lurid saga of *Doctor Lamb*, a serial-killer exposé that begins as a stylish police procedural and ends up in a whirlwind of free-floating flashbacks, jiggling body parts, and pure dementia that attempts to set new standards for the far end of HK's nugget-blowing, Category III extremes.

It stars Simon Yam, HK's suavest chameleon—a baby-faced ladies' man one minute, a scalpel-wielding flesh freak the next—as Lam Gor-yu, the mild-mannered cabbie with a particularly nasty private pastime. Director/producer Danny Lee plays a determined detective, and rotund Kent Cheng appears as his persuasive sergeant.

When a photo-processing lab discovers a suspicious batch of snapshots (a nude woman, stained with blood, her corpse twisted into a grotesque position), the police are alerted. They quickly capture cabbie Lam and begin their merciless interrogation. By hammering a phone book against Lam's chest and whipping the soles of his feet with a belt, the police are unable to produce a confession. Only Detective Lee, with whom Lam is inexplicably obsessed, can coax the cabbie into the confession that makes up the film's second half.

Dr. Lamb (Simon Yam) ponders surgical options for a group of inpatients in the sawbones's eponymous movie.

trates on mainland China, exploring the quaint habits of the various tribes inhabiting the Middle Kingdom. Narration is conducted in jabbering hyper-Cantonese, punctuated with the drawn-out exclamation "Waahhhh!" whenever the live monkey main course's head gets cut off or the wedding veil parts to reveal a toothless old crone.

AMAZING MARRIAGE CUSTOMS

A fascinating look at courtship rituals among the Chinese tribes who haven't yet been dragged into the modern world. Bright costumes, mating dances, tee-heeing young brides. A maiden reclines on her bed; potential suitors announce themselves outside the house, then poke a straw through a hole in the wall. She grabs the straw of her favorite.

Amazing Marriage Customs features plenty of this sort of diversity, including the public trial of a couple accused of adultery. They're convicted by the headmaster, and the punishment is administered in full view of the assembled village: They must walk three times around the fire holding

continued on next page

freshly hacked water buffalo parts above their heads. The woman gets the head and the man gets the hind part, but we've no idea if this is significant.

THE SEX LIFE OF THE ANIMALS

Did you know that the male tiger bites the back of the female's neck (in lieu of giving candy or flowers)? That a snake pecker looks like the drill bit on an oil rig? Or that female lobsters must crawl completely out of their bony shells to make little lobsters? No subtitles, but it makes no difference. Entertainer Charo once used clips from this film in her nightclub act.

SHOCKING ASIA

This monstrous shockumentary is difficult to top. *Shocking Asia* got its stateside press in the seminal fanzine *Sleazoid Express* when it first hit 42nd Street grindhouses in 1984: "Phrases like 'shock value' or 'extreme' tire when describing it," wrote editor Bill Landis.

This thing kicks off with the Hindu festival of Thaipusam, where devotees skewer themselves with metal spears and put

It turns out that Lam, a loner who lives in a crowded apartment with his father and assorted adult half siblings, was emotionally scarred as a child by the death of his mother and the cruelty of his stepmother. One rainy night, a drunken hooker pukes and passes out in his cab. Lam becomes aroused by the scent of corruption, begins yipping at the moon, and garrotes the hooker. He hides her body inside the family's breakfast table, and once the apartment is empty, proceeds to dismember her body. Thank heaven for those convenient Mongkok hardware shops: where else would he have gotten a circular saw on such short notice?

The mutilation of the whore (one of many, it transpires) is a macabre tour de force: Lam manipulates the body like a marionette, antically squeezes and jiggles her breasts, then saws her into pieces, spattering his face, the room, his fishtank, and the camera with geysers of gore. Expressively underlit, Lam's miniature charnel house becomes a theater of blood for Yam's manic performance: he twitches, minces, puckers his lips like a fruity goldfish, and pathetically barks at the moon. Eventually, Lam (himself a virgin) finds a naive nursing student on which to enact his darkest desire: the (sweaty, grunty, lovingly filmed) necrophiliac conquest of a fellow innocent.

Perhaps more bizarre than Lam's over-soaked shenanigans, however, is director Lee's insistence on intercutting the gore with his cops' comic clowning. The high point of this (hilarious? sick-making?) counterpoint arrives when, during a search of Lam's digs, a severed female breast is dumped, wiggling and withered, out of a formaldehyde vat onto Kent Cheng's head, who then tosses it onto the back of a mortified female officer. So goes much of the movie: dark and harrowing one minute, a ridiculous gross-out the next. Somewhere under the slapstick and saw-torn limb stumps is a commentary about HK's overcrowded living conditions and one family's failure to communicate. Don't look too hard for the subtext—you might just find that other breast.

—CS

Man Behind the Sun

1990
Starring Wong Kong, Wong Ying Git, Cheung Kwok Man
Directed by T. F. Mous

Occasionally, something comes along to challenge the acceptable limits of cinema verité. *Mondo Cane, Medium Cool,* and *Faces of Death* all generated controversy for their increasingly graphic portrayals of misery and bloodshed. Add to this tradition *Man Behind the Sun.* The film is already legendary among gore aficionados and has been banned in England. Even viewers used to the hack-and-bleed, head-exploding effects of George Romero and David Cronenberg find *Man Behind the Sun* shocking.

A cat is thrown into a room full of rats. We see it bound around, trying to defend itself against the horde of rodents, eventually collapsing as the rats chew at the head and neck of the dying feline. In the film's most spectacular scene, we see hundreds of flaming rats leaping and writhing in agony, trying to escape immolation.

Killing even properly trained stunt animals is gratuitous; that said, *Man Behind the Sun* is not a cheap attempt at exploitation. It is based on the true story of the Manchu 731 Squadron, a horrifying Manchurian concentration camp built by the Japanese during World War II for the purposes of developing new biological weapons and studying the effects of extreme conditions on human subjects.

Lt. General Jiro Ishii, the camp's commander, was a seriously twisted man, using Chinese and Russian peasants for his test subjects. With Japan on the ropes in the latter stages of the war, Ishii's main goal was to develop a plague-dispersing bomb (that explains all the rats). *Man Behind the Sun* suggests that Ishii achieved his goal, but not in time to help the war effort.

The film does not try to hide its anger over the Japanese behavior. Chinese prisoners are called *maruta*, or kindling wood, and members of the Japanese youth corps stationed at the camp are slapped when they refer to the prisoners as human beings. Still, the

World Video & Supply

Shocking Asia is our favorite travelogue continent, where what's exotic is lunch and what's outrageous is just another street scene.

burning Sterno lozenges on their tongues. The Japanese present dwarf-wrestling and Nazi-drag S and M spectaculars. Chinese restaurants dish up so-fresh-it's-still-alive snake, bat, and turtle, and the gory hell-statues of Tiger Balm Gardens are showcased.

A look at back-alley transvestites in Singapore culminates in the sex-change operation of one of them—five minutes of lunch-losing surgical footage. As

continued on next page

Sleazoid put it: "By this point, the audience is one long groan." *Shocking Asia* is a masterpiece of sorts and will either enthrall your friends or drive them screaming from the room.

SHOCKING ASIA 2

More of the same, but not as memorable as the original. A visit to a Thai monastery shows their emetic cure for heroin addiction. Filipina go-go dancers shake their tailfeathers. A Japanese salaryman is shown visiting various sex establishments: a "no-pan" coffee shop, a dominatrix who dresses him in diapers and tucks him into a crib, and a "Lucky Hole" emporium best left undescribed.

TIBET

Although Tibet is officially part of China, the "Roof of the World" is worlds away from the central authority of Beijing. This documentary presents pilgrims, prayer wheels, and chanting monks in the mountainside Potala Monastery. A horrifying ceremonial funeral—where the corpse is consumed by vultures—is not always included in video copies.

Japanese are not portrayed as plain old evil. Takamura, the camp's security chief, is portrayed as passionate but misguided, believing in his heart that the camp's work is worthwhile. Doctor Ishii is sick and cruel, but the film portrays him as mentally ill, a victim of chemical unbalance, rather than merely demonic.

Man Behind the Sun is well made, which makes it all the harder to take. Scenes of the camp's destruction seamlessly blend stock footage with staged shots, and the autopsy of a living boy looks disturbingly real. In one scene, the last remaining survivor among the prisoners—a boy who has hidden among the corpses—is killed while a Japanese woman gives birth. The movie flits back and forth

Flayin' alive: The Greater East Asia Coprosperity Sphere is explained by one WWII Japanese scientist to a Chinese coprosperer in *Man Behind the Sun*.

between the two events with a disquieting rhythm. The symbolism is obvious but effective. The brutality may prove too realistic for many viewers, but the subject matter demands it.

—JM

Remains of a Woman

1993
Starring Carrie Ng Kar-lai, James Pak, Loretta Lee Lai-chun, Jacqueline Law Wei-kun, Melvin Wong, Dennis Chan, Kenneth Tsang
Directed by Clarence Ford (Fok Yiu-Leung)

Remains of a Woman is based on an actual murder case that rocked Hong Kong in the early 90s. An overseas Chinese man returns to Hong Kong and gets involved in a basic love quadrangle: boy meets girl; boy meets other girl; boy gets original girl to help dismember other girl; boy pretends to find salvation in jail because of third girl and gets sprung, leaving original girl to take the murder rap.

The story unfolds in herky-jerky flashbacks as Billy Chan (James Pak) prepares for his retrial on the charge of dissolving the body of air hostess Lisa (Jacqueline Law) in an acid bath. When a younger Billy meets Judy (Carrie Ng), he recognizes her as an easy fish to land. Judy's addictions fire on all cylinders—love, sex, cocaine, and codependence—and soon she's embezzling from work and turning over the cash to Billy.

Then, when Billy adds Lisa to his string, the women fight over him with coke-fueled inner-child intensity. It's a hard day's night for the creep; if he's not busy betting on the ponies or sticking stuff up his nose, he's indulging in fluff-porn with Lisa or S and M with Judy.

When the flashback clock arrives at the air hostess death scene, it's presented as a *Sid & Nancy*–type screwup, followed by *Grand Guignol* mayhem. Billy is too freaked and shivery to dispose of the

HEX ERRORS

GOOD QUESTION

More fractured English subtitles from your favorite Hong Kong movies (see chapter 3 for a full explanation).

What's a kid-corpse, grandpa?
—*Hello Dracular*

You're a bad guy, where's your library card?
—*Enforcing the Law*

You're a deranged snooper or what?
—*Queen of Temple Street*

Gun wounds again?
—*Rich and Famous*

How can you use my intestines as a gift?
—*The Beheaded 1000*

A red moon? Why don't you say blue buttocks?
—*The Holy Virgin Versus the Evil Dead*

Miss, shall we make it?
—*Ghostly Vixen*

continued on next page

Guns! You think I'm meaning
   puppy?
—*Madam City Hunter*

how can I make love without TV?
—*Brother of Darkness*

You cheat ghosts to eat tofu?
—*The Ultimate Vampire*

How can a bullet be breathless!?
—*Saviour of the Soul*

No ripping off? How about jerk-
   ing.
—*Queen of Temple Street*

Oh, are they chewing gums or my
   hearing's wrong?
—*City Hunter*

Why don't you do something else
   but to pick up the dead men's
   bone?
—*Amazing Stories*

Don't you feel the stink smell?
—*Operation Pink Squad 2*

You circumcised me because of
   my cold. Now my appendix
   because of my headache?
—*Doctor Vampire*

Can the few of you blow up the
   hanging coffins?
—*Bury Me High*

body, so Judy must do it herself. She shoots cocaine in her tongue, than screams "Don't look at me!" into Lisa's wide-open eyes before commencing hacksaw corpse-disassembly.

Once arrested and jailed, Billy seems the perfect candidate for pious redemption, and he hooks virginal, Bible-toting prisoner-visitor Annie Cheung (Loretta Lee). Annie helps authorities see that the new-leaf Billy deserves to get another trial. What he really deserves, though, is a short dance on the end of a long rope.

The spine and soul of *Remains* is Carrie Ng's performance as a woman manipulated over the edge. Her sans-makeup close-ups in the courtroom (as Billy is let off the hook) scream of twisted romantic obsession. Ng's sensual creepiness won her the 1993 Best Actress award at Taiwan's Golden Horse Film Awards.

The scariest thing about the movie is not its gore, but the way Billy turns women into putty by feeding them cocaine or religious beatitudes. Good-looking and soulless, Chan is the sort of heartless bastard that otherwise-rational women crawl over broken glass for while nice guys like us shrug our shoulders in resigned disbelief. In *Remains of a Woman*, they crawl over a lot worse.

The Story of Ricky

1991
Starring Fan Siu Wang, Yukari Oshima, Frankie Chin, Gloria Yip, Kuo Chui
Directed by Lan Nai Kai

Over-the-top gore offerings often end up being tedious voyeuristic voyages, trying to top their predecessors by having more gallons of reddened corn syrup spray-painting the walls, and more stuff chopped off and wiggled. That's not the case with *The Story of Ricky*, which instead resembles some sort of deranged Japanese comic book. There's good reason: this twisted tale of incarceration is, in fact, based on a deranged Japanese comic book

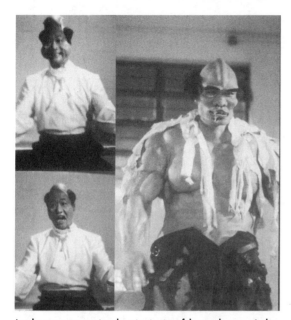

Another argument against the privatization of the penal system. At the end of *The Story of Ricky*, the head warden stuffs a prisoner into a meat grinder, shoots his toady subordinate with a puffs-you-up-and-explodes-you bullet, then, after smoking a cigar, turns into a big snot-nosed monster.

Body-shredding, however, does not seem to faze Ricky, who displays but slight annoyance at having sharp metal objects rammed into his body. He can certainly dish it out as well; a mentally defective, sumo-sized sadist is sent to squash Ricky in the shower, but our boy plunges his bare hand into the goon's ample abdomen and rips out his intestines.

This stunt earns Ricky an audience with the

(a *manga* called *Rikki Oh*). Its chops have been ground and pounded here into one mighty stew of grue.

It's the twenty-first century, and prisons have been privatized, presumably to provide even scummier administrative personnel. Our hero, Ricky Ho, is a lithe muscle dude (played with blockheaded insouciance by Fan Siu Wang) jailed for killing the drug kingpin responsible for his girlfriend's suicide. His fellow inmates are a heinous lot (they like drug kingpins) and threaten him with bodily injury.

After enduring assorted beatings, stabs, slaps, pokes, wrench whippings, razor-blade trail mix, shocks, live burial, rebar rack jobs, steam burns, and blunt and penetrating traumas of every ilk, Ricky decides to punch his own ticket out of Dodge. From *The Story of Ricky*.

assistant warden, a loathsome, carnivorous churl who stores breath mints in his glass eye and whose bookshelves are comprised solely of dozens of luridly boxed porno videos. Unimpressed by prison authority, Ricky duels with the wicked boss of the North wing, Hai—covered in muscles and tattoos—in the prison courtyard. A hard slap to the back of Hai's head pops out an eyeball, which is immediately eaten by predatory birds. The brute hastily attempts *seppuku*, but only so he can attempt to strangle Ricky with his outpouring innards!

Hai's demise forces the other three prison bosses to deal with Ricky. This unlikely trio of inmates—a creepy simian needle-hurler, a huge galoot with Elvis sideburns, and a very butch Yukari Oshima—start to make life difficult, but a touch of comic relief is provided by the arrival of the head warden and his pudgy spoiled brat of a son.

This terrible kid is the movie's worst monster—until the warden works voodoo to transform himself into a nine-foot-tall rubber-bladder beast. In a final-reel battle that recollects Ted V. Mikels's *The Corpse Grinders*, the warden/beast is fed directly into an enormous . . . you know.

The comic book viscera are impossible to take seriously; at one point, a skull-crusher punch is revealed as precisely that by X ray. This isn't a movie one bumps into; this is a movie one seeks out and devours . . . if you're looking for this sort of thing.

The Untold Story: Human Meat Roast Pork Buns

1993
Starring Anthony Wong Chau-sang, Danny Lee Sau-yin, Julie Riva
Directed by Herman Yau Lai-to

Some things are lost in translation. Take, for example, the title of this movie. The English title—*The Untold Story*—is innocuous enough. But the Chinese title translates as *Eight Immortals Restaurant: Human Meat Roast Pork Buns*. Frankly, that's a far more enlightening title for this picture, which is guaranteed to make you look twice at the next pork bun you purchase.

Chan Chi Leung (Anthony Wong) moves from Hong Kong to Macau after a fight in which he kills a man who accused him of cheating at *mahjongg* (he *was* cheating, but that seems irrelevant to Chan). He adopts a different name and gets a job working in the kitchen of the Eight Immortals restaurant in Macau, cutting up pigs and making buns. When the restaurant owner also accuses him of being a *mahjongg* cheat, Chan slices and dices the man and his family, grinds them up for pork bun fixings, then takes over the restaurant.

The Untold Story combines low humor and high gag without blinking. The Chief of Homicide (Danny Lee) always shows up with a different call girl on his arm, and a love-struck but ignored female detective finally dresses as one to get his attention. Chan originally earns police benevolence by being extra-generous when filling squad orders for pork buns. Long, lingering

Yack! It's Anthony Wong making victuals from victims in this Thai poster for *Human Meat Roast Pork Buns*.

washes up on the beach a few days later, the police follow the trail back to Chan. He is arrested, but it is only after days of constant psychological and physical torture that Chan finally tells the story of what really happened that night at the Eight Immortals restaurant.

The Untold Story is a pretty good character study, evoking sympathy for the murderer (at least at first) without ever asking you to like him. Anthony Wong's killer is repugnant and insane, but he still comes across as a human being. Wong's impressive performance won him 1993's Hong Kong Film Award for Best Actor (the Hong Kong Oscar equivalent).

—JM

shots of policemen gorging themselves on free human meat roast pork buns (they have no idea, but the audience does) elicits an abundance of "Eeeuuu's" in unison.

As soon as the jokes stop, it's right back to rape, mutilation, torture, beating, and murder. When bagged restaurant-owner-and-family offal

DON'T BE FOOLED

If you take a liking to Hong Kong films—and we hope that you do—sooner or later you will be fooled. Sooner or later you will run across a movie with a video box, poster, or title that just says, "I'm great." But it will not be great. It will suck.

It's happened to everyone. It's happened to us. It'll happen to you. Here are some especially tempting examples to avoid.

THE AVENGING QUARTET

Take one look at the poster—four potent action heroines holding down bad motorscooters and holding up sleek weaponry. But *TAQ* is a tame melodrama,

CATEGORY

RATINGS

Hong Kong films are divided into three rating categories. Each category is denoted by a roman numeral set in a simple geometric symbol, which grows increasingly angular as it becomes more restrictive. Nobody much cares about the difference between Category I (a single stick in a cute round circle) or Category II (two sticks in a less-friendly square). But the Category III rating (three sticks in a sharp-edged triangle) means under-eighteen types are verboten.

Public service announcements in HK depict teenagers unceremoniously ejected from theaters showing such fare, not to mention the life-sized cardboard cutout of a stern-faced police constable often present in the lobby.

Most Category III films are cheap, rapidly made, soft-core ninety-minute wonders, usually featuring instantly forgettable starlets. These are manufactured and

with Moon Lee and Cynthia Khan gooning inexplicably over nerdo painter Waise Lee. Yukari Oshima and Michiko Nishiwaki appear only peripherally as villainesses, and a dorky cop mooning over Moon gets far more screen time. Action is slow and sporadic.

BLACK PANTHER WARRIORS

Unhinged director Clarence Ford assembled a great cast—including Carrie Ng, Tony Leung Kar-fai, Simon Yam, and Brigitte Lin—in what appears to be a rockin' action flick. Lobby cards of Carrie Ng and her pet Beretta drag you into the theater. But this half-baked pseudosuperhero movie degenerates quickly into a grating, dysfunctional comedy. Skip it.

BLACK MAGIC WITH BUDDA

Horror flick about a Hongkie who smuggles a bleeding, breathing, dis-embodied brain from Indonesia. Sounds good, but this cheapie (directed by Shaw Brothers veteran Lo Lieh) veers from ghoulie lunacy into a $1.98 Hollywood snooze-o-rama. One keeps watching, hoping for something, anything . . . gratuitous nudity, bewitched subtitles, exploding vermin . . . until one just gives up and . . . EJECT.

CROCODILE EVIL

The video box cover art is tempting, and a Thai bar girl does have to make love to a large rubber crocodile. But . . . we have yet to see a subtitled version, and there are far too many scenes devoid of either crocodiles or evil.

LABORATORY OF THE DEVIL

The sequel to the highly disturbing *Man Behind the Sun*, a dramatic presentation of experiments in germ warfare conducted by Japanese troops in occupied Manchuria toward the end of World War II. But while *MBTS* balanced the horror by maintaining a sense of purpose and

李建興 李建生 李建興 連煥勳

Snacks from the dark side: Gruesome, cheap, and sick . . . too bad *Malevolent Mate* is such a lousy flick.

consumed with the fanfare of a bowl of instant noodles: boil water and scarf 'em down. Sometimes gore is added to the mix to spice things up. Much as we salute the exploitative spirit—the "ghoulie, roughie, kinkie" mantra—most of these films are a waste of time.

The catchall category also serves as an "NC-17" category, and some worthwhile films do end up with the stigma of the Triangular Triple-I, like Jacob Cheung's award-winning *Cageman*, a sensitive look at life in Kowloon's infamous Walled City. The film features no sex, violence, or nudity, but was rated Category III solely because of its inventive use of Cantonese slang!

reason, *LOTD* has no such compunctions. Based around a ho-hum love story between a Japanese officer and the kimono-clad gal he left behind, *LOTD* uses the gruesome details merely as an excuse to make a movie. Yuck.

MALEVOLENT MATE

The cartoon poster depicts a pair of skeletonized arms (with batter-fried hands) perched on a Japanese sushi plate, against a backdrop of flames and under a blood-spattered half-visage with off-staring eyes. Lobby cards of Bonnie Fu (the slutty thief from *Full Contact*) in full creep-on mode look good. But the film is an uninspired rip-off of *Human Meat Roast Pork Buns*, and its aimless brutality is truly brutal. Here, the cops beat their suspect and torture her with electricity to obtain a confession (and it's not even 1997 yet). But that's not all; they torment the suspect's daughter by setting fire to her teddy bear!

MY BETTER HALF

The poster makes this look like it could be some sort of feminist *Doctor Lamb* rip-off: a blood-splattered trollop Bobbitting a kielbasa with an enormous French blade; chainsaw and ominous stockpot perched on the kitchen counter, *MBH* is a triptych of stories unconnected save by tedium, and you must sit through over an hour of peekaboo nonsense before getting to "The Saw." Even then, it ain't that good.

NINJA KIDS

You know it has no subtitles going in, but a Category III film with that title's gotta have something, right? Nope, P.U! Too little fighting and too little sex. Lame, lame, lame, even with a ninja devil-mask villain.

RAPED BY AN ANGEL

Promoted as *Naked Killer II*, but lacking *NK*'s frolic and nostalgic paeans. Even worse, *RBAA* lacks the presence of Carrie Ng, *Naked Killer*'s Princess. Instead, we get Mark Cheng as a condom-sportin' serial rapist lusting after Chingmy Yau, the star of a "Fitty Milk" commercial. Sleazy but pointless.

SEXUAL DEVIL

Well, the box looked good.

ULTRACOP 2000

The poster has the marvelous Yukari Oshima in fetching, flat-black, paramilitary drag. However, this shot-in-Manila corker is short on action and long on idiotic scenarios. Worse, the incomprehensible plot (something about aliens coming to Earth to fight, and the only thing that scares the bad alien is a gay guy suffering from AIDS) will just make you mad.

UNDER THE ROSE

Supposed to be a mondo-style documentary of HK's, uh, seamier side. Relentlessly staged and very, very dorkacious. Host James Wong bubbles and rebubbles over with each new "undercover exposé" of topless bars in Wanchai, phone sex services, etc. All of this is unenlivened by amusingly cracked subtitles or, indeed, any subtitles at all.

Access

14

wailo access to HK films continues to improve as the market develops. Specialty video stores are beginning to stock HK product, and some (like Kim's Video in New York City and Le Video in San Francisco) have very impressive selections.

If your town has a Chinese neighborhood, chances are good that there is at least one video outlet stocking Hong Kong fare. In smaller neighborhoods, the Chinese grocery market will often also carry videos for rent. In bigger neighborhoods, there is usually a first-run Chinese theater as well.

Chinatowns have not always been the simplest places for *gwailos* to rent tapes. However, we have included an appendix that gives the Chinese characters for the title of each of the films that we have reviewed. This should help you hurdle any language barrier.

Increasingly, independent "art house" theaters and film societies in major metropolitan areas and large college towns sponsor Hong Kong film festivals or Hong Kong movie nights.

The Art Institute of Chicago holds a yearly Hong Kong Festival that is the best known of the lot. Call (312) 443-3733 for more information. Others that we can recommend first- nor second-hand include The Laemmle in Santa Monica, California; Cinema 21 in Portland, Oregon; and The Roxie Theater in San Francisco, California.

The point is, it's not even close to impossible to find good Hong Kong films in America.

Renting Videotapes and Laser Discs

Here are some places around the United States and Canada to rent HK videos and laser discs. By no means is it a complete list, nor is it up-to-date. In fact, it has been very difficult to track down rental outlets in a number of areas, and we apologize in advance if the nearest place we have listed is five hundred miles from your home. Understand that there probably is someplace to rent HK videos closer to you; we just couldn't find it. So ask around. Other HK fans in your area probably know the score.

If you still draw a blank, you can contact either of the two main U.S. video suppliers, whose addresses appear below, and tell them where you live. We've checked with them, and they will be happy to send you the contact information for your nearest rental shop. And if there's still a long way to go, we've included mail order information, too.

Tai Seng Marketing
170 Spruce Ave.
Suite 200
South San Francisco, CA
    94080
Telephone: (415) 871-8118
Fax: (415) 871-2392

World Video & Supply Inc.
150 Executive Park Blvd.
Suite 1600
San Francisco, CA 94134
Telephone: (415) 468-6218
Fax: (415) 468-1381

Video Rental Locations

ALASKA

Anchorage
Asiana Video Rental
343 W. Benson Blvd., #10
Anchorage, AK 99503
(907) 561-2289

ARIZONA

Phoenix
Asia Video
753 S. Alma School Rd.
Mesa, AZ 85210
(602) 833-2933

China Express
1501 S. Rural Rd.
Tempe, AZ 85281
(602) 966-7633

Tucson
Grant-Stone Inc.
2026 E. Speedway Blvd.
Tucson, AZ 85719
(520) 884-0775

Kim's Oriental Market
2205 S. Craycroft
Tucson, AZ 85711
(520) 790-6945

Kimpo Oriental Market
5595 E. 5th St.
Tucson, AZ 85711
(520) 750-9009

CALIFORNIA

Albany
Albany Hong Kong Video
    Company
919 San Pablo Ave.
Albany, CA 94706
(510) 524-7438

Berkeley
Movie Image
64 Shattuck Sq.
Berkeley, CA
(510) 649-0296

Tower Video
2589 Telegraph Ave.
Berkeley, CA
(510) 849-0900

El Cerrito
Best Video
10777 San Pablo Ave.
El Cerrito, CA 94530
(510) 526-8094

Long Beach
Hong Kong Video
1210 E. Anaheim St.
Long Beach, CA 90813
(310) 591-2668

Los Angeles Area
Chinese Video Center
727 N. Broadway, #210
Los Angeles, CA
(213) 680-1871

and
288 W. Valley Blvd., #108
Alhambra, CA
(818) 281-9055

and
27 N. Garfield Ave., #G
Monterey Park, CA
(818) 571-5583

Entertainment Superstore
288 West Valley Blvd.
Alhambra, CA
(818) 281-9055

Happyland
988 N. Hill St., #108
Los Angeles, CA
(213) 680-4010

and
141 N. Atlantic Blvd.
Monterey Park, CA
(818) 458-9857

and
685 N. Spring, #E
Los Angeles, CA
(213) 687-3721

and
711 N. Broadway, #110
Los Angeles, CA
(213) 689-3692

Jerry's Video Reruns
1902 N. Hillhurst
Los Angeles, CA

Laser Wave
302 W. Valley Blvd.
San Gabriel, CA
(818) 458-5651

Odyssey
11910 Wilshire Blvd.
Los Angeles, CA
(310) 477-2523

and
4240 Lincoln Blvd.
Marina del Rey, CA
(310) 823-2780

Vidiots
302 Pico Blvd.
Santa Monica, CA
(310) 392-8508

Sacramento
Hong Kong Video
6021 Stockton Blvd.
Sacramento, CA 95824
(916) 421-7950

San Diego
Shin Hua Video
4620 Convoy St.
San Diego, CA 92111
(619) 560-5476

San Francisco
Laser Pacific
1433 Bush St.
San Francisco, CA 94109
(415) 673-0191

Le Video
1239 9th Ave.
San Francisco, CA 94122
(415) 566-3606

Naked Eye
533 Haight
San Francisco, CA 94117
(415) 864-2985

One Stop Video
3250 Geary
San Francisco, CA 94121
(415) 386-8680

Tam's Video [and Laser]
2204 Irving [2101 Irving]
San Francisco, CA 94122
(415) 759-1589 [759-1610]

and
612 Clement St.
San Francisco, CA 94118
(415) 751-1399

San Jose
East West Video
175 S. Capitol Avenue, #I
San Jose, CA 95127
(408) 929-9319

Great Hong Kong Video
1828 Tully Rd.
San Jose, CA 95122
(408) 270-3028

COLORADO

Denver
Pacific Ocean International
 Supermarket
2200 W. Alameda Ave.,
 #2B
Denver, CO 80223
(303) 936-4845

Truong An Video
Far East Center
333 S. Federal Blvd.
Denver, CO 80219
(303) 936-5004

DISTRICT OF COLUMBIA

Heng Kang Company
730 7th St., NW
Washington, DC 20001
(202) 783-6030

FLORIDA

Fort Lauderdale
Hong Kong Market
5371 N. State Road 7
Tamarac, FL 33319
(305) 485-6688

Miami
Trung My
N.E. 167th St.
N. Miami Beach, FL

Orlando
Hong Kong Video
1102 E. Colonial Dr.
Orlando, FL 32803
(407) 422-2025

GEORGIA

Atlanta
Blast Off Video
1133B Euclid Ave.
Atlanta, GA 30307
(404) 681-0650

Comedy Plus Video
5389 New Peachtree Rd.
Chamblee, GA 30341
(404) 458-3874

ILLINOIS

Chicago
Asiana Video
3246 W. Lawrence Ave.
Chicago, IL 60625
(312) 539-3566

Bang Bang Video
2337 S. Wentworth
Chicago, IL
(312) 326-5770

Beauty Video
2126A S. Archer Ave.
Chicago, IL 60616
(312) 326-0724

Chinatown Bookstore
2214 Wentworth St.
Chicago, IL 60616
(312) 225-5009

Video Express
1139 W. Argyle
Chicago, IL
(312) 878-2914

Schaumburg
Laserland Video Shop
1039 N. Roselle Rd.
Hoffman Estates, IL 60195
(708) 490-0088

Westmont
Laserworld
International Plaza
665 Pasquinelli Dr.
Westmont, IL
(708) 323-9600

MARYLAND

Baltimore
Po Ting Trading Company
312 Park Ave.
Baltimore, MD 21201
(410) 685-8828

Video American
3100 St. Paul
Baltimore, MD
(410) 889-5266

and
400 W. Cold Spring Ln.
Baltimore, MD 21210
(410) 243-2231

Columbia
Shin Shin Market
9042 Old Annapolis Rd.
Columbia, MD
(410) 730-0078

Rockville
Angus Books, Gifts and
    Video
460 Hungerford Dr.
Rockville, MD
(301) 251-1301

Wheaton
New My-A Video Company
11216 Georgia Ave.
Wheaton, MD
(310) 946-6146

MASSACHUSETTS

Boston
Chum Video
145 Brighton Ave.
Allston, MA 02134
(617) 782-8960

Universe Video
5 Knapp St.
Boston, MA 02111
(617) 451-9442

Yes Station
28 Kneeland St.
Boston, MA 02111
(617) 482-1022

MICHIGAN

Detroit Area
Thomas Video
122 S. Main
Clawson, MI 48017
(810) 280-2833

Evergreen Supply Company
20736 Lahser Rd.
Southfield, MI 48034
(810) 354-8181

Happy Laser House
1893 E. Wattles Rd.
Troy, MI 48098
(810) 524-4742

MINNESOTA

Minneapolis
Asia Import Food and Video
1840 Central Ave., NE
Minneapolis, MN 55418
(612) 788-4571

Asian Movies and Music
2750 Nicollet Ave.
Minneapolis, MN 55408
(612) 870-3548

Intercontinental Video
521 Cedar Ave. S.
Minneapolis, MN 55454
(612) 333-4101

St. Paul
Lee's Video and Rental
315 University Ave., W.
St. Paul, MN 55103
(612) 292-1518

Oriental Video
422 University Ave., W.
St. Paul, MN 55103
(612) 225-1908

MISSOURI

Columbia
Big Lizard Video and Laser
    Disc
21 N. 10th St.
Columbia, MO 65201
(314) 875-4014

Kansas City
China Books and Video
400 Grand Ave.
Kansas City, MO 64106
(816) 221-1311

St. Louis
Kim Thanh
3224 S. Grand Blvd.
St. Louis, MO 63118

Viet Nam Hong Kong
    Movie Rental
3238 S. Grand Blvd.
St. Louis, MO 63118
(314) 773-8400

NEW JERSEY

East Hanover
Tsaix Oriental Import, Inc.
200 State Route 10
East Hanover, NJ 07936
(201) 515-2028

Iselin
Glory Oriental Video Rental
1328 Oak Tree Rd.
Iselin, NJ 08830
(908) 283-4350

NEW MEXICO

Albuquerque
Wavy Brain
2221 Lead SE
Albuquerque, NM 87106
(505) 256-3686

NEW YORK

Buffalo
Mondo Video
1109 Elmwood Ave.
Buffalo, NY 14222
(716) 881-1953

New York City
Chinatown's Laser World
13 Chatham Sq.
New York, NY 10038
(212) 964-8881

The 43rd Chamber
43rd St. (between 8th and
      9th Ave.)
New York, NY 10036
Specializes in kung fu films

Hong Kong Emporium
3703 74th St.
Flushing, NY 11372
(718) 426-0330

Kim's Video
85 Ave. A
New York, NY 10009
(212) 529-3410

and
6 St. Marks Pl.
New York, NY 10003
(212) 598-9915

and
350 Bleecker St.
New York, NY 10014
(212) 675-8996

and
144 Bleecker St.
New York, NY 10012
(212) 260-1010

Lucky Video
1388 Bushwick Ave.
Brooklyn, NY 11207
(718) 919-1126

Sally' Music [laser disc]
89 Bowery
New York, NY 10002
(212) 925-6380

TMC Asian Music [laser disc]
151 Canal St.
New York, NY 10002
(212) 226-6696

NYUE Enterprises (Main
      Address)
61A Walker St., #A
New York, NY 10013
(212) 219-8880

and
109 East Broadway
New York, NY 10002
(212) 619-0800

and
124 Mott St.
New York, NY 10013
(212) 219-0327

and
29 Catherine St.
New York, NY 10013
(212) 227-5632

and
153 Centre St.
New York, NY 10013
(212) 226-1894

NORTH CAROLINA

Carrboro
Dave's Videodroma
405 Main St.
Carrboro, NC 27510
(919) 968-8482

Cary
K K Video
103 Nottingham Dr.
Cary, NC 27511
(919) 460-0940

Charlotte
Hong Kong Fashion &
      Video
2727 South Blvd.
Charlotte, NC 28209
(704) 527-0005

OHIO

Cincinnati
Home Cinema
3234 Jefferson Ave.
Corryville, OH 45220
(513) 221-4499

Columbus
Yao Lee Oriental
      Supermarket
2848 N. High St.
Columbus, OH 43202
(513) 262-7631

OREGON

Portland
Asia Television and
      Video
328 S.E. 82nd Ave.
Portland, OR 97216
(503) 256-0866

Soho Video
1000 S.W. Jefferson
Portland, OR 97201
(503) 221-7079

Trilogy Video
2484 N.W. Thurman
Portland, OR 97210
(503) 229-1884

Video Station
502 S.E. 82nd Ave.
Portland, OR 97216
(503) 255-1266

PENNSYLVANIA

Philadelphia
DTV
207 N. 11th St.
Philadelphia, PA 19107
(215) 625-4720

TLA Video
1520 Locust St.
Philadelphia, PA
(215) 735-7887

U E Enterprise
1015 Race St.
Philadelphia, PA 19107
(215) 627-2033

Pittsburgh
Asian Merchandise
705-09 Penn Ave.
Wilkinsburg, PA

SOUTH CAROLINA

Goose Creek
Redbank Video and
      Oriental Mart
1217 Redbank Rd.
Goose Creek, SC 29445
(803) 572-3567

TEXAS

Amarillo
Thong's Oriental Video
5621 E. Amarillo Blvd.
Amarillo, TX 79107
(806) 381-8813

Austin
Dong Yang Video
5610 N. Lamar Blvd.
Austin, TX 78751
(512) 467-1916

Bruce Lee movies are still high in demand at video rental centers around the country. Rest in peace, man.

I Luv Video Pizza
4631 Airport Blvd.
Austin, TX 78751
(512) 450-1966

Skyline Book and Video
8557 Research Blvd.
Austin, TX 78758
(512) 873-0585

Dallas
Jade Video
10560 Walnut St.,
#650
Dallas, TX 75243
(214) 276-7027

Houston
Asia Video and Gifts
1010 W. Cavalcade St.
Houston, TX 77009
(713) 863-8913

United Chinese Video
9258 Bellaire Blvd.
Houston, TX 77036
(713) 272-6565

Video City
11330 Homestead St., #A
Houston, TX 77016
(713) 590-0176

McAllen
Asia Mart and Video
2516 Pecan Blvd.
McAllen, TX 78501
(210) 682-6750

San Antonio
Century Video
7015 Bandera St.
San Antonio, TX 78238
(210) 684-0804

Sugar Land
Home Laser Entertainment
3536 Highway 6
Sugar Land, TX 77478
(713) 265-3399

UTAH

Salt Lake City
Tower Theater
900 South and 900 East
Salt Lake City, UT
(801) 328-1645
Big-screen venue, but videotape rental also available

Thuy Hang Video and Gift
3590 S. Redwood Rd.
West Valley City, UT 84119
(801) 973-4163

VIRGINIA

Alexandria
Video Vault
323 S. Washington St.
Alexandria, VA 22314
(800) VAU-LT66
Video Vault also sells and
rents by mail. Call for
catalogue.

Falls Church
Universal Books and Video
Corner
Eden Center in Seven
Corners
6763 Wilson Blvd., No. 5
Falls Church, VA 22044
(703) 241-7070

Springfield
Eastern World Supermarket
7040 Spring Garden Dr.
Springfield, VA
(703) 569-1824

WASHINGTON

Lynnwood
Oriental Video
18904 Highway 99
Lynnwood, WA 98036
(206) 775-8890

Seattle
Scarecrow Video
5030 Roosevelt Way NE
Seattle, WA
(206) 524-8554

Video West and China
Warehouse
1043 S. Jackson St.
Seattle, WA 98104
(206) 860-4051

WISCONSIN

Appleton
Oriental Video
216 W. Wisconsin Ave.
Appleton, WI 54911
(414) 738-7440

Milwaukee
Asia Video Store
1308 W. Mitchell St.
Milwaukee, WI 53204
(414) 672-1677

Lanexang
3508 W. Burnham St.
Milwaukee, WI 53215
(414) 384-0573

CANADA

ALBERTA

Edmonton
Asian Girls Video Ltd.
15104 Stony Plain Rd.,
   NW
Suite 1
Edmonton, Alberta T5P 3Y3
(403) 481-4610

BRITISH COLUMBIA

Delta
Asian Video Rentals Ltd.
9329 120 St.
Delta, BC V4C 6R8
(604) 589-3553

Vancouver
Dragon Video Inc.
1394 Nanaimo St.
Vancouver, BC V5L 4T6
(604) 253-2380

ONTARIO

Markham
ACESONIC Laser and
   Electronics Centre
4350 Steeles Ave. East
P.O. Box 1
Markham, ON L3R 9V4
(905) 513-7577

Toronto
Asian Video Movies
   Wholesale
685 Lansdowne Ave.
Toronto, ON M6H 3Y9
(416) 530-0517

Golden Classics Cinema
186 Spadina
Toronto, ON M5T 2C2
Hotline: (416) 504-0585
Telephone: (416) 504-
   0012

Wilson Laser Disc Co. Ltd.
19 Milliken Blvd.
Toronto, ON
(416) 754-1283

QUEBEC

Montreal
Wah Shing Video Ltd.
Place du Quartier Chinois
990 St-Urbain St., G-05
Montreal QC H2Z 1K6
(514) 861-3615

Mail-Order Video

Ordering videos by mail is never as straightforward as simply buying a movie ticket or renting tapes or discs at a rental outlet. And the infrastructure you purchase—original video box art and the option to watch your favorite films as many times as you like—may not be worth the price.

Here is a guide to some of the better mail-order firms that deal in HK videos. We haven't included titles or prices; you should write or call and request a catalog first.

Da-Wei Films
P.O. Box 24513
Los Angeles, CA 90024

Eastern Way Films
P.O. Box 291655
Los Angeles, CA 90029

Far East Flix
59–13 68th Ave.
Ridgewood, NY 11385
Phone/Fax: (718) 381-
   6757
Mon-Sat: 12 P.M.–7 P.M.
   EST

Foxx Entertainment
   Enterprises
327 West Laguna Dr.
Tempe, AZ 85282
(602) 829-1365

JARS Collectibles
14 St. Johns Rd.
Ridgewood, NY 11385
(718) 456-0663
Mon-Sat: 7:00 P.M.–10:30
   P.M. EST

Ng Hing Kee of LA
518 W. Garvey Ave.
Monterey Park, CA
   91754
Phone: (818) 284-4861
Fax: (818) 284-6978

Something Weird Video
Department FUN
Box 33664
Seattle, WA 98133
(206) 361-3759

Video Search of Miami
P.O. Box 16-1917
Miami, FL 33116
(305) 279-9773
E-mail: VSoM@aol.com

Video Vault
323 S. Washington St.
Alexandria, VA 22314
(800) VAU-LT66
Also has a retail store.

White Lotus Video
P.O. Box 7594
Tacoma, WA 98407

Fanzines

Fan magazines ("fanzines") are the best way to stay up-to-date with Hong Kong cinema. We've ranked them according to quality/usefulness, but true diehards will (naturally) subscribe to every single one. Before sending money, make sure to check and see if these people are still in business.

CINERAIDER

Consistently delivers the goods: timely, well-written reviews, and intriguing sidebars. Look for Gere LaDue's "F-Stop" columns, which provide the latest gossip. Chinese characters for each film are listed. Indispensable.

Published: 2–3 times a year
Subscription rates USA/Canada: $10 for 3 issues
 (payable to "Richard A. Akiyama")
Subscription rates foreign: $18 for 3 issues
Cineraider
P.O. Box 240226
Honolulu, HI 96824-0226

FATAL VISIONS

Australia's best movie magazine has had a "Chinatown Beat" feature since 1990, covering the HK scene in Melbourne and Sydney. Slick, glossy, appropriately trashy, and beloved by "freakers" (Aussie gorehounds).

Published: 2–3 times a year
Subscription rates USA/Canada: please write
Subscription rate foreign: please write

Fatal Visions
P.O. Box 1184
Thonbury, BIC 3071
Australia

HONG KONG FILM CONNECTION

Packed with information and reviews. Editor Clyde Gentry III loves HK movies and puts in as much info as he can get his hands on, including Chinese characters for film titles—a big plus. Contributing writers include HK Internet denizen Lars-Erik Holmquist.

Hong Kong Film Connection
P.O. Box 867225
Plano, TX 75086-7225

ASIAN TRASH CINEMA

Many HK film fans object to a pejorative term like "Asian Trash." We're not opposed to trashiness, but we don't like to lump all Asian movies together. That said, *ATC* does a good job covering HK cinema's mix of horror, sex, and other delights. *ATC* is closely affiliated with the mail-order firm Video Search of Miami, described in our section on mail-order videos. The same company also publishes *European Trash Cinema*.

Published: quarterly
Subscription rates USA/Canada: $20 for 4 issues
Subscription rates foreign: $40 for 4 issues
Asian Trash Cinema
P.O. Box 5367
Kingwood, TX 77325

ORIENTAL CINEMA, SHE

A pair of fanzines published by Dra-culina Publishing, who also put out a slew of "scream Queen" 'zines. *Oriental Cinema* covers mostly Hong Kong and Japanese cinema. Lots of excellent info and photos. *SHE-The Magazine of Femme Fatale Cinema and Culture* is dedicated to celluloid bad girls, with strong emphasis on HK eyescratchers. Heaps of information, photos, filmographies.

Published: quarterly
Subscription rates USA/Canada:
    (OC): $15 for 4 issues, (SHE): N/A
Back issues: $4.50–5.50; write for specifics
Draculina Publishing
P.O. Box 969
Centralia, IL 62801

The Internet

The Internet contains some invaluable sites for those interested in making contact with other HK film fans or tracking down specific information. The following information was current as we went to press, but online communications are volatile, and users should be prepared for sources that have blossomed and died like flowers in the spring.

A patented Hong Kong stunt in the midst of going wrong. An outtake from *Aces Go Places*.

NEWSGROUPS

The granddaddy of 'em all is "alt.asian-movies," which is about 80 to 90 percent HK films—oriented. You might also want to check "alt.cult-movies," "soc.culture.hongkong," and "soc.culture.hongkong.entertainment."

WORLD WIDE WEB PAGES

Believe it or not, the best Hong Kong film Web page is in Sweden, but you may set your browser toward any of these:

The Hong Kong Movies Homepage:
  http://www.mdstud.chalmers.se/hkmovie/
The Hong Kong Cinema page:
  http://egret0.stanford.edu/hk/ba.html
Mandrake's Hong Kong Movies Page:
  http://metro.turnpike.net/metro/Mandrake/
Jackie Chan Trivia & Gossip Page:
  http://www.ios.com/~sahpngyi/dinying2.
  html
The Rumble Page: http://www.rumble.com

Apocalypse at 5:15, 7:30, and 10:00: Hong Kong Movies in Asia

We made an extended pilgrimage into the heart of darkness, looking for HK films. Our passports acquired the multicolored patina of immigration stamps and curry stains.

THAILAND

At the huge outdoor Marine Bar in Chonburi, hordes gambol while the billboard-sized Cinemascope screen writhes with chopping goons and yellow snake scratches. Music wails from the Thai boxing matches taking place in a ring just sixty meters distant, competing with the peak-volume movie soundtrack rattling the scarred PA speakers.

Cats roam under the tables, searching for cockroaches and random bits of cartilage and durian shell frags. Bats fly across the screen

Huge, lurid, and designed to suck in patrons like a Dustbuster, a Thai painting for a Hong Kong actioner beckons outside Bangkok's Rama Theater.

Stefan Hammond

scooping up flying snacks, cutting temporary black shapes in the lightplay. A trio of tattooed Thai trollops giggle and catcall as onscreen, actresses Cynthia Khan and Moon Lee rearrange the spleens of assorted poltroons.

Hong Kong filmgoing in Asia is its own thing.

Of course, in some Asian cities, rapid economic growth has created gleaming glitter of chrome and concrete; you're just as likely to be heading for a mall theater in Singapore as you are in Kansas City.

But venture out of the built-up areas and you'll find that a night at the movies is as wild and weird as you like: from gorgeous colonial-era theaters in Malaysia to obscure Thai parking lots turfed out with corrugated-tin drive-in screens. Hollywood plays here, but Hong Kong's gun-mongering and ghoulhopping is coin of the realm.

The view of the future—the Pacific Century—as Japanese *animé* sheen and HK Gucci/Benz glitz is the iceberg's tip; most of Asia is still dusty at best and rotting at worst. Whether a particular country is newly industrialized or preindustrial, travel in Asia is fraught with peril and delight.

Tourist infrastructures come equipped with varying degrees of ornery transport, nutritional toxins, discomfort, annoyance, and crawling skittering things. "Lite" and "sugar-free" are concerns only for the privileged; most want as much sugar, caffeine, and cholesterol as they can get. Against this backdrop, films are viewed as treats, and as such, ought to be as luridly colored, sweet, and loud as possible.

Thailand would be a happy hunting ground for HK *sanuk* (fun) except that the films are usually dubbed into Thai with no subtitles—the exception being in Bangkok's cavernous Rama Theater, where English subtitles are sometimes added. But you don't need subtitles to enjoy something like *Iron Monkey*.

Thai towns of any size have a cinema: a wooden shopfront in the smaller towns or the top floor of the department store in the larger ones. Take the escalator and check out the posters. Multiple films will be on offer (usually HK) and the ticket prices may tempt you into a subtitle-free experience: typically US$1–2.

Category III films do make it into Thailand, but how much T and A survives Thailand's censorship board (who routinely use Vaseline screens to blur nudity, following censorship codes written in the 1920s) is unknown. Hanuman—the *Bangkok Post*'s acerbic film critic—routinely rails against the archaic censorship codes; his fellow critic Poon Choke reviews the HK stuff.

A more elemental form of viewing is provided by Thailand's innumerable open-air theaters. Found at regional fairs, in abandoned lots, or more permanent installations, proprietors reel out whatever they've got. Admission prices run forty cents or so, but mosquito repellent, raingear, and snacks (fiery, sweat-inducing ones are best) are not included. We once saw two projectors playing simultaneously on different screens: a mixture of Thai pop videos, HK hyperviolence trailers, and God-knows-what. Both soundtracks, natch, cranked to the nines . . . awe-inspiring.

Labor is cheap and movies need advertising, so why not hire locals to paint huge billboards, strap 'em to a pickup truck, light 'em up and equip 'em for audio terror, then blast 'em around town? Thailand makes the best MALAHOPTs (Movie Advertising, Loud As Hell, On Pickup Trucks), and your sidewalk Thai iced tea may well be enlivened by one howling past.

Curiously, the expensive seats in Asian theaters are in the balcony! Sometimes, the two-tiered pricing system demarcates main floor and balcony; save money by sitting closer! Just don't sit in the twenty-*baht* seats at the Rama . . .

PENINSULAR MALAYSIA

Malaysia has excellent HK film distribution, due to its large ethnic Chinese population. The films are shown not only with their original Chinese and English subtitles, but with additional Malay subtitles; lengthy phrases can fill the bottom half of the screen with trilingual verbiage. In keeping with Malaysia's state religion of Islam, films are censored for sex, nudity, violence, whatever. Head-tossin' witches, though, don't seem to pose any theological problems.

The peninsula has some funky colonial-era theaters loaded with charm, such as the Ruby in Ipoh and the Rex in Penang. Malacca has a magnificent grindhouse, the Capitol, where we caught a gruesome cheapie called *Curse of the Zombi*. Ceiling fans stirred the warm, sepulchral air as the lone fluorescent light cut out; there was complete darkness until the advertising slides

kicked in. Wiggly pink letters touted "Mr. Rajoo's Films" and reminded us that *dadah* (drugs) is equivalent to a hangman's noose in Malaysia. As slices of heavenly, pale-green melon sent juice running down our arms, the Zombi hopped mightily, delighting the local kids.

As in Thailand, when the bad guy dies, everyone stands up to leave; credits are curtailed in favor of house lights and mass exodus.

EAST MALAYSIA (BORNEO)

Home to the Wild Man, acres of rain forest (swiftly being chopped down, to the dismay of rock stars everywhere), and ethnic Chinese traders who've sought their fortune in the wilderness, Borneo is a big tropical island just south of the Philippines. Divvied up by three countries, it contains tiny, oil-soaked Brunei; the Indonesian state of Kalimantan; and the Malaysian states of Sabah and Sarawak.

Sarawak's local tribes pioneered the curvilinear black tattoo work and privates-piercing techniques later parroted by rich-kid "modern primitives" (*ampallang* is a Malay word). They also preserved dead relatives in jars and kept them in their homes, but this custom has yet to catch on with today's youth.

Most of Sabah's capital city, Kota Kinabalu, was bombed to splinters during World War II, but Sarawak's capital, Kuching, survived intact. Kuching is superfine. Enjoy your bread-and-curry breakfast with a cup or two of aviation-strength Malaysian coffee. Afterward, spend some time at the Police Museum (featuring life-size dioramas of executions and opium dens). Finally, check out the Golden Harvest production at the marvelous Capitol Theater, a jewel of a colonial cinema crumbling grandly in the tropical sun.

Sadly, most of Borneo's crusty grindhouses are moribund. The newly opened Riverside Mall cineplex in Kuching is an example of things to come: four dinky theaters with meat-locker air-con, air-freshener sprays that robotically pop off every fifteen minutes, and (of course) Malaysia's highest admission prices. But at least they run film through a projector. Cut-rate establishments use videotapes on projection TVs, and features are preceded by lengthy karaoke segments.

Heading upcountry, Sarawak's principal out-posts contain both the old theater shells and the new concrete video-projector bunkers that sup-plant them. Our lone night in Sibu took us to the Palace Theater, still showing films despite slow demolishment. Bored by some halfhearted com-edy about imperiled Imperials, our smuggled-in *char siu bao* (roast-pork buns) but a memory, we searched for the exit along the rain-soaked out-side balcony. In the surreal, humid night, we bumped into a huge pile of folded Malaysian movie paintings; handmade sail-sized canvas adverts with alarming imagery and jagged cryp-tographs. Treasures awaiting the junkman. Like giggling buzzards, we carted off all we could carry, our celebration muted by the tragedy of movie-palace entropy.

SINGAPORE

This city-state popped into the Media Window a few years ago, when a spoiled American brat got his butt officially paddled for vandalism. But most of the temporary experts on Singapore's judicial system still couldn't locate it on a map (tip o' the Malay peninsula), nor give an ethnic breakdown of its population (about three-fourths Chinese).

S'pore's continuing experiment in social engineering has permitted R-rated movies since 1991, and some Hong Kong Category III films get shown. Certain salacious nuggets like *Naked Killer* have been prohibited, but Singapore is one of the best places outside of HK to view Hong Kong's cinematic exploits and exports.

Cinemas in Singapore—like everything else—are newly built and squeaky-clean. Ticket prices are high for Southeast Asia (US$2.80–4.35), and the air-conditioning may well freeze you solid—bringing a wrap or jacket is a good idea.

The *Straits-Times* newspaper gives theaters and showtimes, but no clue as to locations. Of course, you can always call the theater; everyone speaks English in Singapore. Taking a night ride via the amazingly sterile MRT out to the Tampines theaters is recommended as you get panoramic views of Singapore's monolithic hous-ing estates—evocative and spookycool.

Some Singaporean cinemas use a computer-ized seat-reservation system. It looks like a video game as it marks a little X on the seating schematic and automatically prints out your ticket. A cute bit of cyburbia, although we'd have

(Left) Beloved throughout the world for his perilous passions: A plywood Jackie dangles from a no-brownout Manila cinema awning in *Police Dragon* (aka *Crime Story*). (Right) In this Tokyo painting advertising *City Hunter*, Jackie is paired not with Hong Kong superstars Joey Wong or Chingmy Yau, but with Japanese teenybopper Kumiko Gotoh.

preferred that they hadn't knocked down all the gorgeous old theaters that make Asian movie-going so much fun.

JAPAN

Jackie Chan is the most popular HK film star in Japan, revving up many a rabid teenybopper. Another big hit with the Rising-Sun crowd are those cute hopping child-vampires, known as *kyonshi*. But Japan is not the best place to catch up on Hong Kong movies. Ticket prices are outrageous, even by Japanese standards: $25 as we go to press. Really. Video rentals are (relatively) reasonable, and a wide range can be found at a new store called Cine City Hong Kong, but HK product is usually dubbed in Mandarin and subbed in Japanese.

THE PHILIPPINES

The history of this archipelago has been aptly described as "three hundred years in a Spanish convent and fifty years in Hollywood." The effects of Catholic indoctrination (with its resulting population *tsunami*) has not been kind to Manila, which bears a stronger resemblance to Los Angeles then to any other Asian capital.

True to their guncrazy Yankee pseudocolonial roots, Manilan criminals tend to fill themselves with street drugs and dogcheap booze, then shoot each other. So while Manila's daily papers are not much use in gleaning HK film information, they are great sources for stories of insane violence featuring gangster squabbles and juvenile fireworks mishaps.

The 'Pines is the only country in Asia where HK films are routinely dubbed into English, although other media often alternate between the native Tagalog language and English, a loopy system that assumes bilingual ability on everyone's part! Fortunately, Filipino ticket prices are extremely low—about sixty cents—but the dubbing is annoying, and projectionists' competence is never assured.

Filipino audiences must be complimented on their fondness for Hong Kong's cinematic warrior-heroines; maybe it's a mutant Blessed Virgin complex. Japanese actress Yukari Oshima, a veteran of HK action cinema, has a large following in the Philippines under the name Cynthia Luster, and Moon Lee appears on more Filipino movie paintings than Stephen Chow or Chow Yun Fat.

MACAU

Five centuries ago, the baddest-ass sailing Catholics weren't Spanish, but Portuguese. Though Portugal's imperial ambitions in Asia were eventually squelched by other similarly minded Occidentals, the plucky Iberians may have had the last laugh. The tiny country of Macau, a short boat ride from Hong Kong, is the oldest European colony in Asia and is slated to be the last. Macau reverts to Chinese rule in 1999, two years after Hong Kong does.

Even with its legal casinos and a dog-racing track called "The Canidrome," Macau has escaped HK's rush to affluence; its narrow, winding streets are more suited to bicycles than Benzes. Stroll along Avenida Infante De Henrique and turn onto Rua Santa Clara, where you'll find Macau's fave longtime movie palace, the Cineteatro. Although now split into a triplex, it's still a stately place to catch a flick. Also of note is the lovable Capitol at Rua Pedro Nolasco da Silva and Travessa dos Anjos. Macau's proximity to the source ensures that the latest HK product will be on offer—at prices comparable to those in HK.

HONG KONG

Money-mad, crowded as hell, and moving at a pace that makes Manhattan look like Albuquerque, Hong Kong itself is one terrific urban-Asia experience. However, the rampant economy has fueled building frenzies, leading to the replacement of many groovy old theaters with multiscreen cinepods. Still, a few hang on, mostly

In Hong Kong, posters on the streets of this movie-mad Asian capital last about a week.

on the Hong Kong Island side, east of Causeway Bay—where tourists seldom venture.

The English-language media in Hong Kong covers the local industry quite well; critic Paul Fonoroff of the *South China Morning Post* also hosts an on-again/off-again TV show on HK movies. Fonoroff, an authority on the Shanghai film industry of the 30s and 40s, does the show in both English and Cantonese—no mean feat.

Late-night shows are also common, some beginning at 3:00 A.M.! Like everything else in Hong Kong, movie schedules change like the wind.

Glossary

animé Animated cartoon version of *manga*, a Japanese comic-book form known for its stylized presentation of often violent and explicit subject matter. Some HK films (*The Story of Ricky, Wicked City,* Jackie Chan's *City Hunter, Saviour of the Soul*) are based on or styled after existing *animé* or *manga* works.

"bitchy" Seen in subtitles. Adjective describing flirtatious female behavior.

Cantopop Formulaic pop music sung in the Cantonese dialect. Film stars often have Cantopop careers on the side and may even be more famous for their music (Jacky Cheung, Andy Lau, and Leon Lai are notable examples). Cheung, star of *A Chinese Ghost Story II* and *Bullet in the Head*, once sold out the cavernous Hong Kong Coliseum *twenty-four* nights in a row! Cantonese, with at least nine tones per written character, is tough to sing. Reproducing the tones for meaning—while sticking to the melody—caused Cantopop superstar Sally Yeh to say that "singing in Cantonese is like singing in prison."

char siu bao *Roast pork buns*

chi The breath of nature. *Chi* symbolizes a cosmic force that created the universe, whose duality (yin/yang) is expressed in many ways, like inhalation/exhalation. Martial arts are about learning how to concentrate one's *chi* energy and apply it (often with a loud yell).

"comfortable" Seen in subtitles. Adjective describing female sexual satisfaction.

durian A football-sized fruit with a hard, spiked exterior. If you wanted to grab a tropical fruit to bash in the head of a bad guy, you'd pick a durian. Cut one open, and a durian will yield a unique combination of delectable flesh and rotting garbage stink: "the taste from heaven with the smell from hell." Most Asians love the fruit, but most Asian hotels and public conveyances ban the durian from their premises.

eunuch In Imperial China, males who voluntarily subjected themselves to castration became eligible for top political posts, which were denied the betesticled. Known as eunuchs, they wielded considerable power within their areas of influence. Voluntarily ceding male "essence" often leads to an increase in supernatural power in HK movies, making older eunuchs fearsome adversaries.

face Respect. Extremely important in Chinese society. Debates over a lack of face given by one to another often lead to cinematic free-for-alls between the two parties.

feng shui The art of arranging objects (buildings, furniture, etc.) so that disharmony with natural elements is avoided. Determining proper *feng shui* requires a geomancer to scope out the surroundings, often with the help of a divining wheel. Bad *feng shui* will motivate believers to rearrange furniture, knock down walls, even wall off building entrances to correct matters. When Bruce Lee moved into Kowloon Tong (a place notorious for bad *feng shui*), he had an enormous *feng shui* mirror put on the roof of his house to deflect the evil energy. A typhoon blew the charm off his roof, and Lee died soon thereafter.

feng shui mirror Octagonal mirror whose round reflective center sometimes has a yin/yang symbol. Rectangular block diagrams around the edge represent the I Ching. Can be used as a weapon against ghosts.

grindhouse An inner-city theater—often a faded Golden Age movie palace—which was often the only U.S. venue for HK fare. Your feet would stick to the floor and lycanthropic drunks howled in the seats behind you. Today, very few remain, supplanted by mallplex corporatia and video superstores.

gwailo A foreigner of American, British, or European extraction. Literally "foreign ghost" or "foreign devil." Some controversy over whether *gwailo* is a derogatory term or not. Depends on how you say it.

Hongkie Semi-derogatory term for a person from Hong Kong.

kimono The classic garment worn by Japanese women. When you see a kimono in an HK movie, it usually means Japanese crunch-princess

Michiko Nishiwaki is about to shed it, showing off her tweaked physique just prior to cracking some heads.

Kyonsi A Chinese vampire. These "hopping ghosts" hop up in many a spooker.

Madam A policewoman, not a brothel owner. In some HK films, though, policewomen comically portray brothel owners and hookers to catch criminals.

mahjongg A table game much loved in Hong Kong, *mahjongg* is played with oblong blocks (tiles) with Chinese characters on them. Four players square off, and the game is usually played for money. *Mahjongg* is the socially acceptable way for women to gamble; men may use the ponies.

manga See *animé*.

Méliès, Georges Early twentieth-century French director who single-handedly invented every special effect in film's predigital past. Méliès created nothing but flights of fancy, and is best known for *A Trip to the Moon* (1902), a film that depicts an Earthly rocket that flies directly into the eye of the Man in the Moon. Although the Frenchman never traveled to the East and died a pauper, we can't help but think that the unheralded Father of Special FX is sitting on a cloud somewhere, his wings shaking with laughter over *Mr. Vampire* or *Zu.*

Mongkok Poor, triad-ridden area of northern Kowloon favored by HK filmmakers seeking that cluttered, depressing, urban look. At one person per nine square meters, it is one of the most crowded places in the world.

ninja Japanese assassins. Not part of the Chinese warrior tradition, but in the pan-Asian glare they turn up in HK films, often as heinous villains.

PRC The People's Republic of China.

RHKP Royal Hong Kong Police. Hong Kong's police force functions under the auspices of the Queen of England; in practice, only the occasional desk jockey is British. In movies, Chinese beat cops have to suck up to these arbitrary lunkheads. Even when beat cops talk to Chinese supervisors in Cantonese, the conversation ends with "Yes, sir," said at attention. After 1997, who knows what the force's acronym will be?

sanuk Thai word meaning "fun."

seppuku Ritualistic Japanese suicide involving evisceration. Sometimes known as "hara-kiri."

Shaolin Temple Famous temple in southern China where, over the centuries, monks refined a special martial arts style.

sifu A respected teacher of martial arts or Taoist technique. *Sifus* can be either male or female, but are usually portrayed as older men with eyebrows out to here. (See pages 78–79.)

swastika Buddhist symbol used for more than 8,000 years. Recently misappropriated by mid-twentieth-century Europeans.

triads Chinese gangster societies. More than forty are reported to have operations in Hong Kong, though there are only two or three market-share leaders. Triad societies participate heavily in traditional crime enterprises, such as gambling, loansharking, and prostitution, and they have also branched out into legitimate businesses, such as film and the popular music industries. The triad lifestyle—money, guns, and girls—is prime film fodder.

The Walled City of Kowloon When the Chinese ceded HK to the Brits in the nineteenth century, they walled off a small portion of the territory and declared it part of China in a face-saving gesture. Since HK laws did not extend to this enclave, it became a haven for criminals, who turned it into a seamy rabbit warren of illegal businesses and overcrowded residence for unde-sirables. The Walled City was demolished in the early 1990s.

wirework A technique in which actors are suspended from wires, giving the illusion of defiance of gravity or outright flight. A staple in supernatural films, but often derided by aficionados of martial arts films who view it as cheating.

yakuza Japanese gangster and gangster syndicates.

"You're bad!" Seen in subtitles. Teasing condemnation used by females when males are sexually suggestive.

Appendix

Renting Videos in Chinatown

The best selection of Hong Kong movies can be found at the Chinese-owned video stores located all over North America. But a "Chinatown" video store is bewildering for the first-time *gwailo*. Shelves groan with hundreds of video boxes, their spines either bereft of English or bearing cryptic titles like *I Hate You Deeply* or *A Group of Awful Tigresses*. The staff seems perplexed by your presence, and requests such as "Excuse me, do you have the new John Woo movie?" are met with a curt "No!" or a dismissive wave of the hand.

The staff is not being rude; they simply assume you've wandered into the wrong place by mistake. Many are owned and operated by new Americans, for whom English is a second or third language. They're not used to dealing with *gwailos*. Even in shops where proprietors are friendly and speak good English, they often will not know the English titles of films, which can be very different from the literal translation of the Chinese titles; nor may they be familiar with the Anglicized names of the actors and directors.

Fortunately, there's an easy solution to this problem, and you now hold it in your hands. Below are the Chinese characters for each of the main movie titles we have reviewed. Next time you visit one of these stores, bring the book along and just point to what you want. Presto!

However, a number of Shaw Brothers titles are not included because they are much easier to find in the martial arts section of your local video store under their English titles.

Chinese Film Titles

Armour of God
龍兄虎弟

Armour of God II: Operation Condor
飛鷹計劃

As Tears Go By
旺角卡門

The Assassin
殺人者唐斬

A Better Tomorrow
英雄本色

A Better Tomorrow 2
英雄本色2

The Big Heat
城市特警

Black Cat
黑貓

The Bride With White Hair
白髮魔女傳

Bullet in the Head
喋血街頭

Burning Paradise
火燒紅蓮寺

A Chinese Ghost Story
倩女濺魂

A Chinese Ghost Story II
倩女幽魂2-人間道

A Chinese Ghost Story III
倩女幽魂3-道道道

Chungking Express
重慶森林

City Hunter
城市獵人

City on Fire
龍虎風雲

Deadful Melody
六指琴魔

Descendant of the Sun
日劫

Doctor Lamb
羔羊醫生

Dragon Inn
新龍門客棧

Dragons Forever
飛龍猛蔣

Drunken Master II
醉拳2

Eastern Condors
東方禿鷹

Encounter of the Spooky Kind 2
鬼咬鬼

Erotic Ghost Story II
聊齋豔譚2

Fantasy Mission Force
迷你特攻隊

The First Time Is the Last Time
弟一繭

Fong Sai Yuk
方世玉

Full Contact
俠艷談盜高飛

Gangs
童黨

God of Gamblers
賭神

Green Snake
青蛇

Gunmen
天羅地網

Hard-Boiled
辣手神探

Hello Dracular
合曬撈屍

The Heroic Trio
東方三俠

Holy Flame of the Martial World
武林聖火令

In the Line of Duty 3
雌雄大盜

In the Line of Duty 4
直擊證人

It's Now or Never
飛女正傳

A Kid from Tibet
西藏小子

The Killer
喋血雙兒

Legacy of Rage
龍在江湖

Long Arm of the Law
省港旗兵

Magnificent Warriors
中華戰士

Man Behind the Sun
黑太陽731

Mr. Vampire
殭屍先生

My Heart Is That Eternal Rose
殺手蝴蝶夢

My Lucky Stars
福星高照

Naked Killer
赤裸羔羊

On the Run
亡命鴛鴦

Once a Thief
縱橫四海

Once Upon a Time in China
武狀元黃飛鴻

Painted Faces
七小福

Peacock King
孔省王子

Pedicab Driver
群龍戲鳳

Peking Opera Blues
刀馬旦

People's Hero
人民英雄

Police Story
警察故事

Police Story 3: Supercop
警察故事3:超級警察

Prison on Fire
監獄風雲

Prison on Fire 2
監獄風雲2

Project A
A計劃

Project A Part II
A計劃2

Queen of Temple Street
廟街皇后

Red Spell Spells Red
紅鬼仔

Remains of a Woman
郎心如鐵

Righting Wrongs
執法先鋒

Robotrix
女機械人

Rock 'n' Roll Cop
省港一號緝犯

Rouge
胭脂扣

Royal Warriors
皇家戰士

Satin Steel
重金屬

School on Fire
學校風雲

Seeding of a Ghost
種鬼

A Serious Shock: Yes Madam '92
92末路狂花

The Seventh Curse
原振俠與衛斯理

Sex & Zen
玉蒲團

She Shoots Straight
皇家女將

The Story of Ricky
力王

Swordsman II
笑傲江湖2東方不敗

Taxi Hunter
的士判官

Tiger on Beat
老虎出更

To Hell With the Devil
摩登天師

The Untold Story: Human Meat Roast Pork Buns
八仙飯店之肉叉飽

Wheels on Meals
快餐車

The Wicked City
妖獸都市

Wild Search
伴我闖天涯

Zu: Warriors from the Magic Mountain
蜀山

Index